the
dauntless
dive bomber
of world war two

D0904324

the dauntless dive bomber of world war two

by barrett tillman

naval institute press
annapolis, maryland

The latest edition of this work has been brought to publication with the generous assistance of Marguerite and Gerry Lenfest.

Naval Institute Press
291 Wood Road
Annapolis, MD 21402

© 1976 by Barrett Tillman

All rights reserved. No part of this book may be reproduced or utilized in any form or by any means, electronic or mechanical, including photocopying and recording, or by any information storage and retrieval system, without permission in writing from the publisher.

First Naval Institute Press paperback edition published 2006
ISBN 978-1-59114-867-8 (paperback)
ISBN 978-1-61251-543-4 (eBook)

The Library of Congress has cataloged the hardcover edition as follows:
Tillman, Barrett.
  The Dauntless dive bomber of World War Two / by Barrett Tillman.
    p. cm.
  Originally published: Annapolis, Md. : Naval Institute Press, 1976.
  Includes bibliographical references and index.
  ISBN 1-59114-867-7 (alk. paper)
    1. World War, 1939-1945—Pacific Ocean. 2. Dauntless (Dive bomber) 3. World War, 1939-1945—
Aerial Operations, American. 4. World War, 1939-1945—Naval operations, American. I Title.
  DS559.5.F35 2010
  959.704'37—dc22

                                                                        2005027285

♾ Print editions meet the requirements of ANSI/NISO z39.48-1992 (Permanence of Paper).
Printed in the United States of America.

19 18 17   7 6 5

To the Memory of
William A. Cantrel
Colonel, USMCR

Legends for two-page photographs follow:

Frontispiece: Nearly identical to the SBD-3, the SBD-4 differed mainly in its improved electrical system. This Dauntless sports the 1943 tri-color scheme which later that year became standard in the Pacific. (U.S. Marine Corps)

Pages 2–3: The *Saratoga* air group preparing to launch on a prewar mission. The SBD-2s of Bombing Squadron Three are in the foreground. (U.S. Navy)

Pages 18–19: At the command, "Prepare for launching planes," this carrier flight deck, in early 1942, became as busy as a mid-town street crossing. (U.S. Navy)

Pages 30–31: Tokyo-bound, *Enterprise* trails *Hornet* enroute to launching Colonel Jimmy Doolittle's B-25s against the Japanese in April 1942, three weeks before the Battle of the Coral Sea. (U.S. Navy)

Pages 56–57: Loaded with heavy caliber bombs, these SBD-3 dive bombers stand ready for takeoff, early in 1942. Even in heavy weather and with rain making the carrier deck slippery, wartime operations proceeded on schedule. (U.S. Navy)

Pages 92–93: The ever-present mud of Henderson Field is evident in this late 1942 photo as SBDs and TBFs start their engines in preparation for a mission from Guadalcanal. (U.S. Marine Corps)

Pages 126–27: An SBD-3 returns to Guadalcanal after a late patrol. (U.S. Navy)

Pages 144–45: Dauntless Scout bombers, with the aid of auxiliary gasoline tanks, range far ahead of their carriers in late 1942 to act as the "eyes" of the task force. (U.S. Navy)

Pages 162–63: Composite Squadron No. 29 aboard the escort carrier *Santee* (VC-29) provided antisubmarine patrol for Atlantic convoys in 1943. (U.S. Navy)

Pages 172–73: An SBD-5 of Bomber Squadron 16 is launched from *Lexington* (CV-16) in early 1944. This was the namesake of CV-2, the carrier which was sunk at the Battle of the Coral Sea. (U.S. Navy)

Pages 188–89: A VMBS-231 Dauntless roars over an American fleet anchorage somewhere in the Pacific in 1944. (U.S. Navy)

Pages 210–11: Spraying mosquitos in Portland, Oregon, about 1963. This aircraft, A-24A, is now in the Naval Aviation Museum at Pensacola, Florida. (B. Tillman)

foreword

When Barrett Tillman asked me about the markings on one of my World War II airplanes, I learned that he and his father, a former Marine pilot, had found a surviving SBD and were restoring it to extremely fine condition. Then came the desire to write a book, the first to be devoted exclusively to the Dauntless dive bomber; it records the SBD's contribution to winning the war, particularly in the Pacific.

A notation in my flight log book dated 27 December 1940 says that "Lt. Cdr. H. D. Felt is thoroughly familiar with the equipment, controls and operating procedure for the SBD type aircraft he is about to fly." Bombing Squadron Two was being outfitted with a new dive bomber. For a year, SBD-2, number 2105, provided my steady seat as we trained to fight a real war. The SBD was a joy in a search, a find, and in a dive. During this prewar year, all VB squadrons in *Lexington, Saratoga, Enterprise,* and *Yorktown* replaced their older dive bombers with Dauntlesses.

The last days of 1941, starting 7 December, were frustrating searches for the Japanese, who were off and running. I waited dockside for *Saratoga's* arrival at Pearl Harbor. SBD-3, number 4592, had the Air Group Commander marking 00 on her side. But we missed Coral Sea and Midway by reason of a torpedo in "Sara's" side and instead took some SBDs to North Island, where we had to correct a pilot-to-seat ratio of one-to-one.

Meantime, the Dauntless proved what we knew could be true. When we limped off to Bremerton one of "Sara's" squadrons (VB-3) was left behind in Pearl Harbor, then transferred to *Yorktown* and performed creditably at Midway, Max Leslie in command.

Later came Guadalcanal and the Battle of the Eastern Solomons, where number 03213, Radioman Snyder and I were baptized. "Queen Bee" was the sobriquet given by flight and ready rooms to 03213. In 1943 the Queen, having survived but suffering too many patches, was retired with ceremony; she was eased over the side.

At that time, SBD-4s and -5s were carrying new pilots being trained at dive bombing in the Operational Training Command. And finally, as I was on the way from Moscow to Okinawa, SBD-6, number 54978, eased me off and onto Ford Island.

So for a span of five years, the Dauntless and I were friends. Many who flew, fed and tended SBDs surely have similar feelings, which the author has revitalized in this book.

Harry Don Felt
Admiral, U.S. Navy (Retired)
Former Commander in Chief,
U.S. Pacific Forces

preface

The year 1942 changed forever the traditional concepts of naval warfare, and the rise of the aircraft carrier coincided with the decline of the battleship. Before that critical year was out, there was no longer room for doubt as to the relative effectiveness of capital ships and aircraft. Exclusive of destroyers and submarines, the U.S. Navy sank only one Japanese battleship and one cruiser in 1942 without the aid of carrier-based aircraft.

Dive bombers accounted for over 70 percent of all hits made by both sides in the four carrier battles of 1942, and I therefore contend that the most important aerial antagonists of the Pacific War were the Douglas SBD Dauntless and the Aichi D3A, called "Val" by the Americans. Their mortal struggle to destroy each other's respective roosts was the axis around which sea combat revolved in the Pacific.

Behind this deadly new form of air-sea warfare were two decades of design, development, and experimentation on both sides. The Japanese aerial torpedo capability far exceeded that of the United States up to 1943, but dive bombing—if not actually of U.S. Navy origin—was at least perfected in this country between the wars. It might be said that the SBD came to embody the concept, doctrine and execution of precision dive bombing just as the Boeing B-17 represented the Army Air Force's faith in the concept of daylight strategic bombing.

The difference is that the glamorous, well-publicized Flying Fortress gained worldwide acclaim for its accomplishments. The Dauntless remains largely unheralded and perhaps even unappreciated, despite the absolutely crucial role it played throughout the Pacific War. The names of Coral Sea, Midway, and Guadalcanal speak for themselves, yet the old axiom that "dive bombers don't make headlines" seems as true now as it did over 30 years ago. Hopefully this book will help change some of that.

A brief note to the layman is in order as to the style in which this military history is written. I could have avoided the use of technical terms and references, but thought a wholly "civilianized" style would detract from conveying the SBD's personality and the flavor of the times.

As a pilot I've stayed pretty much within the aviator's frame of reference. Most distances are given in nautical miles unless otherwise noted. Positions of latitude and longitude, where given, are included for the benefit of serious students of the Pacific War.

On the personal level my motivation for this project is largely sentimental. With two or three other owners and pilots of antique aircraft I invested one year of my life and a bit of my soul in restoring one of five remaining Dauntlesses to original condition. Before that Dauntless went to the Marine Corps Museum, I made a few flights in it with my favorite SBD pilot—my father. And though the plane was six years older than I, there was no generation gap; I came to love that old Douglas like an overgrown pet.

In fact, I found that if you're not careful, you might end up writing a book about it.

Barrett Tillman
Athena, Oregon
May 1975

contents

the
dauntless
dive bomber
of world war two

chapter 1
birth of
the dauntless

Dauntless dive bombers, the SBDs, the most successful and beloved by aviators of all our carrier types . . .

Samuel Eliot Morison
History of United States Naval Operations in World War II

Dive bombing may or may not have been an American innovation; its origin is attributed to various times and places. Some authorities contend it began in the First World War, but what was then described as dive bombing was probably little more than what later became known as glide bombing.

It is known, however, that dive bombing was first used by American aviators in 1919 when Marine pilots experimented with the technique. But nobody knew exactly what to call the tactic of releasing a bomb from a steeply diving aircraft, and one Navy summary noted that "dive bombing emerged as an established fact almost before anyone knew enough to call it by name." It was variously called light bombing, strafing with light bombs, and diving bombing before the final terminology came into wide use.

The U.S. Navy's interest in dive bombing took an upward turn with the commissioning of USS *Langley* in 1922—a former collier converted into America's first aircraft carrier. In the pioneering days of carrier aviation it quickly became apparent that the number and type of aircraft available for sea duty would be sharply limited. The torpedo plane was a natural, as was the fighter. But carrier planes could not possibly carry as heavy or as many bombs as land-based aircraft, so a method of delivering ordnance with the greatest possible accuracy was needed. That method was dive bombing.

Dive bombing had a quasi-official status until 1926 when the Chief of Naval Operations decided to include it in the fleet exercises that year. Most of these early tests were conducted with Vought 02U Corsair biplanes, practically the only aircraft then suitable for the role. But most dive-bombing tests up to that time had been done against stationary targets, so in October of 1927 Fighting Squadron Five completed a series of tests against target platforms towed by destroyers at 20 knots. The targets, moving at a realistic pace, were reported "easy prey for the diving planes," and it was judged the planes' speed was a deterrent to antiaircraft fire.

But it wasn't long before the continued existence of Navy dive bombing was seriously threatened. Several aircraft were struck by their own bombs upon releasing them in steep dives, with damage to propellers or landing gear. No planes were lost as a result of these accidents, but it was plain that protective measures were required. Therefore, in 1929 all dives were restricted to shallow angles and the use of live bombs was prohibited until the Bureau of Aeronautics and Bureau of Ordnance could arrive at a solution.

At length the answer was found: a bomb-displacing gear, sometimes called a bomb fork or crutch. When the bomb was released, the displacing gear swung the bomb safely away from the aircraft, clearing the propeller and wheels. The device was flight-tested and approved for all dive bombers in early 1931.

During the summer of 1934, the Bureau of Aeronautics held design competitions for the types of aircraft it had recently standardized for carrier operations. There were four: single-seat fighter, two-seat light scout-bomber, two-seat heavy dive bomber, and three-seat torpedo plane and horizontal bomber. The Navy wanted its carrier aircraft of the next generation to be all-metal monoplanes with retractable landing gear in order to keep pace with developments in military aviation. The scout and dive bombers, as an additional requirement, were to have some form of speed brake to inhibit airspeed in a dive and thus provide a better aiming platform.

One of the competing companies was the Northrop Corporation, a progressive and imaginative firm based at Inglewood, California. The company's founder was John K. Northrop, one of the outstanding aeronautical engineers of all time. His Alpha, Beta and Gamma mailplanes had utilized innovative construction features which revolutionized the aircraft industry. The Alpha, which appeared in 1929, featured a monocoque fuselage with duraluminum sheets, stringers and bulkheads. The craft's smooth exterior covering carried most of the aerodynamic load, allowing a lighter weight due to minimal interior bracing. With a top speed of 170 mph the six-passenger Alpha was a sensation, and inspired production of the smaller but similar two-seat Beta sportplane. But both were eclipsed in 1933 by the Gamma, a larger single-seat fast mailplane capable of 220 mph. Though few of these Northrops were built, their influence on aviation was to be immense.

Northrop examined the Navy's specification for the dive-bomber contract and his experimental bomber was one of three designs selected for final evaluation. The leading entry was Brewster's XSBA-1, with an internal bomb bay and a top speed of over 250 mph. But the Brewster model met a dead end, for the parent firm had built few aircraft previously and lacked the facilities for producing enough dive bombers to fill the Navy's order.

The second finalist was from Vought, a long-time supplier of Navy aircraft. The SB2U-1, later christened Vindicator, was built more along the lines of a light scout-bomber than a true dive bomber. It had folding wings and fully retractable landing gear but its intended speed brake, a device which would flatten propeller pitch in a dive, was never perfected. Furthermore, according to a Marine pilot with ample experience in the type, "It had no performance with a 1000-pound bomb."[1] Over 50 SB2Us were eventually ordered by the Navy, but the Northrop was clearly the only fullfledged dive-bomber design.

A racy-looking aircraft designed by chief engineer Ed Heinemann, the XBT-1 (experimental bomber by Northrop) embodied many of the construction and engineering techniques perfected in the Alpha-series mailplanes. Though Northrop decided against installing a folding mechanism in the wings as a weight-saving consideration, and the landing gear was only semiretractable, there was an offsetting factor. A set of split dive flaps mounted at the trailing edge of the wing was standard on the XBT, whereas only the abortive Brewster and an export model of the SB2U had similar arrangements. After consultation with the National Advisory Committee on Aeronautics, the XBT-1's dive performance was improved by drilling large holes in the flaps to allow air to pass through relatively undisturbed. This eliminated tail buffeting and permitted a steeper diving angle.

Powered by an 825-horsepower Pratt and Whitney, the XBT-1's top speed was only 212 mph as a more powerful engine was not readily available. But the plane went through Navy tests in 1935, and in April of the following year an order for 54 production models was placed. By late 1937 Bombing Squadrons Five and Six were equipped with the BT-1, which was destined to go aboard the U.S. Navy's new carriers *Yorktown* and *Enterprise* the next year.

Landing a BT-1 aboard a carrier was a tricky matter, with the plane's relatively poor lateral stability and tendency to torque-roll upon sudden power application at low airspeed. Ed Heinemann examined the BT-1's drawbacks and concluded the rudder needed modification. This and other changes resulted in the XBT-2.

But the new model did not enter production—at least not under the Northrop banner. It was agreed in 1937 that Douglas Aircraft Company,

The SBD's predecessor: Northrop's XBT-1 in flight during 1935 (National Archives)

An SBD-5 shows off its distinctive perforated dive flaps as it rolls away from the photo plane. (R. M. Hill)

which John Northrop had been associated with early in his career, would take over the Navy contract. When Northrop sold his El Segundo, California, plant to Douglas in January of 1938 most of the BT personnel stayed with the project, including Heinemann.

The XBT-2 was in many ways a different airplane from the production BT-1. Controls were almost completely redesigned, with a dozen different sets of ailerons being tested. A new engine was found for the "dash two," Wright's R-1820-32, which produced 1000 horsepower. The Cyclone engine, combined with the addition of fully retractable landing gear, boosted the dive bomber's top speed by 35 mph. The new airplane also possessed markedly improved stability and low-speed control over the

BT-1. A primary factor in improving the plane's flying qualities were the "letter-box" antistall slots in the leading edge of each wing. They in effect provided the wing with a second chance to keep flying when approaching the stall speed of 78 mph. Test pilots were highly enthusiastic about the XBT-2's handling characteristics, particularly the light control responses.

The XBT-2 was completed in August of 1938 and Douglas made the changes asked for by BuAer, which included more equipment, such as an autopilot. Normally the designation would remain the same as the prototype, simply dropping the X which indicated experimental status. But since the design now bore the Douglas stamp the XBT-2, BuAer number 0627, became the XSBD-1: the Scout-Bomber by Douglas. The production version, in accordance with Navy wishes, was altered somewhat to achieve the classic silhouette which would eventually become famous.

The Douglas plant received an order for 144 SBDs in April of 1939; 57 SBD-1s for the Marines and 87 SBD-2s for the carrier squadrons. As was the custom with Douglas aircraft, an alliterative name was chosen for the SBD. The Army's B-23 bomber was to become known as the Dragon and the TBD torpedo plane became the Devastator. Even the workhorse C-47 transport followed suit, being named Dakota in British service. And so it was for the SBD, which became popularly known as the Douglas Dauntless. Seldom has any airplane been better named.

The Dauntless production line at El Segundo, California, was under the direction of Eric Springer, with Ed Heinemann remaining as project engineer. But they weren't the only old hands involved with SBD production and testing. During the summer of 1940 a number of well-known aviators were on the Douglas payroll, including Vance Breese, who did numerous dive tests, and Frank Sinclair, who conducted roll tests. James H. Haizlip, famous as a prewar air racer in the fabulous Gee Bees, mostly test-flew the twin-engine DB-7 which later became the Army's A-20, but did occasional production flight testing in Dauntlesses.

Early SBD production was unusual in that the Marines rather than the Navy received the initial deliveries of a new first-line aircraft. This was attributable to the rapid changes being made in Navy requirements for combat planes, and it was not deemed advisable to put SBD-1s aboard carriers when SBD-2s were much better suited for the job with 50 percent more fuel capacity. Pilots' armament was increased from one to two .50 caliber machine guns, though the gunner retained a single .30 caliber in the SBD-2. Armor plate and bullet-proof windscreens were also added.

The Marine Corps received the first Dauntlesses. This SBD-1, carrying a 1,000-pound bomb, is the squadron commander's aircraft of VMB-2. (U.S. Marine Corps)

The Dauntless entered squadron service in June 1940, when Marine Air Group One at Quantico, Virginia, received the first SBD-1s. In November of that year the Navy got its initial batch of SBD-2s, and all 87 were delivered by the following May. Bombing Squadron Two aboard *Lexington* was among the earliest recipients of Dauntlesses and was the first carrier squadron completely equipped with the new type. Under the leadership of Lieutenant Commander H. D. Felt, VB-2 ran up an impressive record prior to December 1941, when Felt left to assume command of the *Saratoga* Air Group. Bombing Two participated in Army maneuvers at Lake Charles, Louisiana, and made a two-day "attack" on Oahu in May 1941. Felt, who later rose to command the Navy's Pacific Forces in the Vietnam era, commented that *Lexington*'s SBDs were instrumental in "demonstrating to the Japanese Consul General, resident cross-channel from Ford Island, how it could be done."[2]

Deliveries of SBD-3s began in March of 1941, heralding the arrival of the one aircraft model which would truly become the workhorse of the Pacific War in the year following the Japanese attack on Pearl Harbor. By paring 180 pounds from the airframe, all the dash-two modifications became standard in the SBD-3 with no appreciable increase in weight, though the new model was sardonically called the "Speedy Three" for its rather low maximum speed of 216 knots, or 250 mph. But it carried the burden of the Navy's aerial offensive in 1942 almost entirely by itself, as the SBD-2 largely disappeared from combat after the Battle of the Coral Sea. The dash four, virtually identical to the dash three except for an improved electrical system, was slowest of the entire Dauntless series with a top speed of 212 knots or 245 mph.

The workhorse of the Pacific War in the year following Pearl Harbor was the SBD-3. This brand-new aircraft was photographed at El Segundo, California, March 1942. (Peter M. Bowers)

By the end of 1941 Douglas was turning out 20 dive bombers a month, but in the monumental buildup of production from peacetime to sudden war, all previous records were shattered. This was accomplished despite the fact that during the critical period of 1942 Dauntlesses suffered from shortages of several important components while still on the assembly line: notably armor plate, fuel valves, and propellers. But to its ever-lasting credit, Douglas Aircraft always managed to scrounge up the parts and keep turning out Dauntlesses when they were needed most. Some 1,600 SBDs had been delivered or ordered by late 1942, and after Douglas got tooled up to peak efficiency the El Segundo plant was rolling dive bombers off the line at the rate of 11 a day.

This expansion took time, of course, but it accounted for the bulk of Dauntless production, as embodied in the penultimate version, the SBD-5. The dash five was equipped with an improved version of the Wright Cyclone engine, the 1820-60, which produced 1200 horsepower on take-off. It was built in response to reports that when fully loaded the SBD-3 and -4 were operating at nearly maximum power all the time. The dash five was also the first Dauntless which came with a twin .30 caliber machine gun mount in the rear cockpit. Previous models with twin .30s had been fitted after delivery.

Over 3,000 SBD-5s were ordered, delivery beginning in May 1943. The final version, the dash six, was produced in moderate quantity with only 450 being built before SBD production ended in July of 1944. The

SBD-6 had the 1820-66 engine which put out a maximum 1350 horse-power. Many, if not most dash sixes, went to the Marine Corps.

Douglas Aircraft Company built nearly 30,000 aircraft during World War II, including the A-20 and A-26 medium bombers, the C-54 cargo plane, plus the B-17 and B-24 under contract from Boeing and Consolidated. But with the notable exception of nearly 10,000 C-47 and R4D transports, the Dauntless was the most numerous Douglas product. From 1940 to 1944, 5,936 of the rugged dive bombers were accepted by the government. Some 950 of these were delivered to or built specifically for the Army Air Force under the name of Banshee, so called for the wailing shriek the plane made in a dive. Built at the Douglas Tulsa plant, the Army variants were A-24 (SBD-3), A-24A (SBD-4), and A-24B (SBD-5). There was no equivalent to the SBD-6.

Solidly committed to strategic bombing, the Army had almost completely neglected dive bombing until the Luftwaffe's stunning success in Europe with the Junkers 87 sparked a renewed interest. Turning to the Navy for help, the Air Force quickly learned how far behind it had fallen. Banshees, in fact, were little used in combat by the U.S.A.A.F., and even then very seldom as true dive bombers. Glide-bombing and skip-bombing were the usual Army techniques.

One pilot caught unawares by the Army's need for expertise with the new dive bomber was William C. Lemly, a Marine staff officer at San Diego. Burdened with paper work, Lemly hadn't yet flown a Dauntless when his commanding officer directed him to provide a group of Army pilots with cockpit checks in the SBD. Lemly boned up well enough to herd his new-found pupils through the intricacies of flying the Dauntless without telling them he hadn't logged so much as one hour in the type. But he had ample opportunity afterwards, and flying a modified SBD, Lemly completed a photo-mapping session of San Diego in one day.

As much as the SBD was an improvement over previous dive bombers, it was still not the airplane the Navy counted on to fight the Pacific War. The big, brutish Curtiss SB2C Helldiver was the dive bomber BuAer hoped would be ready when war came, but the "SB Deuce" suffered an uncommonly long gestation period with more than its share of bugs. Built to the 1938 design specifications, the Curtiss was to have outshone the Douglas in every capacity, with twice the bomb load, 60 mph greater speed, and longer range.

The Helldiver finally did outperform the Dauntless, though not by the margins desired. Its maximum speed was 30 to 40 mph more than the SBD, and the SB2C-5 cruised about 22 mph faster than the SBD-5. But the Helldiver most often carried a single 1000-pounder in its internal bomb bay, and in operational conditions was often shorter-ranged than the Dauntless. In other words, the SB2C offered relatively little over the Dauntless where it really mattered; hauling a large bomb load over an appreciable distance at high speed. The plain fact was, by the time Helldivers reached combat in November of 1943 their virtues and improvements had no great effect upon the outcome of the war. The critical period was past.

It is ironic that the majority of dive-bomber pilots who stressed the need for a replacement for the Douglas during 1942–43 were disappointed when they finally got hold of the Helldiver. With its much lighter and more responsive controls the SBD was, when lightly loaded, a fun airplane to fly. It had none of the SB2C's adverse stall characteristics nor the 2C's rather marginal handling at low airspeeds. The SBD's only bad habit was the tendency to snap inverted without warning while in a tight vertical left-hand bank, after which the nose fell through the horizon and the aircraft would spin. In a right-hand vertical bank the reaction was less pronounced. But all military aircraft exhibited similar tendencies owing to the powerful left-hand propeller rotation, so it was not a problem unique to the SBD.

Another highly important feature of the Douglas was that it required fewer maintenance man-hours than the Curtiss. The SB2C's Curtiss-Electric propeller caused a good deal of trouble both in the air and on the ground, a problem the SBD's Hamilton-Standard prop never gave. And though the Dauntless was designed well before the concept of the 30-minute turnaround, mechanics rated it easier to work on than the significantly larger Helldiver.

Still, nobody with experience in the SBD would claim it was free of fault. The Dauntless was inherently noisy and drafty; it was relatively slow and widely considered underarmed. The sluggish performance of early SBDs under full bomb and fuel loads gave rise to such nicknames as the Barge and the Clunk. But it should be remembered that Helldiver pilots called their plane the Beast, and mechanics swore that SB2C stood for S.O.B. Second Class.

The best-remembered description of the Dauntless was an acronymic play on its designation. "Slow But Deadly" was the way many SBD pilots thought of their airplane, and certainly it was accurate, for the Dauntless was the most successful and the best dive bomber of the war. Its inherent stability made it the steadiest possible sighting platform in a dive, and its light control responses made corrections easy when lining up a target.

The SBD-1 through the -4 were equipped with a three-power telescopic sight, a holdover from the open-cockpit aircraft of the thirties. The pilot looked through the tube, lining up the crosshairs on the target

"Hook down, wheels down, flaps down." An SBD-4 prepares to land aboard the Independence, *early 1942. Because their wings did not fold, Dauntlesses were not taken into combat on the crowded hangar decks of these light carriers. (R. M. Hill)*

while keeping a ball much like that of a turn-and-bank indicator centered in its groove. The centered ball told him the aircraft was level in the dive, otherwise the bomb would go off on a tangent when released. The drawback to the telescopic sight was its tendency to fog over in a dive from high altitude because of a sudden change of temperature, and the resulting condensation clouded the lens. The windscreen was also prone to fogging, and pilots said the tubular sight was inadequate for aerial gunnery since it severely limited the field of vision.

The answer was a reflector gunsight nearly identical to those used in fighter aircraft. Beginning with the SBD-5, Mark VIII reflecting gunsights were installed, as were heaters for the windscreens. These measures eliminated the problem and were instrumental in improving bombing accuracy. But they were not available until 1943.

During 1942 dive-bomber squadrons usually consisted of 18 aircraft, flying in three divisions of two three-plane sections. Each section flew an inverted V formation with one wingman on each side and slightly behind the leader. The squadron flew in stairstep fashion, beginning at the top with the entire formation stepped down by sections and divisions. This arrangement presented a formidable defense against enemy fighters and served as a guide to spacing each aircraft in its dive.

Visual contact with enemy ships was usually made between 30 and 40 miles in clear weather at the normal cruising altitude of 18,000 feet.

Once the squadron commander picked out his target and maneuvered into a favorable position—ideally down-sun and upwind—the formation was down to pushover altitude of about 15,000 feet. The rearseatmen were facing aft with their canopies open and machine guns cocked in anticipation of fighter interception.

The attack began from the top of the formation with the squadron commander leading the way down. As each aircraft pushed over into its dive the pilot allowed enough space between the plane ahead of him to retain a good view of the target. By the time the last plane started down the formation was spaced vertically over some 1500 feet.

The mechanics of diving a Dauntless were not too complicated. The pilot retarded his throttle, pulled the plane's nose slightly above the horizon and activated the diamond-shaped handle on his right. There were three levers, marked D, L, and W. The L handle opened the bottom set of landing flaps; W lowered the wheels. But the D lever opened all the flaps, both dive and landing flaps as the two systems were interrelated. The pilot then half-rolled into his dive and settled the Dauntless on an angle of 70 degrees, which was nearly straight down.

An SBD seldom achieved much in excess of 240 knots (276 mph) in a prolonged dive, which was not really very fast. From 15,000 feet the pilot had 35 to 40 seconds to pick out his target, line it up, steady the aircraft, judge the wind drift, and release in time to pull out. Most corrections in a dive were made along the lateral axis of the aircraft, requiring use of the ailerons.

When satisfied the plane was level and the crosshairs properly placed, the pilot reached below the throttle quadrant on his left and pulled the double-handled manual bomb release. By selecting one of three slots in the bracket he could drop all three bombs at once or just one of the 100-pounders mounted on a small rack under each wing. Selecting the middle slot, marked "salvo," would release the heavy centerline bomb and both small, wing-mounted bombs simultaneously. Partway through SBD-3 production, electrical arming and release circuits were installed and this became standard in subsequent models. A red button marked B on top of the stick controlled the release mechanism though the manual system was retained as a back-up.

Releases were generally made between 1,500 and 2,000 feet with a five or six G pullout made low on the water at high speed. But the dive brakes had to be retracted before the pullout, as the Dauntless could not easily maintain level flight with the upper set of flaps extended.

For strike missions SBDs usually carried a 1,000-pound, general-purpose bomb under the fuselage, and may or may not have bothered with the 100-pounders under the wings. Fuze settings were varied among the bombs in order to achieve a variety of above-deck and below-decks damage if ships were the intended target. Instantaneous settings would detonate a bomb as soon as it hit anything, while those with delay settings could penetrate armor plate and explode inside the hull. The most common fuze settings were 1/100 and 1/250 second delay.

As its designation indicates, the SBD was a scout as well as a bomber. Until well into 1943 the standard U.S. carrier air group consisted of four squadrons, with SBDs equipping the bomber and scout squadron. Scout units as such disappeared by the end of that year, but in the four great carrier battles of 1942 the scouts played a critical role, both as reconnaissance and strike aircraft. In less hectic times they performed more mundane tasks, such as antisubmarine patrol.

Depending upon the tactical situation, a carrier might launch a comprehensive 360-degree search beginning at dawn. More often only a portion of the circle was to be searched, but in either case an imaginary line of 200 to 250 miles radius was drawn around the proposed launch position. The search segment was then divided into pie-shaped wedges of usually ten degrees width, so a 360-degree search required a number of bomber and torpedo planes as the 18 scouts could not cover the entire area without widening each sub-sector to twenty degrees.

Generally teamed in pairs, the scouts flew at 1,000 to 1,500 feet to conserve fuel otherwise consumed in a long climb to altitude. Armed with a 500-pound G-P (general-purpose bomb), scouts were not expected to bomb enemy ships unless the circumstances were favorable. Their primary mission was reconnaissance, and notifying the carrier of enemy vessels took precedence over attacking. Besides, a single 500-pounder or even a pair of them could not sink a warship larger than a submarine. But they could possibly knock a carrier deck out of action, and flattops were always the priority target for any attack, followed by battleships and cruisers.

Upon making contact with an enemy surface force the pilot had his rear-seat man send a preliminary report, usually by Morse Code, as voice radio was not entirely efficient in 1942, and the dot-dash of "CW" was more reliable and longer-ranged. The standard abbreviated form of a typical contact report might read, "One CV, two CA, five DD, Lat 08-45S, Long 163-20E, Cus 160, Spd 15." This meant that one carrier, two cruisers, and five destroyers were sighted at 8° 45′ South Latitude, 163° 20′ East Longitude, course 160° True, speed 15 knots. Most contact reports were supposed to be encoded before transmission, but this was a time-consuming job and a really crucial report could be sent "in the clear." The radioman-gunner was to keep sending the message until acknowledged by his ship, but atmospheric conditions and the state of existing low-frequency radio equipment sometimes prevented ships or other aircraft from receiving the information.

When possible, other scouts would leave their sectors to join the aircraft in contact with the enemy in hopes of making a combined attack. But this rarely occurred and if any attack were made at all it was usually by the team which made the discovery. Keeping up-sun of the hostile ships, using available cloud cover, the scouts got as close as possible before initiating standard dive-bombing attacks. During the approach the gunners had their canopies open, machine guns deployed and ready, ever alert for the combat air patrol bound to be over any carrier force. But the scouts' greatest ally was surprise, and once an attack had been made it was usually impossible to remain in the vicinity because of aroused enemy defenses. For this reason the scouts usually refrained from attacking too soon, as Japanese warships did not have radar until well into 1943. By keeping their distance and using sun and clouds, scout teams could remain undetected for quite some time.

Like all World War II aircraft, the SBD was experimented upon to find how much "stretch" was built into the design. The fact that the Dauntless airframe remained almost completely unchanged throughout the entire series speaks well for the original concept, but a wide variety of ordnance and equipment was tested for suitability on the SBD. This included .50 caliber gun packs under the wings, zero-length rocket rails, multi-shackle light bomb racks, and even radar in some late model aircraft.

At one point shortly after the Battle of Midway BuAer gave serious consideration to building a single-seat Dauntless adapted to carry a torpedo. Fortunately the Grumman TBF proved a fine torpedo plane, and BuAer's drastic suggestion was never acted upon.

Though Dauntlesses flew innumerable antisubmarine patrols, ground-support missions, and utility and training flights, the SBD's major contribution was the search-strike role for which it had been designed. In dollars and cents the SBD surely earned its way and even paid dividends: the XBT-1 was designed and built at a cost of $85,000. Nearly ten years later the last SBD-6, minus military-supplied equipment, cost the United States $29,000.

Considering what happened in between, the Dauntless was a bargain.

Hit hard, hit fast, hit often.
Admiral William F. Halsey

For the men of the carrier *Enterprise*, sea duty under Admiral Halsey in 1941 was a twilight zone between peacetime routine and wartime readiness. This morning was no exception, for the "Big E" was returning to port after delivering F4F fighters to the Marine garrison on Wake Island. The other Pacific Fleet carrier, *Lexington*, was engaged in a similar mission, taking 25 aircraft to Midway. *Saratoga* was still on the West Coast undergoing repairs.

Two hundred miles out from Hawaii, *Enterprise* was due to dock at 0730, but rough seas had prolonged the refueling of her escorting destroyers. The sailors would be hours late making port, but the fortunate aviators of Scouting Squadron Six would arrive well before anyone else. By 0630, 18 Dauntlesses had been launched; 13 from VS-6 augmented by four from Bombing Six, all led by Commander Howard Young, the *Enterprise* air group commander.

Normally it was an easy hour and a quarter flight, but Halsey was taking neither the normal nor the easy course of action. *Enterprise* and her air group were operating on a wartime footing, and the unusual procedure of a full search to the east before entering port was established. The 18 SBDs fanned out to search the eastern horizon.

Two hours dragged by when the duty watch attending *Enterprise*'s radio shack was startled by the voice of Ensign Manuel Gonzales in Six-Baker-Three: "Please don't shoot! This is an American plane!"[1] Nothing more was ever heard from him.

The time was about 0800 on Sunday, 7 December 1941.

Commander Young and his Dauntlesses had flown straight into the opening moments of World War II in the Pacific. With Lieutenant Commander Bromfield Nichol of Halsey's staff in the rear seat, Young was about ten minutes ahead of the other SBDs. Approaching Ewa Marine Corps Air Station with his wingman, Young noticed several aircraft overhead and assumed they were Army fighters up for practice. But that was peculiar for a Sunday, and so were the black bursts of antiaircraft fire over Pearl Harbor. It was all much too realistic for a drill.

The situation became a good deal more authentic moments later when one of the fighters peeled off and initiated a gunnery pass on the CAG's Dauntless. The leading edges of the stranger's wings lit up with yellow lights and pieces of aluminum were hacked out of the SBD's wing as the tracer shells found their mark. When the attacker pulled up, the dull red rising sun insignia of Japan was visible under both wings.

Young and his wingman simultaneously dived towards Ford Island. They eluded the Zero, but were immediately fired upon by numerous "friendly" ship and shore-based guns. The surprise attack had been in progress long enough for men on the ground to assume every aircraft was hostile. Intent upon his landing, Young had no time to call a warning to the SBDs behind him. He virtually had to stand on his brakes in order to bring his speeding Dauntless to a halt.

For some, the reality of the situation was almost too much to comprehend, but others sheltered fewer doubts. One was Lieutenant (jg) F. A. Patriarca, who accurately assessed the circumstances at once and turned back towards *Enterprise*. But Halsey, with responsibility for preserving the precious carrier, changed course and was running under radio silence. Unable to find the "Big E," Patriarca once more reversed his heading. But his fuel situation was nearing the critical point and he decided upon a wheels-up landing in a Kauai pasture.

Ensign John Vogt's Dauntless was probably the one sighted by Marines at Ewa, which became engaged in a low-level dogfight with two—some said three—Japanese fighters. Witnesses said the SBD clung tenaciously to the tail of one Zero, firing constantly until the Mitsubishi pulled its nose up and stalled. The Dauntless collided with its victim and both exploded.

Another lone SBD pilot who experienced a violent set-to with the swift Zeros was Ensign E. T. Deacon. Nursing a wounded leg and a badly riddled airplane, he attempted to glide into Hickam Field but had to ditch just offshore. Deacon made his way to Ford Island where several other *Enterprise* pilots had gathered. They noted with a professional eye that the Aichi D3A dive bombers did not dive as steeply as the SBDs. They estimated that the Japanese "Vals" came down at about a 50-degree angle—much shallower than the Americans.

Lieutenant Clarence E. Dickinson and his wingman, Ensign Bud McCarthy, were jumped by two Zeros at 4,000 feet near Barbers Point. McCarthy maneuvered his plane to support Dickinson's, but was hit by the Zeros and fell away in smoke and flames before either gunner could open fire. Dickinson saw McCarthy's chute open but the gunner didn't get out.

Four more Zeros appeared and lined up astern of the lone SBD. Though Dickinson's gunner, Roger Miller, was wounded early in the combat he shot down one fighter in flames. Turning constantly, trying to throw off the other Zero's aim, Dickinson couldn't evade them all. A burst of cannon fire hit one wing, which was soon burning. Miller was killed at this same time, and Dickinson found he had lost control of his Dauntless. In a right-hand spin at only 800 feet he unbuckled his seat belt and bailed out. He heard his Dauntless spin into the ground and explode on impact and then he landed, falling backwards on a newly graded dirt road.

Shortly after the third Japanese attack ended, Lieutenant Commander Halstead Hopping of Scouting Six had his plane refueled and went on a solo reconnaissance flight. Japanese transports had been reported off

Barbers Point—just one of many incredible rumors which had to be checked out. Gunning his Dauntless down the runway, Hopping was subjected to a maddening send-off by what appeared to be every gunner for miles around. The morning's events had convinced most people that all airplanes over Pearl Harbor were made in Japan. But Hopping got off without being hit and scouted to a distance of 30 miles. He found nothing and returned to Ford Island, landing about 1100.

Nine of the SBDs—seven of Scouting Six and two from Bombing Six —were servicable upon Hopping's return. Each was fueled and fitted with a 500-pound bomb. Hopping led them off on another search just after noon with orders to scout two hundred miles to the northwest. By that time, though, the six Japanese carriers were long gone. The weather thickened and the SBDs returned to base. They arrived at 1530 to be greeted by the now-familiar welcome of friendly gunfire, but all landed safely. Ensigns Bucky Walters and Ben Troemel of Scouting Six returned after dark from an equally unsuccessful search. Painfully aware of the confusion at Pearl Harbor, they elected to land at Kaneohe instead. The field was blacked out and they got no response from the control tower, but Walters figured this was a security precaution. Both pilots made normal landing approaches but had to take violent, last-second avoiding action to clear a variety of vehicles parked on the darkened runway. Walters screeched to a halt under the boom of a mobile crane; Troemel slewed to a stop with his plane nose-to-nose with a cement mixer. The two scout pilots incurred the displeasure of the base commander who was convinced his obstacle course runway would prevent any airplane from landing.

So ended the SBD's first day at war. It had not been an auspicious beginning. Seven Dauntlesses from *Enterprise* were shot down or crash-landed, with the loss of three pilots and five gunners. Marine Air Group 21's two squadrons of SBD-1s—VMSB-231 and 232—lost 17 of their aircraft and all the remaining 10 were damaged. The final tally was some two dozen Navy and Marine SBDs destroyed on 7 December.

Enterprise remained in Hawaiian waters as a precaution against the possibility of a follow-up attack. It did not materialize, of course, but Japanese submarine activity had been reported within 200 miles north of Pearl Harbor, and on 10 December the morning patrols reported three large submarines on the surface, one of which was attacked. At 1130 three SBDs were launched to follow up the earlier contacts.

One was piloted by Lieutenant Dickinson, who had been shot down by Zeros three days before. The contact he was to pursue had been reported 125 miles north of Pearl, so he had only to fly 75 miles south to

This early 1942 photo of Dauntlesses warming up on Enterprise's *flight deck was taken during a period of change for aircraft markings. Note that S4 has not yet received its large national fuselage star. (R. M. Hill)*

reach the sub's position of 0600. But in nearly six hours a surfaced submarine could be a considerable distance away, so Dickinson decided to fly a rectangular search pattern. Reasoning that the sub would have headed north or east, he flew 20 miles south, turned on a leg of 30 miles east and finally 40 miles north.

As he reached the northern corner of his search pattern he spotted his quarry on the surface, 15 miles to starboard. The submarine was driving northeast at high speed as Dickinson radioed his contact report to *Enterprise.*

The sub was *I-70,* measuring 343 feet in length and displacing 1,400 tons. She had evidently been damaged in the morning attack but carried sufficient antiaircraft guns to defend herself, and opened fire as soon as the plane was in range. From a search altitude of 800 feet, Dickinson had to climb to at least 5,000 in order to have enough time for an accurate dive.

Nearly ten minutes after his sighting, Dickinson was ready. Settling in his descent, he saw the Japanese gun crews through his telescopic sight and remembered to lay his bomb close alongside the sub to cause maximum damage. Grasping the manual bomb-release lever, Dickinson pulled the knobbed handle as far back as it would go.

Pulling out of his dive, Dickinson looked past his SBD's tail and saw his bomb had exploded close aboard the submarine, amidships. Turning back towards the sub, he saw she had stopped dead in the water and was settling on an even keel. Since there was no forward motion, Dickinson knew the sub wasn't diving, especially when she settled more by the stern. In less than one minute she had disappeared completely from view. An oil slick and unidentifiable debris was all that remained.

Dickinson was careful to claim only a probable sinking, but for once the conservative claim was not the most accurate. As confirmed by post-war Japanese records, I-70 went down 180 miles north of Pearl Harbor on 10 December 1941. The Dauntless had accounted for the first enemy fleet submarine of the war.

Enterprise spent a month near Hawaii before Halsey decided upon a more aggressive position. But first the Pacific Fleet needed its carrier strength reinforced in order to carry out the series of raids planned over the next three months. *Saratoga* was some five hundred miles southwest of Oahu on 11 January 1942 when a Japanese submarine put a torpedo into her port side aft. After temporary work at Pearl she was sent to Bremerton, Washington, for permanent repairs and modernization. "Sara" would be out of the war until summer, but her Air Group Three stayed in Hawaii.

Meanwhile, *Yorktown* had been transferred from the Atlantic and was ready to undertake operations, as was *Lexington*. But it was up to *Enterprise* to strike the first blow. In late January she departed Samoa, bound for Kwajalein Atoll in the Marshalls.

Beginning at 0445 on 1 February, *Enterprise* launched her first strike force of the war. Commander Young was in overall command of the attack group on Kwajalein, which numbered 36 SBDs and nine TBD torpedo planes.

After a harrowing predawn launch and form-up, which included several near-collisions, Commander Hopping led Scouting Six's first division down on Roi Island at 0700. Lieutenant Earl Gallaher and Lieutenant Dickinson followed with their six-plane divisions in low, shallow glide-bombing runs but the vital element of surprise was lost. Antiaircraft guns opened fire as Mitsubishi A5M Claudes and Zero fighters took off to intercept. Hopping bored in, heading for the airfield and dropped his bombs at less than 1,000 feet—another record for the SBD, as these were the first bombs dropped on Japanese-occupied soil in World War II.

Three sections of SBDs in right echelon. Dive bombers flew in three-plane sections and six-plane divisions, with eighteen to a squadron. (U.S. Navy)

But moments later Hopping's Dauntless was hit by AA fire and engaged by fighters. Most of Scouting Six saw their CO's plane hit the water and sink almost immediately; neither crewman got out. The other aircraft pressed the attack on Roi's facilities.

About 20 minutes later Commander Young was on the air notifying Bombing Six that targets suitable for heavy bombs were at Kwajalein anchorage. Commander Hollingsworth led Bombing Six in the SBD's first true dive-bombing attack of the war, but results were largely un-observed because of the thick smoke and flames from damaged vessels and shore installations.

Though three Japanese fighters were claimed shot down over Roi, four SBDs were lost, and Lieutenant Gallaher was designated to take command of Scouting Six.

But there was still work for the Dauntless. Large numbers of enemy bombers were based on the Taroa airfield, which had not yet been hit. Hollingsworth was back in the air for a second time that day, leading nine SBDs with orders to destroy the Japanese bombers. Lieutenant Richard Best, also of Bombing Six, led another nine-plane formation off the "Big E's" deck to handle whatever Hollingsworth missed.

He didn't miss very much. Hollingsworth led his flight down out of the sun and personally destroyed seven grounded bombers with his three bombs. The other eight SBDs wrecked hangars and more aircraft. Passing Hollingsworth's formation outbound, Best's small group had to fight its way through more Japanese fighters to reach the target. A few SBDs became embroiled in dogfights with the enemy planes, claiming two for the loss of Ensign Jack Doherty who was last seen battling three A5M Claudes.

Enterprise recovered her aircraft by 1300 and departed the area under harassment by several surviving bombers, but escaped safely. The Kwajalein raid was successful in that it resulted in the sinking of an enemy transport and heavy damage to nine other ships. Many aircraft were destroyed, and buildings and facilities were hit, in exchange for the loss of five SBDs, their crews, and two Wildcats. Objectively analyzed such raids could not affect the outcome of the war, but for the moment it was nearly all the United States could do to strike back.

The Kwajalein raid, coming less than 60 days after Pearl Harbor, set the stage for U.S. carrier operations for the next three months. *Lexington's* turn came next, in an attack on Rabaul in the Solomons on 20 February, followed four days later by *Enterprise* led by Halsey attacking Japanese-occupied Wake Island. It resulted in the destruction of large quantities of gasoline stored by the Japanese, but cost Scouting Six two SBDs and three men.

Before returning to Hawaii *Enterprise* diverted to hit Marcus Island on 4 March. *Yorktown* and *Lexington* turned up at New Guinea on the tenth, attacking Lae and Salamaua, where their SBDs helped sink a minesweeper and two 6,000-ton transports.

After returning to Pearl Harbor in early March, the Big E's air group spent over a month re-equipping and rebuilding to full strength. Scouting

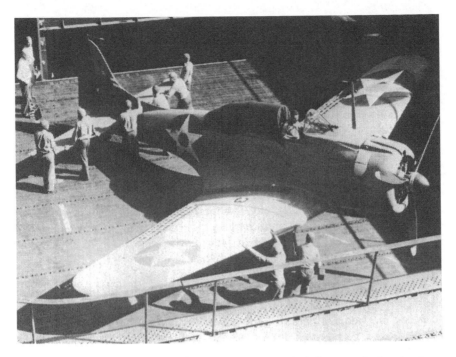

A Bombing Six SBD-3 is brought up from Enterprise's *hangar deck prior to the strike on Wake Island, 24 February 1942. (U.S. Navy)*

Six was assigned two successive batches of 18 new SBDs only to lose them after making them operational. Gallaher's squadron finally kept the third batch, but wouldn't be making the next cruise. Its place was taken by Bombing Three—one of the displaced *Saratoga* squadrons—under Lieutenant Commander Maxwell F. Leslie.

When *Enterprise* put to sea on 8 April, barely a soul on board knew her destination. Four days later she joined up with *Hornet*, newest carrier in the U.S. Navy. There was an important difference in *Hornet*'s air group, for she carried 16 Army B-25 medium bombers on her deck. Lieutenant Colonel Jimmy Doolittle, long America's number-one pilot, was going to lead the Mitchells on the first bombing raid against Japan.

The Dauntless played an important part in this dramatic event, for at 0715 on the eighteenth a Bombing Six SBD came in at low level and dropped a message notifying Halsey that a Japanese picket boat was 50 miles ahead. Even worse, the Dauntless pilot was certain he'd been sighted. Radio silence was strictly enforced, for obvious reasons, thus the information could not be called in. The discovery resulted in Doolittle's

B-25s being launched earlier than planned and threw the schedule off. Arriving over the Chinese coast in darkness, very low on fuel, all 16 Mitchell bombers were lost when their crews either bailed out or crash-landed. The few bombs dropped on Tokyo, Yokohama, and other Japanese cities caused very little real damage but the psychological and strategic impact of this small raid would be immense.

For years the Japanese public had been told the home islands were sacred and inviolate but there was no way to conceal the fact that bombs had fallen and several Americans, captured in China, were put on trial as "war criminals." And despite President Roosevelt's jaunty remark that Doolittle's planes had launched from the Shangri-La of James Hilton's novel *Lost Horizon*, the Japanese concluded the B-25s could only have come from a carrier. Clearly, the U.S. carrier force would have to be destroyed quickly, and plans were laid which would bring the remainder of the Pacific Fleet to final combat in Hawaiian waters.

The first quarter of 1942 had seen little accomplished towards the goal of redressing Japanese dominance in the Pacific. For the Dauntless it was merely a breaking-in period, as it was for many of the aviators. But the hectic period had served to provide a testing-ground for the climactic summer and fall months which would decide the ultimate course of the Pacific War. The SBD was about to enter the most critical period in its entire operational life.

Scratch one flattop.
Lieutenant Commander Robert Dixon

When Admiral Chester Nimitz, as commander in chief of the U.S. Pacific Fleet, learned through intelligence sources of Japan's intended thrust towards Australia, his carrier forces were widely scattered. Planned for early May 1942, the Japanese operation would begin with an assault on Port Moresby, the allied stronghold on New Guinea's southeastern coast. The Japanese already held most of New Guinea, and acquisition of Port Moresby would put them in position to launch operations against northern Australia, already well within air range of bases at Lae and Salamaua. A transport invasion force was assembled for the assault, and would have carrier-based air cover.

Only two American carriers were readily available, as *Enterprise* and *Hornet* were returning from the Doolittle raid and *Saratoga* was still on the West Coast undergoing repairs. Nimitz' only means of countering the threat was the two-carrier task force under Rear Admiral Frank Jack Fletcher, flying his flag in *Yorktown*. Though not a flier, Fletcher had previous experience with carriers. He had led the *Saratoga* attempt to reinforce Wake Island but had turned back, worried about his destroyers' fuel supply. The other flattop was *Lexington*, flagship for Rear Admiral Aubrey W. Fitch. An experienced naval aviator, Fitch had commanded three carriers before reaching flag rank.

Pitted against the American carriers would be two Japanese veterans of Pearl Harbor, *Shokaku* and *Zuikaku*. A third carrier, the smaller *Shoho*, would operate independently as part of the Port Moresby invasion support group.

The enemy force was still to the north when Fletcher and Fitch joined forces on 30 April. They cruised the Coral Sea for two days until it became known that the Japanese had occupied Tulagi Harbor in the Solomons and were building a seaplane base in addition to the anchorage. Left alone, Tulagi could pose a threat to U.S. naval operations in the area, situated as it was on the eastern flank of the Coral Sea. *Lexington* had a date with a refueling group but Fletcher dashed towards the southern Solomons with *Yorktown* to launch air strikes against Tulagi.

The *Yorktown* Air Group was still intact at this early stage of the war, and its four squadrons were reasonably experienced. They included Bombing Five under Lieutenant Wallace C. Short and Scouting Five under Lieutenant Commander William O. Burch. Both units had 19 SBDs, mostly dash twos, while VF-42 and VT-5 flew the usual F4F-3s and TBD-1s. Throughout the night of 3 May, as *Yorktown* approached her launch point for next morning, air staff and pilots scrambled to assemble as much data as possible on Tulagi. Almost no one had ever heard of it before, and no reliable charts or maps existed. At length somebody found an old issue of the *National Geographic* which included some dated photos of the harbor. It was about all the fliers had to go on.

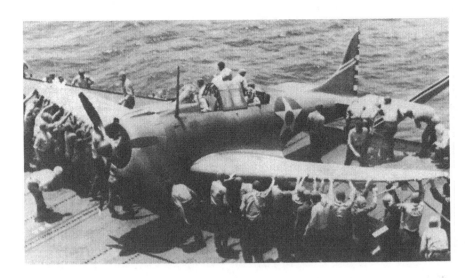

Taken aboard Yorktown *on 4 May, only three days before the Battle of the Coral Sea, this photo shows an SBD being pushed on an outrigger, allowing more aircraft to be stored on the flight deck. (Peter M. Bowers)*

Yorktown commenced launch at 0730 on 4 May, putting up 28 Dauntlesses and 12 TBDs while retaining her fighters for protection. Crossing the mountains of Guadalcanal, the carrier planes approached Tulagi from the south and found the harbor full of enemy shipping. Shortly before 0900, Burch's planes attacked what appeared to be a light cruiser with two destroyers moored alongside, but fogging of windscreens and sights prevented observation of any results. Short's 15 SBDs encountered identical problems and only two hits were claimed. Bombing Five gunners shot down a Rufe floatplane near the rendezvous point, however.

All 40 planes were safely back aboard by 1000 but a second strike was deemed necessary. Little more than an hour later Wally Short was winging north again with 14 Dauntlesses, followed separately by Burch with 13 scouting planes. By the time they arrived over the target there was no trace of enemy shipping in the harbor. But VB-5 located three vessels identified as gunboats (probably minesweepers) and left at least two sinking. Scouting Five dived on a destroyer and claimed two hits, then had a hassle with a Japanese floatplane. Burch's planes expended almost 3,000 rounds of machine gun ammunition before the two-seat Mitsubishi went down.

Though a TBD and two F4Fs had ditched during the day, no SBDs were lost. The fliers claimed a major victory, believing they had sunk 14 naval vessels. Actual Japanese losses were the destroyer *Kikutsuki*, three minesweepers, four barges, and a destroyer run aground. Five floatplanes were also destroyed, in the air and on the water. These losses were nearly inconsequential to the enemy, but served to boost morale among the fliers, who honestly thought they had dealt the Japanese a serious blow. *Yorktown* then steamed south to rejoin *Lexington*.

Two days later, on 6 May, Army B-17s found the Moresby transports and their covering group. At least there was now positive knowledge that the Japanese were on the move. It was fairly certain the next day would bring combat with Japanese carriers, and the aviators were anxious for a crack at them.

No aircraft carrier had ever fought a genuine battle against another. True, Admiral Nagumo's carrier-based dive bombers had sunk the British carrier *Hermes* in the Indian Ocean on 9 April, but that was a completely one-sided affair. *Hermes* hadn't even been carrying any planes at the time; they were all ashore on Ceylon. Whatever happened after sunup, the fliers knew, would go a long way towards proving or dispelling so many of the early carrier advocates' theories about naval aviation.

Pilots, gunners, mechanics, and plane captains worked as long as necessary to make sure everything was ready for the morning launch. In Bombing Five's readyroom aboard *Yorktown* the squadron gunnery officer, Lieutenant John J. Powers, expounded on his pet topic, a low release altitude to insure a hit.

Over on the "Lex," Lieutenant Commander Weldon Hamilton checked the status of his SBDs and noted with satisfaction that all 18 were in commission as he posted the flight assignments for the morning. Hamilton would be flying his own plane, since the deck crews had managed to spot the Dauntless with 2-B-1 on its fuselage at the head of the VB-2 formation.

Everyone in the American task force was up an hour before dawn on Thursday, 7 May, only to find the ships steaming through drenching rain under a thick overcast. But weather conditions had improved somewhat by 0645 when ten SBDs were launched to search from northwest through east to a distance of 250 miles. That was the area in which Fletcher expected the Japanese would be found. As the planes left *Yorktown*'s slippery deck, a totally new concept of war at sea commenced. In this, the first carrier battle in history, no ship of either side would even come within visual range of the enemy.

The scouts were silent as they spread out along their search patterns, probing the watery expanse of the Coral Sea for some sign of the Japanese. There was no development for nearly an hour until, at 0735, a scout reported two enemy cruisers far to the northwest of *Yorktown*. The next report came only ten minutes later when Lieutenant John Neilsen, in another search sector, came upon a cruiser floatplane which was also probably on a scouting mission. Neilsen wasted little time in shooting down the enemy snooper, nor did Ensign Lloyd Bigelow who also found a Japanese search plane. But this type of information didn't tell Fletcher what he needed to know: where were the Japanese carriers?

That information was provided by another *Yorktown* scout at 0815. The pilot reported sighting two carriers and four cruisers 180 miles to the northwest of the American task force. It had to be the Carrier Striking Force with *Shokaku* and *Zuikaku*. Enemy scouts had been shot down in the vicinity of Fletcher's force, so he proceeded on the assumption that the Japanese knew where he was. Actually they didn't at this point, for an erroneous report by an enemy scout sent 78 of Nagumo's planes well to the south to sink the U.S. oiler *Neosho* and the destroyer *Sims*.

At 0925, when the distance was down to around 175 miles from the contact, *Lexington* began launching her strike. Commander William B. Ault, a tall, fiftyish Oregonian, headed up the formation. As "Lex's" CAG he would lead her strike group with a plane from VB-2 on either wing, while Lieutenant Commander Hamilton followed with 15 more SBDs.

Lieutenant Commander Robert Dixon was next with ten scouting planes, then came ten Wildcats and finally a dozen TBDs of Torpedo Two. In all, 50 *Lexington* aircraft were climbing and circling, joining into tactical formation.

Half an hour later *Yorktown* commenced launching 43 aircraft, including 17 Scouting Five SBDs and eight of Bombing Five. One of Short's pilots, Lieutenant J. W. Rowley, almost aborted with a balky engine but at length he coaxed it into life. It took awhile for all 93 planes of the two air groups to organize, but it was accomplished by 1030 when both groups headed northwest, climbing slowly, with Commander Ault and his *Lexington* squadrons ahead of the *Yorktown* group. The only pilots remaining aboard the carriers were those on standby for Combat Air Patrol, or the unfortunate few who had not been assigned to fly on this day. Eight *Lexington* scouts stayed home for Inner Air Patrol and antitorpedo plane defense.

As the strike groups cleared the task force, the weather became increasingly better and the SBDs climbed to 15,000 feet while the torpedo planes stayed low at 4,000. It turned into a perfect day for hunting ships, with unlimited ceiling and excellent visibility. Both groups were settled on a true course of 324 degrees, headed for Tagula Island and the Japanese force which lay beyond.

Well to the north of the carrier planes, at 1022, a B-17 was flying over a group of ships identified as a carrier, ten transports, and about 15 other vessels. The news, relayed to Admiral Fletcher, prompted some speculation. Was the report accurate, and if so, was this the larger portion of the same group of ships the morning scout had reported? The Army contact placed the ships 60 miles north of the *Yorktown* scout's message. If both reports were accurate, that meant the 93-plane attack group was headed not for just two carriers, but for all three the Japanese were known to have in the Coral Sea. But Fletcher's intelligence sources told him the two big carriers, *Shokaku* and *Zuikaku*, were operating apart from the Moresby invasion group.

The puzzle was solved several minutes later when the ten morning scouts began returning to *Yorktown*. The pilot who made the carrier contact quickly reported that a serious mistake had been made; he'd found two cruisers and four destroyers, not two carriers and four cruisers as reported. In his rush to get off the report and the need to maintain a lookout for Japanese aircraft, the pilot had mismatched the sliding portions of his circular message encoding board. The error resulted in cruisers being coded as aircraft carriers and destroyers as cruisers.

Greatly relieved, *Yorktown* signaled the corrected message to the strike group, still on its way northwest at 1053. By that time the *Lexington*

Scouting Squadron Six SBDs over the Enterprise *in 1941 (U.S. Navy)*

pilots, and probably those in the *Yorktown* formation, could clearly see the islands of the Louisiades, stretching out from the eastern tip of New Guinea. Tagula Island was passed close to port shortly after *Yorktown*'s revised contact report, and a few minutes later Lieutenant Commander Hamilton, at the head of the Bombing Two formation, led his planes in a crossover turn above Scouting Two, ending up behind Bob Dixon's squadron. This was the planned procedure; the scouts would go in first when contact was made while the bombers held back to watch the progress of the attack and then pounce at the best moment.

Hamilton lifted his 7x50 binoculars and studied the horizon. He scanned across the nose of his Dauntless and continued swinging to the right when his movement stopped. There, off to starboard about 40 miles to the north, were several barely discernible wakes far below. The enemy was located.

Hamilton called out the sighting to Dixon, and the *Lexington* squadrons banked to starboard, steadily closing the distance. At 25 to 30 miles the wakes were clearly visible from 15,000 feet, and Dixon was also studying them through his glasses. The ships were about 35 miles southeast of the first contact report as Dixon radioed Lieutenant Commander James Brett, far below with the torpedo planes. But Brett was still too low to see the ships from that range and relied upon Dixon, at 12,000 feet, to direct him towards them. Within minutes the entire *Lexington* air group was pointed at the wakes.

Commander Bill Ault, out in front with his two wingmen, began a descent towards the ships in order to size up the situation. The bright morning sunshine made for excellent visibility, reflecting a polished yellow from one of the vessels below. It was the flight deck of the light carrier *Shoho*, the prime target. She was escorted by four cruisers and a destroyer, all of which were giving her ample maneuvering room, remaining at 4,000 to 6,000 yards' distance.

Ault's CAG section of three SBDs approached at 10,000 feet for its run-in to the carrier but fell afoul of one of the cruisers. The enemy gunners' first salvos bracketed Ault's planes, jarring them badly. Ault made a full-circle turn over the cruiser prior to diving on the carrier, but the escort maneuvered to keep up a heavy volume of AA fire. The CAG then peeled off to initiate the first dive an SBD would make on Japanese aircraft carriers.

The best Ault and his two young wingmen managed was a near-miss, their aim spoiled by the large amount of AA fire directed entirely at them. But 50 more dive bombers were waiting to take their turns, and first in line was Scouting Two. Lieutenant Commander Dixon began a high-speed approach of 180 knots while making a gradual let-down to pushover altitude. The ten Dauntlesses turned to the right, following their leader to a favorable attack position downwind and down-sun along the carrier's course.

As Dixon positioned his squadron at 12,500 feet immediately before reaching the pushover point, enemy opposition picked up dramatically. Orange-yellow lights began blinking along the edges of the carrier's flight deck, indicating her antiaircraft guns were joining those of the escorting cruisers. Simultaneously two Zeros began a pass at Dixon's lead section. But it was too late, as at 1105 Dixon came back on his plane's throttle, nosed up and moved the flap selecter to open all the dive brakes.

The two Zeros flashed by overhead, thrown off by the SBD's deceleration as Dixon rolled into a 70-degree dive. Other enemy fighters snapped at the rearmost Bombing Two planes, which were still approaching the diving point. But the lead SBD pilots were already lining up the carrier in their sights as they strained forward against their shoulder harnesses, hands and feet gentle on the controls while studying the target through their three-power lenses.

At the time, and for long afterward, *Shoho* was identified as "*Ryukaku*," a puzzling development as no carrier ever bore such a name, nor did any Japanese warship during World War II. But below Scouting Two's plunging Dauntlesses a Japanese carrier, regardless of her name, was making a frenzied turn to port in hope of evading the bombs which had already begun to fall. And the tactic evidently succeeded as the enemy commander, by turning his ship crosswind, greatly compounded the bombing problem. The carrier offered VS-2 a much narrower target because the SBDs were diving in from one side instead of from astern. In dive bombing, range errors always exceed deflection, especially in a brisk wind. Of the ten 500-pounders dropped by Scouting Two, only three hits were claimed, and of course it is possible that fewer were actually scored. But Dixon's pilots did reasonably well, as at least six bombs were laid close aboard for near misses, knocking five planes off *Shoho*'s flight deck.

The fourth Scouting Two Dauntless was flown by Ensign John Leppla with ARM3/c John Liska in the back seat. Two Zeros tried to follow Leppla's SBD during its dive and closed to minimum range at high speed. But Liska was ready for them and drove off both with his rear-firing .30 caliber.

While the gunner was protecting his own plane, another Zero went past with all the speed built up in a prolonged dive, since it had no speed brakes. The Zero overshot Leppla's plane and went after the number three Dauntless flown by Ensign Smith. Leppla momentarily rolled off the carrier target, sighted in on the Zero ahead of him, and triggered his two .50 calibers. As the fighter appeared to fall away Leppla rolled back into his dive on *Shoho,* released his 500-pounder and scored a near miss. The pilot and gunner claimed three Zeros in about 30 seconds.

Shoho's 12 fighters couldn't do much damage to the SBDs in their near-vertical dives but several of them tried. The Zeros attempted to compensate for their lack of dive flaps by dropping land gear and stunting to avoid overshooting the dive bombers, mostly to no avail. But after releasing their bombs and recovering from the 12,000-foot dive a few Dauntlesses ran into trouble. Scouting Two's Lieutenant Edward H. Allen, became separated from the rest of the squadron and his Two-Sail-Ten was seen shot down. Ensign A. J. Quigley, a young reservist, radioed that his Sail-Nine wasn't responding well to aileron control and that he was heading for Rossel Island "to do a stretch of beach-combing." Quigley and his gunner were rescued 18 days later.

Dixon and Scouting Two cleared the area to observe the progress of the attack, for Lieutenant Commander "Ham" Hamilton was maneuvering Bombing Two into position for the heavy blow. *Shoho* was proceeding generally northwest as the scouts approached, and Hamilton had moved to intercept her even while Dixon's pilots were in their dives.

Shoho was just completing her second evasive circle when Hamilton dived. He had a good view of the 11,000-ton carrier, noting she was maintaining a high speed and was apparently not badly damaged; he saw no smoke or flames. As he dived through 2,000 feet Hamilton had everything lined up just the way he wanted. He gripped the black-knobbed manual bomb release with his left hand and, satisfied he could do no better, gave it a good tug. The 1,000-pounder fell away from the SBD's belly, but the abrupt, jerking motion of Hamilton's left hand caused an involuntary reflex in his right hand, triggering his two .50 calibers. The instantaneous result was a fearsome vibration and rattling of the propeller. The Cyclone engine threatened to shake itself out of its mount.

Hamilton's forward-firing machine guns, normally synchronized to fire through the propeller arc, had slipped out of timing and shot holes in the propeller blades. He quickly throttled back to reduce vibration and turned for home.

There was more than adequate compensation, however, as most of the pilots saw Hamilton's bomb drill straight through *Shoho*'s flight deck, aft of amidships. The other 14 Dauntlesses, strung out in a vertical line behind Baker-One, were dropping out of the sky over the carrier. Four more direct hits were claimed, all aft and around Hamilton's, causing a great deal of smoke and flame to obscure most of the ship.

Just as the last SBDs pulled out of their dives the *Lexington* torpedo planes went in, using the voluminous smoke to cover their approach. They released their fish, claiming nine hits, and got away unharmed.

The Grumman Wildcat fighter, here in F4F-4 version, was the SBD's stable-mate during 1942–43. But the Wildcat's short range prevented it from accompanying Dauntlesses on many strike missions. (U.S. Marine Corps)

Bombing Two got off almost as easily, with only shrapnel or bullet damage to six SBDs while the gunners fought off more Zeros. One was shot down by ARM2/c F. G. Stanley in Baker-14.

Lexington's squadrons had possibly done enough damage to sink *Shoho*, but the evidence is inconclusive. At any rate, the *Yorktown* Air Group went to work about 15 minutes after Scouting Two had pushed over, and this second wave finished the job for certain. Lieutenant Commander Burch led his 16 Dauntlesses down on *Shoho* just as Torpedo Two was finishing its low-level run. Scouting Five claimed a 75 percent record, with an even dozen hits. Burch's wingman, Lieutenant Stanley Vejtasa, testified that the skipper "laid one right in the middle of her flight deck,"[1] and then put his own bomb close by. Little *Shoho* appeared smothered in a rapid succession of hits.

Finally Lieutenant Wally Short's Bombing Five piled in with eight more SBDs. Half of the pilots thought they'd hit the target, including the energetic Powers and Win Rowley, who almost hadn't gotten his engine started aboard *Yorktown*. The Bombing Five attack went so smoothly that Short was reminded of a peacetime drill. The last man down, in the fifty-third SBD, was Ensign Ben Preston. As he rolled into his dive the carrier was "burning like mad"[2] with smoke and flames almost hiding it from view. Preston continued his dive just the same and was fairly certain he'd scored a hit.

The attack was over barely 20 minutes after it began, with Torpedo Five attacking last. Lieutenant Commander Bob Dixon, still orbiting above, couldn't quite believe what he saw. The carrier apparently slid under the waves still doing about 20 knots. Exultant, Dixon broke radio silence at 1136 to report the success of the combined assault to *Lexington*: "Scratch one flattop! Dixon to carrier. Scratch one flattop!"[3] It was perhaps the first time the now-familiar term had been applied to aircraft carriers. But it was definitely the first time any Japanese warship larger than a destroyer had been sunk since the war began.

The planes of the two air groups were widely scattered in the battle area and started to reform by sections or divisions for the return flight. But some found themselves alone in the sky and had to shift for themselves. Lieutenant Win Rowley spotted a Zero and told his gunner they were going after it. The determined SBD pilot chased off the fighter but by the time he took stock of his bearings he discovered he was alone and running out of fuel. Rowley tried to raise *Yorktown* on the radio but, receiving no answer, headed for Port Moresby. He ran out of fuel and ditched offshore, then paddled to safety in the rubber life raft with his gunner.

Most of the other planes had uneventful flights back to the task force, but Leppla and Liska of Scouting Two weren't quite finished. They were halfway back to *Lexington* when a Japanese floatplane was sighted in the distance. Leppla banked towards it and closed the distance until the enemy, caught at bay, turned to fight. A stiff tussle ensued with each plane scoring hits until the Douglas got in a solid burst and the floatplane tumbled into the sea.

All but three SBDs—two from Scouting Two and one of Scouting Five—were recovered by 1340. Several others were damaged but most could be repaired. Leppla's plane, however, was a borderline case. It had 7.7 and 20-mm holes in the fuselage, tail, wings and most control surfaces but had brought its aggressive crew home. Though the SBD required a major overhaul, Leppla and Liska were ready to fly again.

Commander Hamilton of Bombing Two was also fortunate. He got the last available propeller aboard *Lexington* to replace the one he'd accidentally shot full of holes over *Shoho*.

As the morning's dismal weather returned Fletcher turned his ships south under the cover of low clouds and heavy rain squalls. All the fliers were naturally elated at their success as they recounted various incidents over a late lunch. The Dauntless crews claimed nine enemy aircraft in the course of searches and the strike, six of which were Zeros. The scout-bombers thought they had done better than the two fighter squadrons, as Fighting 42 claimed four kills during the morning and Fighting Two only a pair. In fact, close examination of Japanese records confirms no SBD victories over Zeros.

While *Shoho* had been sunk—the first of six Japanese carriers destroyed in whole or in part by SBDs over the course of the war—the actual results of the massed attack were much overestimated. Japanese evidence at the end of the war put *Shoho's* fatal damage at 13 direct bomb hits and seven torpedoes. In light of postwar knowledge, it appears the *Yorktown* squadrons did most of the damage to the light carrier.

This first attack ever made on a Japanese carrier taught some valuable lessons. Bob Dixon stated in Scouting Two's report, "The necessity of having a group commander in the air is more important than ever before." It was pointed out that all aircraft of both groups—except a plane which damaged a cruiser—had attacked *Shoho* though she was in fact sinking before the *Yorktown* strike ended. Had there been an officer in tactical control he could have diverted one or two squadrons to other targets, and a cruiser might actually have been sunk. This practice was later adopted.

It wouldn't be known for quite some time, but Fletcher's pilots had, by sinking *Shoho*, achieved Nimitz' goal for the operation: preventing the invasion of Port Moresby. Suddenly deprived of its carrier-based air cover, the transport group had no choice but to turn back and await developments.

Aviators on both carriers spent the evening of 7 May rehashing the events of the day and discussing the possibilities for tomorrow. Commander Ault and the *Lexington* squadron commanders recounted their observations of the *Shoho* strike for *Chicago Tribune* correspondent Stanley Johnston's dictaphone before turning in.

The situation was similar aboard *Yorktown*, where in Bombing Five's ready room Lieutenant Powers lectured on point-of-aim and diving technique again expounding his pet theory of a minimum release altitude to improve accuracy. Powers had pressed his dive on *Shoho* almost to the limit that morning, and had scored. He recognized the added danger from antiaircraft fire at low level, plus the hazard of recovering from a dive under 800 feet, which would expose the plane to damage from its own bomb's explosion. But results were all that mattered.

Powers closed his analysis with a short pep-talk. "Remember what they did to us at Pearl Harbor," he said. "The folks back home are counting on us. As for me, I'm going to get a hit on a Jap carrier tomorrow if I have to lay it on their flight deck."[4]

Those words would long echo in the minds of everyone who heard John Powers speak that night.

The eighth of May dawned clear and bright, with the promise of superb flying weather in the area of the American task force. *Lexington's* scouts rose with the sun to seek out the enemy the hard way, a full-circle 360-degree search. Eighteen Dauntlesses—14 from Scouting Two and four from Bombing Two—were launched at 0625 to search the northern semi-circle to 200 miles and the southern semicircle to 150 miles. Fletcher was fairly certain the Japanese carriers were somewhere to the north but couldn't afford to take any chances.

Nearly two hours passed in silence before Lieutenant (jg) J. G. Smith's voice crackled over the radio: "Contact, two enemy CV, four CAs, many DDs."[5] Smith's report informed *Lexington* he'd found two big carriers, four cruisers and several destroyers but there was a delay in transmission while he maneuvered Two-Sail-Two into a more favorable position. It required 20 minutes for Smith to get off the rest of his contact report, and part of the transmission was garbled. The relative bearing of the Japanese force was 006° True from Fletcher's position. The enemy was steaming southeasterly at about 15 knots, but the men in *Lexington*'s radio shack couldn't quite get the range Smith was reporting. All they heard was, "[static] miles from Point Zed,"[6] meaning point of launch.

It was a trying moment. Fletcher's air staff had enough information to launch a strike, though the contact could be at optimum range for heavily loaded attack planes. But there was really no choice. Fletcher had to assume the Japanese knew where he was, and ordered a launch within one minute of Smith's report. The flight decks of both carriers swarmed with the multicolored jerseys of plane handlers, catapult crews, armorers and plane captains who helped their pilots get buckled in for the launch.

Far to the north, Lieutenant Smith had a confusing problem of his own. He'd found the enemy, tracked the big carriers, and provided his ship with the critical information. But he wasn't sure *Lexington* had received his report, as there had been no acknowledgment. The usual procedure was to transmit until acknowledged, but Smith heard no reply because his radio receiver was out of commission. As soon as it became apparent two-way communications had been lost, Smith scooted for home.

Smith didn't know it, but *Lexington* wasn't the only unit trying to talk to him. His skipper, Lieutenant Commander Bob Dixon, was covering the adjoining sub-sector to the west and overheard Smith's report. He also heard *Lexington*'s repeated calls to Smith and surmised his pilot might need assistance. Dixon tried to contact Smith by radio with no luck, and relayed the contact to the ship. Then the Scouting Two CO banked to starboard and headed east to reestablish the carrier contact.

While Smith was heading home and Dixon was on the trail of the Japanese task force, *Lexington* and *Yorktown* were engaged in launching their air groups. Three of Dixon's pilots had remained aboard the "Lex" during the morning's search and were assigned to accompany Commander Ault. Hamilton's VB-2 brought the total number of dive bombers for the strike up to 22, while 12 TBDs and nine Wildcats filled out the rest of *Lexington's* group. Launch began right away, but the SBDs were starting with a handicap. There hadn't been time to top off their fuel tanks, leaving the Dauntlesses about 12 percent under full capacity.

Yorktown's strike force was of similar composition, with 39 aircraft to Ault's 43. Bombing and Scouting Five put up two dozen SBDs while Torpedo Five chipped in nine Devastators and Fletcher dispatched six fighters as escort. The *Yorktown* group departed first, leaving the task force at 0915. *Lexington's* strike was outbound ten minutes later.

On the strength of Smith's original contact and Dixon's repeat of it, the 82-plane attack group steered a true course of 025°. Estimated distance to the target was 175 miles, meaning the big enemy carriers, *Shokaku* and *Zuikaku*, were something over an hour's flight from point of launch.

This mission, the fliers knew, wouldn't be like yesterday's when over 90 U.S. planes jumped one light carrier. Fletcher had a total of 122 planes at his disposal on 8 May, compared to 121 aboard the two Japanese carriers. Today would be the main event, with two heavy fleet carriers and virtually identical air strength on both sides. Under such circumstances, luck and skill counted for about equal importance.

While his friends were winging north under clear skies, Bob Dixon was finding that the enemy's weather luck was not only holding out, but was improving. Arriving in the area of Smith's contact, the scout CO found low-lying broken cumulus clouds punctuated by dense rain showers, which made his job much more difficult. The lone Dauntless began a systematic sweep of the vicinity at low altitude but was hampered by rain and clouds which often reduced visibility to zero from sea level up to 6,000 feet. Dixon knew he'd be fortunate to find anything; it was "like looking for a deer in a forest."[7]

The blue gray SBD continued its expanding search pattern, knifing through the thinner, fluffy tendrils in its way and skirting the thicker ones. The process continued for several minutes until, as he passed over a clear spot and glanced down, Dixon was rewarded with the sight of two large carriers and two destroyers sliding into view. It was 0930 when he reestablished communications with *Lexington*: "Contact, two CV, two DD bearing 000° distance 160 miles."[8] The Japanese had maintained their southerly heading and were now steaming due south at an increased speed of 25 knots.

Dixon dropped down to 150 feet and by skillful employment of rain and clouds remained in contact for over an hour. Between ducking in and out of cloud cover and evading the heavy Zero CAP, Dixon thought he counted 14 ships; the two carriers and 12 escorts. *Shokaku* and *Zuikaku* were actually escorted by six destroyers and two cruisers.

Dixon couldn't tell just how many fighters were bent upon shooting him down, but there seemed to be dozens. He had several brushes with them and noted they weren't too aggressive. The Zeros preferred to stay at near-maximum gun range, possibly in hope of enticing Dixon's gunner into wasting ammunition. But the scout team wasn't buying any of that. With his gunner holding fire until well within range, Dixon used the SBD's fighterlike maneuverability to turn into any close attacks and confront each Zero nose-to-nose. They always broke off, possibly knowing the SBD's two forward-firing .50 calibers had more range and a higher rate of fire than the Zero's two 20-mm cannon and 7.7-mm machine guns.

Dixon remained in contact with the carriers until 1045, when his fuel situation dictated a return to *Lexington*. Way out ahead of him Lieutenant Smith was nearing the task force. Smith came upon the *Yorktown* strike and momentarily reversed course to fly alongside the lead TBD, Five-Tare-One. It was Lieutenant Commander Joe Taylor, skipper of Torpedo Five. Smith signaled the heading to the enemy's last-known position and then banked away to resume his homeward flight.

As the strike groups entered the contact area, only 15 minutes after Dixon set course for *Lexington*, they immediately encountered the same difficulty with weather. Three VF-2 Wildcats got separated from Hamilton's dive bombers and returned to the ship. Torpedo Two, at the CAG's direction, initiated a box search and attempted to maintain radio contact with Bombing Two. At this point things began to deteriorate for the *Lexington* "Minutemen." Hamilton led his squadron in a slow descent attempting to link up with Lieutenant Commander Brett's torpedo planes, but could not find them.

Several minutes later Hamilton radioed Commander Ault that unless the *Lexington* group could reorganize and gain visual contact with the enemy carriers, Bombing Two would have to head for home. That 12 percent fuel deficiency was making itself felt; most of the Dauntlesses on the strike were SBD-2s and they were really missing those 35 gallons. Shortly after Hamilton's call Commander Ault responded that his four-plane CAG section had the carriers in sight, off to port.

Hamilton took Bombing Two down to only 1,000 feet, maneuvering in and out of rain squalls in a desperate effort to find the enemy. *Lexington*'s dive bombers could hear the torpedo pilots preparing to attack, which only heightened their own sense of frustration. Sick at heart, Hamilton finally had to give up and turn around. Twenty minutes later he ordered his pilots to jettison their 1,000-pound bombs to further reduce fuel consumption. They continued the trip in gloomy silence.

Yorktown's dive bombers had better luck than Hamilton's, for they were in the first group this time and arrived before the Japanese ships began taking evasive action. Lieutenant Commander Burch, leading seven VS-5 Dauntlesses, peered over the side of his cockpit at 1032 and saw two big flattops 17,000 feet below.

Burch wanted to coordinate his attack with Torpedo Five but the sluggish TBDs were still some distance away. The SBDs made a couple of circuits to organize into attack formation, but by the time they were ready to push over only one carrier was still in sight. *Zuikaku* had raced for the cover of some nearby clouds. That did it—Burch wasn't waiting for *Shokaku* to elude him, too.

But before all the Dauntlesses could dive, several Zeros with their rocketlike rate of climb scrambled up to their altitude and were upon them in an instant. The fighters struck just as Burch had split his flaps and was nosing into his near-vertical descent, and the gunners fought them all the way down. Every one of the seven SBDs was hit, five in their fuel tanks, but the self-sealing rubber liners performed as advertised, preventing loss of gasoline and possible fire. Scouting Five gave better than it took, though, claiming four fighters shot down during the dive on *Shokaku*.

But Burch's pilots were dismayed to find they couldn't get a proper view of the big carrier. With so much moisture in the air and a fairly rapid descent, windscreens and sights fogged over with condensation. The results were predictable and disappointing: no hits. Even worse, Ensign J. H. Jorgenson had to ditch his heavily damaged plane after a hassle with more Zeros. A destroyer later rescued him with his gunner.

Yorktown's first wave made no hits but Bombing Five was still to be heard from, as Wally Short's 17 SBDs were only minutes behind the scouts. They were so close that Short reined in his planes to execute a 360-degree overhead to size up the situation before diving. As Short's Dauntlesses came around full circle, the gunners blazing away at still more Zeros, they were ready to push over. The SBDs probably knocked down five Zeros during the approach and attack, but were much more concerned with the long, narrow flight deck now fully in view.

Once in their dives, Short's pilots were generally free of fighter attack, allowing them to concentrate on their bombing. But they fared only slightly better than Scouting Five; just one hit of the first dozen bombs dropped. The fourteenth plane was flown by Lieutenant Powers, the squadron's gunnery officer who had vowed to "lay it on their flight deck" if necessary. The last three pilots in line—Guest, Preston, and McDowell— had a good view of Powers' Dauntless as it was hit repeatedly by AA fire, throwing it off course. But John Powers was a determined individual, and though he radioed he and his gunner were wounded, he rolled the

The Japanese carrier Shokaku *under dive-bombing attack on 8 May 1942 at Coral Sea.* Yorktown *and* Lexington *Dauntlesses hit her with four bombs, thus crippling her for action in the Midway operation. (U.S. Navy)*

SBD back on target and continued his dive. The plane was afire as it plunged through 2,000 feet, the normal release altitude, but there was no indication of release or pullout. Bombing Five's tail-end pilots watched intently from above, still in their own dives, as Powers continued his descent through 1,500 feet, then 1,000 and incredibly stayed with it at 500. They didn't see how he could possibly pull out.

At the point-blank distance of under 300 feet Powers dropped his heavy bomb. The 1,000-pounder splintered *Shokaku's* flight deck perhaps two seconds before the mortally wounded SBD crashed into the Coral Sea. Powers' friends hoped he'd known at the last second that he'd gotten his hit. One of them said, "He just decided he wasn't going to miss. And he didn't, God bless him."[9]

Shokaku was afire on the forward portion of her flight deck from the two hits as *Yorktown's* dive bombers cleared out, hightailing it to the northwest and the cover of a thick cloud bank. Lieutenant Commander Taylor's TBDs had a go at the stricken carrier but all their torpedoes missed, ran wild, or failed to detonate.

Only 21 *Lexington* aircraft contacted the enemy: 11 TBDs, six Wildcats and four SBDs. It was only half of the 43 planes launched, and three of the F4Fs were shot down protecting the torpedo planes. The other Wildcats became engaged in a running dogfight with the seemingly omnipresent Zeros.

For nearly 15 minutes the *Lexington* torpedo planes flew an ever-expanding square search pattern under a relatively low ceiling with Commander Bill Ault's four Dauntlesses overhead at 5,500 feet. Ault finally called out a carrier off to port, 15 miles away. This was the call Hamilton had heard just before reluctantly breaking off the hunt as fuel gauges were registering near the danger point. The CAG had found *Shokaku*, still licking her wounds after Bombing Five's attack.

Lieutenant Commander Brett's torpedo planes turned in for their approach, passing over one of two escorting cruisers while Ault's four SBDs nosed into their dives in an attempt to cover the torpedo attack. It was 1136—precisely 24 hours after *Shoho* had gone under—as the TBDs headed towards the water from 3,500 feet and Ault's section rolled in on the target from above. The Japanese gunners were preoccupied with the lumbering Devastators and may not have even known dive bombers were overhead. At any rate, Ault's planes were unopposed as they swooped down on the smoking *Shokaku*. Ault and Ensign Harry Wood both claimed hits, but Ensign John Wingfield's bomb did not release in the dive. After pullout the four Dauntlesses were climbing back to altitude for the return flight when Wingfield was notified his 1,000-pounder was still in place. He immediately turned out of formation and headed back to the enemy carrier but his plane was never seen again.

Brett's torpedo attack had been as unsuccessful as Taylor's, even though VT-2 claimed five hits. The 11 TBDs regrouped and headed for *Lexington* when another large group of Zeros appeared. Torpedo Two's gunners claimed two shot down and chased the others off.

But it was much tougher for the SBDs. A large group of fighters, estimated at 20, pounced upon Ault and the two Wildcats escorting his flight. Both F4Fs were shot down, striving to protect the group commander. Nobody knows for certain what happened in the combat which followed, but apparently the SBDs fought off the attack. Ensign Wood in Two-Sail-Five radioed that he was heading for the nearest point of land. Then Ault reported his gunner was badly wounded, himself hit in an arm and a leg, and he was going to try to ditch his damaged plane. That was the last anyone heard from him. Only one of the four SBDs returned to *Lexington*, but Wood eventually made it to Tagula Island.

Ault's planes had made one solid hit on *Shokaku*, which combined with the two by Bombing Five put her out of the battle. She could neither launch nor recover aircraft with her flight deck badly damaged, and *Zuikaku* assumed full responsibility for carrying on the fight. But it mattered relatively little, for both Japanese air groups were then en route to

Fletcher's carriers, steaming under perfectly clear skies with no weather to hide in.

While the strike groups were away, eight of *Lexington*'s scouts had returned from the early search and were launched to provide additional protection from Japanese torpedo planes. When the 90-plane enemy attack opened at 1118, 23 SBDs without bombs were airborne to augment the 17 Wildcats Fletcher had retained for CAP. The F4Fs would presumably handle the Zeros and Vals while the Dauntlesses were to prevent torpedo planes from getting close enough to take aim on either carrier. This theory was a holdover from prewar days, but it was based upon the assumption that Japanese torpedo planes were of similar performance to the Douglas TBD. Nothing could have been further from the truth. The Nakajima B5N—"Kate" to the Americans—was the best in the world for its specific role. Not only did the Japanese possess a far better aircraft, but their torpedoes were much superior to the U.S. Navy's.

American torpedo pilots had to limit their attacks to 110 knots and 100 feet above the water before releasing their fish. These limitations imposed upon the carrier-based torpedo squadrons made it exceptionally difficult to deliver an effective attack against a well-defended task force. The Imperial Navy labored under no such restrictions, as the SBD pilots were about to discover.

Lieutenant Roger Woodhull spread his eight scouts by sections at 2,000 feet altitude some 6,000 yards from *Yorktown* in anticipation of low-level attacks. But the Dauntless pilots were astonished when a squadron of 18 Kates swept directly overhead at 5,000 feet, straight towards *Yorktown* at 180 knots. The Japanese expertly split their formation and came in on both bows of the carrier, some of them at 500 feet. As the deadly, efficient "Long Lance" torpedoes plunged into the water and streaked for *Yorktown*'s hull, it was painfully apparent the enemy's strike capability significantly exceeded the U.S. Navy's. None of Woodhull's pilots or gunners were able to get a shot at the swift Kates, which attacked unhindered.

Captain Elliot Buckmaster's skillful shiphandling effectively neutralized the well-executed torpedo attack as the 19,000-ton carrier dodged all the fish which came her way, though she was hit by a bomb which damaged several compartments. But Woodhull's pilots were now beset by the escorting Zeros. Two Dauntlesses were shot down almost immediately, leaving six to fend for themselves in the midst of all 18 enemy fighters.

Leading the second division of Woodhull's flight was Lieutenant "Swede" Vejtasa who had put his bomb through *Shoho*'s flight deck 24 hours before. He lost contact with the other SBDs and found himself the center of attraction for eight of the enemy fighters. He shoved throttle, mixture and RPM controls to the firewall and told his gunner to "keep your head and conserve ammunition."[10] It was the beginning of an epic 40-minute exercise in survival.

Vejtasa would later recall that he never felt so alone in his life, knowing it was a fight to the finish. He handled his dive bomber aggressively, always turning into each attack. He triggered his guns in short, economical bursts to obtain maximum results with minimum expenditure of ammunition. With his gunner protecting his tail, utilizing the SBDs responsive handling qualities, Vejtasa fought three Zeroes during the course of his wavetop struggle. His Dauntless received several hits, one of which drove a piece of metal into his leg, but Vejtasa never let up. When it was all over, only three other *Yorktown* SBDs were still in the air. One of them claimed a Zero, too; so four SBDs had been shot down, claiming an equal number of enemy fighters destroyed.

Lexington's scouts also tangled with Japanese aircraft in a similar low-level combat which resulted in a claim of eleven for the loss of three SBDs. Back hunting "meatballs" was the tireless team of Lieutenant John Leppla and his gunner, John Liska. Unable to engage the Kates which put two torpedoes into *Lexington,* they became entangled with a flock of Zeros. Leppla boresighted one and hit it right off. Then, emulating Vejtasa's aggressive tactics in the midst of an undetermined number of Zeros, he attacked another one. But Leppla's plane was heavily damaged, and he broke off with one of his .50 calibers inoperable and the other out of ammunition. The Dauntless was nursing its way back to the "Lex" when a pair of Zeros dropped down, evidently anticipating an easy kill. But Liska saw them coming, knowing his .30 caliber was the only remaining means of defense. He stitched one Zero which turned away trailing a plume of smoke, and its companion withdrew.

Lieutenant (jg) William E. Hall was one of the few scout pilots who came to grips with the Kates, dropping two out of a formation of nine. He was coming around for another pass when five Zeros bounced him. He had no choice but to accept combat, for the fighters were much faster, in addition to having an altitude and numerical advantage.

With throttles against the stops and wings vertical in mind-blurring high-G turns, the six planes chased tails for an eternity. Hall momentarily gained enough deflection on a Zero to squeeze off a burst which seemed to career into the water. The Dauntless was also taking hits, and Hall received painful, disabling wounds to both feet. But there was no opportunity to disengage so he persisted, trying to bring the four-to-one odds down a bit more in his favor. Moments later he got another chance and put a solid burst into a second Zero which he thought went

Lieutenant (jg) William E. Hall receives the Medal of Honor for his defense of Lexington *in the Battle of the Coral Sea. (U.S. Navy)*

down; there was no time to watch it fall. But the remaining three had had enough of the lone dive bomber and, Hall related, they "escaped into a cloud."[11]

There was no guarantee the battered Two-Sail-Eight could stagger back to *Lexington,* and even if it did Hall wasn't sure he could land safely. But the wounded pilot and the crippled Dauntless made it, though the SBD was so badly shot up that it was beyond salvaging, and was pushed overboard.

Another Scouting Two SBD, flown by Lieutenant (jg) C. W. Swanson, suffered the same fate. Swanson barely managed a landing aboard *Lexington* with his gunner dead and rudder controls severed. This plane, Sail-Sixteen, was also pushed overboard.

Remarkably, only one *Lexington* Dauntless had been shot down. Lieutenant (jg) R. O. Hale and his gunner failed to return.

Six VB-2 aircraft were also involved in the defense of *Lexington*, claiming two victories. Lieutenant (jg) R. B. Buchanan, in Lieutenant Commander Hamilton's plane, shot down a Kate after it had dropped its torpedo. Another pilot bagged a Val after it pulled out of its dive. But Two-Baker-Thirteen, flown by Ensign R. R. McDonald, came to grief while attempting to land aboard. McDonald had been wounded in the right shoulder, thus impairing his stick hand. *Lexington* was listing to port from the two torpedoes she'd taken, and McDonald's plane hit the deck at an odd angle. His arresting hook engaged the number two wire, which snapped under the strain, and Two-Baker-Thirteen cartwheeled across the flight deck, plunging off the port side into the water. McDonald suffered a broken arm in the crash but he and his gunner were rescued by the destroyer *Morris*.

In the carrier's ready room, intelligence officers were digesting the pilots' accounts of the hectic and confusing day's activities. SBDs had done the only damage inflicted on *Shokaku*, though many torpedo hits were claimed at the time. The last pilots who saw the big carrier said she was settling fast, and she was presumed sunk. Actually, the three bomb hits had wrecked her flight deck and she turned out of the battle, taking course for Japan.

Dauntlesses had shown they could survive fighter opposition, though their claims were exaggerated in the normal confusion of combat. The SBD squadrons thought they shot down nine Zeros during the strike and six more while defending the task force, losing six of their number to the Mitsubishis. Ten Kates and a Val were also claimed by the SBDs. In fact, it appears unlikely that any Zeros were destroyed by scout-bombers at Coral Sea. During the strike against the U.S. carriers, only one of the 18 Zeros was lost. Dauntlesses did knock down a Val and four Kates, however, while F4Fs splashed four more hostiles. But the Japanese claimed 19 SBDs and 36 Wildcats!

On the other hand, three Dauntlesses went down on 7 May and 13 had been lost on the eighth; six from *Yorktown* and seven from *Lexington*.

But all thoughts of score-keeping ended at 1247 when the first of several internal explosions erupted within *Lexington*'s hull, caused by gas vapors escaping from a fractured fuel line. The big carrier continued air operations, recovering her strike, but a second major explosion occurred at 1445. Thirty minutes later flight operations ceased, and at 1630 that afternoon she was dead in the water. Captain Sherman ordered preparations to abandon ship.

Most of the crew eventually watched from the decks of other ships that night as the 14-year-old, 33,000-ton carrier settled on an even keel.

The carrier Lexington's *last hours. Ruptured fuel lines caused internal explosions in CV-2 after the Japanese air strike on 8 May 1942, TBDs, F4Fs, and SBDs are still on the flight deck. (U.S. Navy)*

She took 36 planes, half her air group, to the bottom—14 SBDs, 13 TBDs, and nine F4Fs. Five of Bombing Two's Dauntlesses had landed aboard *Yorktown* and were saved.

For the next two days *Yorktown* steamed southwards with a full deckload of aircraft armed and fueled. "We were running scared, if the truth were told,"[12] said VB-5 skipper Wally Short. It was not known how closely the Japanese might be pursuing, and the Bombing Five crews almost lived in their aircraft between dawn and dusk. In the event an enemy force had been sighted the dive bombers were to be considered expendable as long as they got enough hits to slow down the Japanese, allowing *Yorktown* to escape. Happily, the enemy had also withdrawn from the Coral Sea.

So ended the most radically different naval engagement ever fought. The Japanese had "scored more points" by sinking *Lexington* in exchange for the much smaller *Shoho*, but were foiled in their attempt to invade Port Moresby. The world's first carrier duel demonstrated how terribly high the attrition could be in this new form of sea combat. Fletcher lost half of the aircraft at his disposal on the morning of 7 May and the Japanese aircraft losses amounted to about two-thirds. Enemy aircrew casualties were also significantly higher.

The Dauntless had come through its first fleet engagement with a good record, but one it would surpass. The overall bombing accuracy for the two-day clash was very near 20 percent—16 direct hits for the 80-some bombs dropped on two carriers by the four SBD squadrons.

Two Dauntless pilots were awarded the Congressional Medal of Honor for their part in the battle. A posthumous award went to Lieutenant John Powers of Bombing Five who demonstrated in tragic, convincing form that his minimum-altitude release technique really worked. The other Medal went to Lieutenant (jg) Hall of Scouting Two, in appreciation of his singlehanded effort in spite of serious wounds, a damaged aircraft, and greatly superior enemy strength.

Lieutenant Wally Short was also recommended for the Medal of Honor, and though he did not receive it he was much too professional to let it bother him. He believed that if anyone should receive decorations it should be the reservists, "because the rest of us were just doing what we were paid to do."[13]

Another SBD pilot honored by the Navy in a different way was *Lexington's* Air Group Commander, Bill Ault. The new Whidbey Island Naval Air Station at Oak Harbor, Washington, was christened Ault Field later that year. Still later, the Navy honored Ault and Powers by naming a destroyer after each of them.

Yorktown was recalled almost immediately to Pearl Harbor for repair of her bomb damage, as a monumental crisis was shaping up in mid-Pacific. Dauntlesses had played a major part in foiling the Japanese expedition against Port Moresby, but their role in contesting Japan's new expedition would be absolutely crucial.

One of the few, the immortal names, that
were born not to die.

Fitzgreen Halleck
Marco Bozzaris

Yorktown entered Pearl Harbor's dry dock on the morning of 27 May, having flown off her aircraft to NAS Kaneohe. But she wouldn't be there long, as Admiral Nimitz said she had to leave in less than three days. And though her scout, torpedo and fighter squadrons were going ashore, Bombing Five under the energetic Lieutenant Wally Short would be going out again almost immediately—just as soon as 1,400 workmen could effect such repairs of the Coral Sea bomb damage as were possible in about 60 hours. At the end of that time *Yorktown* would put back to sea and take aboard VB-5 as part of a new air group.

Commander Murr E. Arnold, *Yorktown's* air officer, explained the reasons behind the seemingly arbitrary move: "First, we had been at sea for some 105 days and the air group was dead tired. Second, we had lost several pilots and aircrew at Coral Sea so individual replacement would have been necessary. Third, and probably most important, a lot of the remaining planes on board with Air Group Five needed replacement. Time could not have permitted drawing new planes and checking them out. So we took VB-5 because only one spare dive-bombing outfit was available. This decision was made by ComAirPac. We on *Yorktown* had nothing to say about it."[1]

About ten of VB-5's SBDs still remained operational but a similar number had to be drawn from the fleet aircraft pool and made combat-ready. As Arnold said, it was a time-consuming job and pilots worked with the mechanics almost around the clock to get the job done.

Short's problems with getting his new pilots operational were even more complicated than readying the new Dauntlesses. Ten veteran pilots stayed on, but almost none of the eight fresh replacements were qualified for carrier landings. They had been drawn from the *Saratoga* air group but since "Sara" was still on the West Coast having her January torpedo damage repaired, her squadrons had not operated together since then. New arrivals consequently hadn't done much flying at all.

The balance of *Yorktown's* new air group also came from *Saratoga*, but at least they were generally more current than the VB-5 replacements. To Commander Arnold, Torpedo Three and Fighting Three looked "raring to go," but no extra scout squadron was available. Instead, Bombing Three under the capable direction of Lieutenant Commander Maxwell F. Leslie was chosen.

Max Leslie was possibly the most experienced aviator in the U.S. task force. He had won his wings in 1929 and reported aboard the battleship *Oklahoma* as an observation pilot. He subsequently flew patrol planes and fighters before converting to dive bombers, and had logged something over 4,600 hours as a naval aviator. Leslie and Bombing Three had replaced Scouting Six aboard *Enterprise* for the Doolittle raid in April, when the "Big E" escorted *Hornet*.

When *Yorktown* sortied from Pearl Harbor on 30 May she was probably the most hastily organized fighting unit the U.S. Navy would put together during the entire war. She had two bombing squadrons, no scouts, a mixed fighter unit and a torpedo squadron which hadn't flown from a carrier in months. The level of proficiency among the pilots ranged from highly experienced squadron commanders like Short and Leslie to the young replacements who had never landed on a carrier. Short's youngsters had been drilled in practice landing by *Yorktown*'s landing signal officer ashore, but their real training began when Bombing Five rendezvoused with the ship. Though nearly half the VB-5 pilots were making their first deck landings they all got aboard safely.

Bombing Five lost more than a uniformly high level of combat readiness, however; it also lost its identity. A couple of days out of Pearl Harbor the *Yorktown* staff became aware of the problems contingent upon having two bombing squadrons aboard. Loudspeaker announcements such as "Bomber pilots to the ready room," or "Spot bombers for launch," were confusing. Whose squadron was involved—Leslie's or Short's?

Therefore, on 1 June Bombing Five was redesignated Scouting Five for the duration of the cruise. Leslie's Bombing Three had more collective experience working as a unit while Short's pilots were more sharply divided between old hands and young fledglings. It would be easier for them to undertake scouting duties than to jump headlong as a dive-bomber outfit into whatever they would encounter on this hastily organized expedition.

In their most ambitious operation yet undertaken, the Japanese intended to occupy tiny Midway atoll, some 1,140 miles northwest of Pearl Harbor. Less than two hundred miles east of the International Date Line, Midway loomed large on military maps because of its strategic position. Admiral Isoroku Yamamoto's thrust at Midway forced Nimitz into battle, lest the Japanese gain a major foothold in the Hawaiian Islands. True, they would have a very long supply line to Midway, even from their advance base in the Marshalls. But the distance from Kwajalein to Midway was less than from Oahu to San Francisco.

Yamamoto assigned all his available carriers to the operation, accompanied by every Japanese battleship and a majority of the heavy cruisers. But the overall plan contained an important flaw. The enemy forces were dispersed in two main units: one as a diversion towards the Aleutians and one as the main thrust at Midway.

The Japanese disposition thus reduced the odds Nimitz would have to contend with at Midway, but those odds were still plenty long. Nearly a hundred Japanese vessels were assigned to the main area of operations, outnumbering the Americans four to one. Only in air strength were the numbers near equal: four Japanese carriers to three American, plus U.S. land-based air power on Midway itself.

But the Japanese carrier commander, Vice Admiral Chuichi Nagumo, felt he had all the strength he needed with four fleet carriers, two battleships, three cruisers and 12 destroyers directly under his control. This was the force Rear Admirals Frank Jack Fletcher and Raymond A. Spruance would have to face.

But Fletcher, in tactical control of the U.S. carriers with his flag in *Yorktown*, and Spruance with *Enterprise* and *Hornet*, had the invaluable advantage of prior knowledge of the enemy's plans. Nimitz' exceptional intelligence staff had monitored most of the Japanese communications about the Midway operation and deciphered the important parts. Spruance, operating as Task Force 16, and Fletcher with Task Force 17 would wait north of Midway for the Japanese to come within range, then hopefully take them by surprise in what amounted to "one of the biggest ambushes in history."

Unlike *Yorktown*'s mismatched air group, *Enterprise* and *Hornet* operated the units they'd had since joining the fleet. Aboard the "Big E," Bombing Six was led by Lieutenant Richard H. Best, the only pilot in his squadron who'd made more than one wartime cruise in carriers. The same went for Lieutenant Wilmer Earl Gallaher, who had taken over Scouting Six after Lieutenant Commander Halstead Hopping had been killed in early February. Lieutenant Commander Clarence Wade McClusky, a former fighter pilot, was the new *Enterprise* Air Group Commander. In order to perform his new duties McClusky had traded in his Wildcat for a Dauntless, but had little time to assimilate dive-bomber doctrine.

Hornet's air group had never been in combat but the unit was more or less used to working and flying together. Bombing Eight was led by Lieutenant Commander Robert R. Johnson and Scouting Eight's skipper was Lieutenant Commander Walter F. Rodee. The CAG, also SBD-equipped, was Commander Stanhope C. Ring.

In all, 112 Dauntlesses were assigned to the three carriers, most of them being new dash threes. But Bombing Eight had a selection of SBD-1s, -2s and -3s, and Scouting Eight had a number of dash twos. In fact, Rodee's squadron had embarked with only 17 aircraft because Lieutenant W. J. Widhelm couldn't get his engine started when Scouting Eight departed Ewa. But he had managed to scramble aboard *Hornet* before she departed with *Enterprise* on 28 May. *Hornet*'s Dauntlesses were further reduced the next day when a scout failed to return from a

Lieutenant Commander C. W. McClusky receives the Distinguished Flying Cross from Admiral Nimitz in early 1942. At Midway, McClusky's tenacious pursuit of the Japanese carriers was instrumental in deciding the battle. (U.S. Navy)

routine patrol. Therefore, 110 SBDs were available to Spruance and Fletcher immediately prior to reaching the Midway area.

Though Admiral Nimitz could count on a total of over 230 carrier planes, Midway itself served as an "unsinkable carrier" which would be packed to capacity with well over a hundred Army, Navy, and Marine aircraft. New planes and pilots for Midway's garrison air force, Marine Air Group 22, had arrived on 26 May, though the pilots were considerably newer than the planes. The 19 second lieutenants were almost directly out of flight training with an average of around 250 hours flying time. Like Wally Short's replacements, these young Marines and their rear-seat men would literally receive on-the-job training.

There was reason for some optimism, however, for arriving with the new fliers were 19 SBD-2s to augment the 21 SB2Us already on hand. The senior Marine aviator, Lieutenant Colonel Ira L. Kimes, determined that the Dauntlesses could be more profitably employed by his few seasoned pilots and therefore relegated most of the newcomers to the old Vindicators. But even as the replacement pilots landed on Midway they were blissfully ignorant of their purpose there. Some of them thought, quite logically, they had seen sent to such a desolate place for dive-bomber training.

Called together for an introduction and briefing, the pilots were very quickly informed of the desperate situation in which they found themselves. Major Lofton "Joe" Henderson would command the reinforced scout-bomber squadron, designated VMSB-241, and he explanied that the young fliers' newly acquired skills would very shortly be put to the test.

Early in the morning of 3 June one of Midway's 32 PBY patrol planes spotted the Japanese transports some seven hundred miles west of the atoll. Though Nagumo's Carrier Striking Force remained undetected, by evening it was clear that the next morning would bring combat. *York-town* would provide the scouts in the form of Wally Short's Scouting (nee Bombing) Five, and orders were posted delegating Ensigns Richey, Gibson and Bridgers to make sure the others were up 40 minutes before flight quarters sounded in the pre-dawn darkness.

Another member of the squadron with a special, though self-imposed duty, was Short's plane captain, Howard W. Johnson. Not being able to fly in combat with his aircraft or commanding officer, Johnson nevertheless had an equity in each flight to the extent of a twenty-dollar bill stashed in the plane.

The pilots sat in their comfortable ready-room chairs, upright or reclining as suited their individual tastes, just waiting. Their plotting boards were filled in with weather and basic navigational data, but by 0500 the most important bit of information—location of the Japanese carriers—was still lacking. Most of the fliers had been up since 0130 Midway time for an extra-early breakfast and many were restless, anxious to get going.

The Task Force 16 crews had to stay in their ready rooms, but Wally Short's scouts were already airborne. *Yorktown* had launched ten SBDs at 0430 to conduct a full hemisphere search over the northern perimeter, west to east. Short's pilots had orders to fly outbound a hundred miles on the possibility the enemy fleet was coming from the north instead of the west, as expected. The long-range PBY Catalinas were responsible for searching the western quadrant, and most ships were tuned in to the PBY frequency. Short's pilots discovered the Japanese were in the area, as they contacted a few scouting floatplanes. Ensign Ben Preston got mixed up with one, but to no conclusion.

Shortly past 0600 a delayed PBY report was handed to Admiral Fletcher on *Yorktown*'s bridge. Thirty minutes previously a Catalina had gained visual contact with a force of Japanese carriers. Little more than ten minutes passed before the patrol plane had amplified its report further: two carriers and many escorts were heading southeast, towards Midway, making 25 knots.

Fletcher was fairly certain from advance intelligence data that more than two carriers would be opposing him, but at least he had the vital position report. He directed Spruance to immediately proceed southwest with *Enterprise* and *Hornet* while *Yorktown* stood by to recover her scouts.

The defenders of Midway were allowed to "sleep in" later than their counterparts at sea; reveille didn't sound until 0300. But less than an hour later all the aircrews were in their planes, ready to go. They sat like that until 0530 when the PBY contact report was picked up and the order was given to start engines. At length the enemy task force was known to be on the way.

It wasn't much longer before those on Midway knew Japanese aircraft were headed in, too. The first warning was a radar blip picked up a little before 0600. Nagumo's four carriers had launched 108 planes, bent on leveling Midway prior to invasion. An officer ran around to each squadron and formation leader with takeoff orders. Shouting to make himself understood over the noise of so many engines he yelled, "Attack enemy carriers. Distance 180 miles, bearing 320."[2] The Japanese task force was steaming straight for Midway at 25 knots.

Taking off immediately behind the Marine fighters, the hodge-podge Midway strike group headed out. It included ten Navy and Army planes in the first wave—six brand new Grumman Avenger torpedo planes and four Martin B-26s—which were the first to attack Nagumo's force. One

TBF and two Marauders returned. VMSB-241 had 27 aircraft in the air, which rendezvoused 20 miles east of the atoll: 16 SBDs under Major Henderson and 11 Vindicators led by Major Norris. Only three of the Dauntless pilots had any appreciable experience in SBDs, so Captain Richard Fleming was assigned as navigator for the lead group. Very few of the Marines were as yet familiar with long, over-water flights.

Heading northwest at 9,000 feet, the SBD crews got their first glimpse of the Japanese fleet at 0755. Making his orders as simple as possible, Major Henderson merely said, "Attack the two enemy CV on the port bow."[3]

With that, Henderson started a spiraling descent towards 4,000 feet when Fleming shouted the first warning. Simultaneously a Zero rocketed vertically past the lead Dauntless, firing as it climbed. The Japanese CAP had found the Marine formation and was wasting no time intercepting. Heavy and accurate antiaircraft fire also beset the 16 SBDs. The hoped-for element of surprise was completely lost.

Joe Henderson's plane was soon afire along the trailing edge of its port wing but he somehow held onto the lead position through repeated attacks by the numerous Zeros. Continuing the prolonged glide was too much, however, as the lead dive bomber rolled over and fell into the sea. Shortly afterwards another SBD went down but at least one parachute was observed this time. Realizing the entire formation would probably be decimated at this rate, Captain Elmer Glidden moved into the lead and headed towards a cloud layer for temporary protection.

The pack of Zeros followed along, anticipating the Marines' intentions, shooting the SBDs full of holes. But the gunners were not entirely amateurs, and kept some of the Japanese fighters at bay. Lieutenant Moore's gunner, Private Huber, had a jam in his machine gun, leaving the plane defenseless. But Huber continued to track the Zeros with such a show of determination that they stayed out of range.

Another rear-seat man, PFC Reed Ramsey in Lieutenant Rollow's Dauntless, used deception instead of bluff. Noting that the Zeros preferred to attack when the gunners were reloading, Ramsey tossed a beer can out of his cockpit and foxed one fighter into thinking it was an empty ammunition box. He thereby suckered the Japanese into close range and waited until he couldn't miss. It is not known whether Ramsey's beer can was full or empty.

Glidden emerged from the cloud base at 2,000 feet to find a pair of Japanese carriers right below, heavily escorted by destroyers. The ten remaining Dauntlesses pushed their vulnerable glides to point-blank range before releasing—nearly all dropped at 500 feet or lower. Then, hounded by the persistent Zeros, the SBDs flattened out as low on the water as they dared and sped from the scene at full throttle. Glancing back over his shoulder, Glidden thought he saw two direct hits and a near-miss on the carrier he'd attacked. But suddenly he was too busy for sight-seeing; he was chased 40 miles by angry fighters.

Though only half of VMSB-241's 16 Dauntlesses returned to Midway, they were convinced they'd scored three hits and two near misses on one of the big carriers. In reality they had dived on *Hiryu*, one of the smaller carriers, and laid five bombs close aboard but inflicted no major damage.

Major Norris fared no better, losing four Vindicators while claiming one hit on a battleship. Thirty-seven aircraft—six TBFs, four B-26s, 16 SBDs and 11 SB2Us—had attacked the Carrier Striking Force, losing 19 of their number, but were unrewarded with a single hit.

Over 60 planes were ranged on the "Big E's" flight deck, a maximum-effort strike. There were 36 Dauntlesses among Bombing Six, Scouting Six, and Lieutenant Commander McClusky's three-plane CAG section. Flying as McClusky's wingmen would be two VS-6 ensigns, Bill Pittman and Dick Jaccard.

Scouting Six would be led by its skipper, Lieutenant Earl Gallaher, with Clarence Dickinson and Charles Ware leading the second and third divisions. Likewise, Lieutenant Dick Best was spotted at the head of Bombing Six, while a lieutenant (jg) named Van Buren took the second division and Lieutenant J. R. Penland led the third. As *Enterprise* swung into the wind at 0700 Midway time to begin launching her strike, all aircraft engines were warming up, props ticking over, pilots checking their instruments. Three Bombing Six planes which wouldn't start were struck below.

Wade McClusky ran up the engine in the lead dive bomber, checked his gauges once more, then released his brakes and was rolling down the deck, gaining flying speed. One by one the other 32 SBDs were launched and began climbing as they formed into sections, divisions, and squadrons.

McClusky had cleared the flight deck at 0706 but half an hour later, with his two SBD squadrons tucked in tight behind him, the TBDs and F4Fs still hadn't launched. From where the CAG sat it appeared as if flight operations had shut down because of some kind of maddening delay. All the while the SBDs circled overhead, burning valuable fuel.

In Scouting Eight's ready room Lieutenant Gus Widhelm, one of *Hornet*'s more vocal aviators, perked up when the command to man the planes came through. "Widhelm is ready," he announced in what would become his battle cry, "now prepare the Japs." He was one of 35 pilots who would fly *Hornet*'s strike under the CAG, Commander Stanhope C. Ring. As the senior Task Force 16 pilot on the mission, Ring would normally command both *Hornet* and *Enterprise* strikes, but there were no plans for coordinating the two. The operation was too hastily organized for such things.

Ring was perhaps the most colorful air group commander in the Pacific, being well known for his immaculately tailored dress uniforms and decidedly British mannerisms. A Bombing Eight pilot, Lieutenant James Vose, had known Ring when both were aboard *Enterprise* before the war. "He had been attached to a British carrier and had an opportunity to personally see the importance of radar, and was carrying the message throughout the Navy," Vose said. "Ring's tour with His Majesty's Forces had certainly made an impression on him . . . Commander Ring was the epitome of the picture of the ideal naval officer."[4]

Hornet began launching at the same time as *Enterprise*, but the former's torpedo planes were the first in the air. Bombing Eight and Scouting Eight's SBDs were kept on the hangar deck while Torpedo Eight's 15 TBDs were launched, as they needed a full deck run to get airborne. Bombing Eight's ready room was just off the flight deck and Lieutenant Commander Johnson's pilots watched the leader of Torpedo Eight, Lieutenant Commander John Waldron, stride past the island towards his Devastator, raising his arm in a salute. It was the last time they would ever see him.

The *Hornet* air staff had decided to launch the torpedo planes first so the dive bombers and fighters could link up with the slower TBDs en route to the target. As soon as Waldron's squadron had departed, 35 Dauntlesses and ten Wildcats were ranged on the flight deck and launch soon commenced.

Commander Ring began a long climb to altitude with his bomber, scout, and fighter squadrons but they eventually became separated from Waldron's low-flying TBDs, which veered off to the west. Waldron followed his instinct and would make contact with the enemy, but the meticulous CAG followed his orders and proceeded according to the PBY contact which placed the Japanese carriers 155 miles distant, bearing 239° True. The *Hornet* Dauntlesses headed southwest by west with Ring leading the two SBD squadron commanders on either wing. The 45 aircraft proceeded in good flying weather with bright sunshine and occasionally thick but scattered clouds lying at about 1,500 feet. Ceiling was unlimited and visibility extended to 35 or 40 miles.

Meanwhile, Wade McClusky and the *Enterprise* Dauntlesses were still orbiting the task force at 0745 without any indication of the fighters or torpedo planes being launched. Admiral Spruance knew that a Japanese scout had detected the American ships, which hastened the necessity of getting the strike underway. Therefore, the 33 SBDs were directed by signal light to "proceed on mission assigned."[5]

Leading his two squadrons in a prolonged climb, the *Enterprise* CAG no longer even had *Hornet*'s strike in sight. Thus, Task Force 16's 68 dive bombers set out on the most important mission ever launched from American carrier decks, without proper fighter escort, widely separated and with no integrated operations plan.

Flying generally southwest, the *Hornet* and *Enterprise* aviators had a spectacular view of the Pacific, stacked as they were between 18,000 and 20,000 feet. The occasional low clouds blocked out some of the 8,000 square miles of ocean visible from that height, but it was too little to

With dive brakes deployed, an SBD-3 releases a 500-pound bomb. (U.S. Navy)

67

hide any force the size of Nagumo's fleet. Off to starboard, roughly paralleling the SBDs' course, was a fairly large bank of cumulus obscuring the western horizon, but otherwise it was good hunting weather.

The 45-plane *Hornet* strike was the first to arrive in the expected contact area, something after 0900. Ring, with his 35 SBDs and ten F4Fs, found an empty ocean where the enemy's Carrier Striking Force was anticipated. The *Hornet* CAG had no way of knowing that at 0918 Nagumo's ships had gained definite knowledge of American carriers and turned from their southeasterly course, directly towards Midway, to north-northeast. The course change, plus much evasive action necessary to avoid the numerous land-based air attacks launched from Midway, had thrown Nagumo's schedule out of kilter. The Task Force 16 pilots had been briefed to intercept the Japanese carriers assuming they maintained course and speed towards Midway.

Stan Ring was faced with two very clear choices. He could turn to the right or to the left to continue the search. If Nagumo had been delayed somehow, or perhaps changed course, he would be off to starboard, probably below the clouds on the horizon. On the other hand, if the contact report had been in error and the Japanese maintained their 0800 heading of 135 degrees they could possibly be on their way towards Midway.

It was actually Ring's fuel gauges which made the decision for him. As Lieutenant Vose related, "Gas consumption was terrific. We flew parade formation and the throttle was in use constantly to maintain position. We arrived at the interception point, no enemy, and the group commander made the only possible decision."[6]

Ring dipped the wing of his Dauntless in a port turn and the *Hornet* strike group followed him on a heading for Midway, off to the southeast. It didn't seem possible for many of the planes to return to the task force because of their depleted fuel state.

What Ring and none of the other pilots knew was that the PBY contact report had been about 40 miles off, and Nagumo had changed course.

As *Hornet*'s SBDs turned southeast, her torpedo squadron was making its final approach to the Japanese carriers. Lieutenant Commander Waldron had led his VT-8 on a course farther west than the dive bombers and found Nagumo heading northeast. All 15 of Waldron's Devastators were shot down, and only one had gotten close enough to launch its torpedo. Several minutes later *Enterprise's* 14 TBDs also went after the Carrier Striking Force and ten were lost. A total of seven separate Navy, Marine and Army air attacks had been made upon the Japanese force so far, still without any success.

Stan Ring arrived within visual range of Kure Atoll, 60 miles west of Midway, not long after Torpedo Eight was decimated. The *Hornet* dive bombers circled briefly on the remote chance some word might come through about their elusive target, but radio silence was being strictly observed. Ring noted his fuel gauges again and directed his three squadrons to return to base independently.

Thirteen SBD pilots decided they didn't have enough fuel remaining to risk a flight back to *Hornet*, and continued east for Midway. They'd refuel and get back to the task force as soon as possible. Twenty other Dauntlesses headed back north and homed in on *Hornet's* beacon, landing aboard as their engines sucked the last vapors from empty tanks. The other 12 *Hornet* planes weren't so fortunate. Two SBDs ditched, one in the Midway lagoon, and all ten F4Fs went down with dry tanks. The aviators were later rescued, but the *Hornet* air group was now effectively out of the battle.

Wade McClusky was getting concerned. Two VS-6 planes had dropped out because of engine trouble, reducing his strength to 31 Dauntlesses. Best's 15 planes were holding formation but Ensign T. F. Schneider seemed to be in trouble. His engine was smoking badly, obviously using much more fuel than it should, though the young pilot kept tucked in tight formation. Up in front Ensigns Jaccard and Pittman kept a watchful eye on McClusky, wondering what he was thinking. If they didn't sight something pretty soon there might not be enough fuel to return to the "Big E."

In the lead, McClusky was scanning the horizon with his binoculars. Visibility could hardly have been better, but the strike was getting close to the anticipated interception point at roughly Latitude 29° 14' North, Longitude 178° 25' West. McClusky checked his clock: almost 0920 Midway time. Yet there wasn't the slightest trace of smoke on the horizon; nothing to indicate the enemy's presence in this quadrant.

The CAG drew out his plotting board from beneath the instrument panel and studied it. The navigation was apparently accurate. The planes were at the anticipated contact point but the Japanese simply were not there. McClusky scanned the horizon yet again, pondering the same intangibles as Stan Ring had not long before. But by allowing a maximum rate of advance, 25 knots, McClusky was certain the Japanese couldn't have already passed by, closing the distance to Midway.

That meant the quarry had to be somewhere off to starboard, to the west or even the north. McClusky didn't know what decision the *Hornet* strike had made, nor was he aware that VT-6 and VT-8 had both located the enemy carriers and were massacred trying to attack them. Fourteen *Enterprise* TBDs under Lieutenant Commander Lindsay had launched much later than McClusky and consequently flew a more direct course to the target.

Furthermore, the intent of the *Yorktown* air group was similarly mysterious to McClusky, so he was acting almost totally in the blind. But regardless of the information available to him, Wade McClusky without exaggeration would win or lose the Pacific Ocean for the United States, depending upon which way he turned. His two SBD squadrons were the bulk of American air power left in the battle.

Deciding he could have things a little of both ways, McClusky elected to continue on the 240-degree heading for another 35 miles, and if nothing showed up he'd turn to starboard and fly up the reciprocal heading of what the Japanese force was last known to be following. He'd fly 315 degrees until 1000, and finally turn northeast back towards *Enterprise*. By then the fuel situation would be near the critical point and he'd have to make a final decision. The Dauntlesses had already been in the air almost two and a half hours.

At 0935, at the end of the extra 35 miles McClusky had tagged on to the original 155, he swung right on the reverse of Nagumo's reported path. Owing to the error in the initial contact report, *Enterprise*'s dive bombers were actually flying about 20 miles west of the enemy's 0800 track. McClusky didn't know it, but when he led his planes into that starboard turn he was only 50 miles due south of his target.

It would be the most important decision of the battle, and it was made not by an admiral but by a lieutenant commander. It was as if a British major had been called upon to decide the crucial moment at Waterloo.

McClusky had made his choice and now he was stuck with it. Continuing his methodical box search he flew northwest for 20 minutes. In five more minutes he'd be forced to turn northeast and, if he still didn't have the enemy in sight, there would be nothing to do but return to *Enterprise*. In Bombing Six, Ensign Schneider was gamely maintaining position while entertaining grave doubts about getting back with dry feet.

At 0955 McClusky got the one break he needed. A single vessel, which he thought was a cruiser, was steaming at high speed crossing his path at almost right angles. She was actually the destroyer *Arashi*, making knots to catch up with the Nagumo force after an ineffective depth-charge attack on an American submarine. McClusky guessed the "cruiser" was on some kind of liason mission between the Carrier Striking Force and the Midway Invasion Force. Checking his compass he noted she was heading northeast. McClusky brought his formation around on the new heading for about 25 miles, and ten minutes after turning to *Arashi*'s course his decision paid off.

Almost straight ahead, a few degrees to starboard, was an ill-defined break in the blue curve of the Pacific. McClusky, peering intently through his binoculars, was looking at the white wakes of the Carrier Striking Force.

Yorktown withdrew southwest after recovering Wally Short's ten scouts at 0645. Task Force 17 was out of sight of *Hornet* and *Enterprise* and Fletcher was anxious to get within range of the Japanese carriers. The other three squadron commanders—Max Leslie, Lance Massey, and Jimmy Thach—conferred with the air group commander, Oscar Pederson, and air officer Murr Arnold about the upcoming strike. *Yorktown's* air staff thought the risk unacceptable for a CAG to fly without strong fighter escort, so Pederson stayed aboard as the fighter director. They planned for Massey's Torpedo Three to be launched first, then the SBDs, and finally the shorter-ranged but faster F4Fs. It was agreed that the three squadrons would rendezvous en route, with the TBDs staying low, watching the whitecaps for wind drift while the dive bombers and fighters steered by reference to Massey's planes.

But Fletcher wanted a reserve strike, either as a follow-up or as an alternate ready for launch in case the first group didn't find anything. Scouting Five would therefore remain aboard, but Short's pilots figured they'd get their chance a bit later.

Meanwhile, Fletcher was awaiting more information on the Japanese carriers. But after several more minutes he made up his mind; he knew waiting could be fatal. The aircrews manned their planes at 0840 and in five minutes 35 aircraft were commencing launch.

The heart of the strike was Max Leslie's 17 SBDs. Massey took off with a dozen TBDs but Jimmy Thach was allowed to take only six F4Fs, which disturbed him deeply. In the first place, they weren't enough to protect the strike planes and secondly, six was an awkward number. It meant he'd have an unbalanced force with one complete division of four and a section of only two.

At 0905, two full hours after Task Force 16 launched its SBDs, an hour and 20 minutes after McClusky actually departed *Enterprise*, the *Yorktown* strike headed out on the briefed course. The cruiser *Astoria* blinkered a farewell message—"Good hunting and a safe return."[7]

Once clear of the task force Leslie signaled his pilots to arm their bombs. He was to preserve radio silence, hence the need of a hand signal. Bombing Three's SBD-3s were equipped with electric arming switches which simplified the method of making the bombs "hot." Leslie flipped his switch and was immediately startled by a sudden, unexpected upward lunge of his Dauntless.

The veteran pilot knew right away what had happened, and it filled him with wild frustration. Somebody had mixed up the wiring between the arming and release circuits, with the result that activation of the arming switch released the 1,000-pound bomb. Leslie consulted briefly with his rear-seat man, Radioman W. E. Gallagher, about returning quickly to *Yorktown*, only about five minutes astern, to get another bomb. But there was a chance Admiral Fletcher wouldn't let them take off again, and Leslie had no intention of missing the most critical mission of the war. He remained at the head of the squadron.

Shortly another bomb exploded far below the climbing planes, and Leslie had to break radio silence to prevent any further needless drops. He ordered his pilots to arm their bombs manually. But it wasn't long before the disconcerting news came to the skipper that the problem was widespread. "I learned en route to the attack that three or four other pilots had prematurely lost their bombs," Leslie would later recall.[8] Roy Isaman, Chuck Lane, and Bud Merrill had all suffered the ignominy of dropping their bombs around the ears of Jimmy Thach and his low-flying Wildcats. It wasn't the pilots' fault, of course, and nobody got hurt, but that didn't change the fact that Bombing Three had lost one-quarter of its striking power.

At 0945 the *Yorktown* air group achieved rendezvous as planned. Leslie's SBDs overtook Massey's Devastators, and Thach's F4Fs were deployed in protective formation. The dozen TBDs flew at 1,500 feet, just below the scattered clouds, while Bombing Three leveled off at 16,000. Two Wildcats stayed low at 2,500 feet to protect the torpedo planes and the other four cruised at about 5,000. The formation continued this way, probing for the enemy ships. The bombless SBD at the head of Bombing 3 was still in command, and though he was sick at heart over the prospect of making an ineffective dive, Max Leslie completely dismissed any thought of relinquishing the lead. He had gotten his squadron ready for combat and, by the fates, he was going to take it down on the biggest carrier he could find, bomb or no bomb.

Fifteen minutes after rendezvous was effected, Lieutenant Commander Massey discerned three faint plumes of smoke on the western horizon. He led his TBDs in a shallow climb for a little better visibility, turning to starboard. Leslie and Thach caught the course change and followed his lead. From high altitude neither the F4Fs nor SBDs could see what Massey was after, but Leslie surmised it was the enemy. He received confirmation within five minutes when Gallagher in the back seat called out wakes ahead. Leslie saw them at almost the same moment, 30 to 35 miles straight ahead, but never did see any smoke.

Massey took his squadron down below more of the low-lying clouds on a course of 345 degrees and was lost from sight forever to Bombing

Three. Leslie tried to raise Massey on the radio but could not establish contact. More frustration; it meant the *Yorktown* squadrons wouldn't be able to initiate a fully coordinated attack, as had been planned. And the element of surprise was lost to the lumbering TBDs when a flock of Zeros hit them about 14 miles from the center of the sprawling fleet. Jimmy Thach's Wildcats, at 6,000 feet, had to fight for their lives and were unable to provide any assistance to the torpedo squadron.

Leslie led Bombing Three down to 14,500 feet and found himself over the northeastern portion of the Carrier Striking Force—three flattops, headed northeast, and the one which seemed to fascinate most of the VB-3 fliers was almost directly below. The large red sun painted forward on her flight deck stood out prominently. She was packed with aircraft, and as Leslie maneuvered his squadron into the sun, Gallagher notified him the carrier was turning starboard, into the wind, apparently ready to launch.

Try as he might, Leslie still couldn't get a reply out of Torpedo Three. Time was running out, and a swarm of Zeros might descend on the unescorted Dauntlesses at any moment. Leslie knew his 17 planes—only 13 of which now carried bombs—had little chance of taking out more than one carrier, especially one as big as this looked; some of the pilots thought she was of the *Akagi* class.

There was no AA fire so far, but it was for certain things wouldn't stay that way, so Leslie signaled he was ready to initiate the attack. A glance at his instrument panel clock showed it was 1023 as he looked over at his wingmen, Lieutenant (jg) Holmberg and Ensign Schlegel, to check their spacing.

Then Max Leslie patted the top of his head in the familiar aviator's "I've got the lead" signal, and rolled into his dive.

Ensign Bill Pittman, one of Wade McClusky's two wingmen, noticed the CAG gesturing. Looking out past the nose of his Dauntless, Pittman saw many wakes on the surface. They were about 35 miles away—the hunt was over.

In the Bombing Six formation behind McClusky, Ensign Schneider's efforts to keep pace also came to an end; his engine sputtered and died, having exhausted the last of its fuel. Schneider nosed down, headed for a water landing. McClusky had now lost fully one-sixth of his original formation, leaving him with 30 Dauntlesses including his own.

But there was no time to contemplate diminishing numbers. McClusky examined the enemy force through his glasses, noting it was dispersed in a circular formation with the four carriers maneuvering independently in the middle, evidently dodging a torpedo attack. Two flattops were in his line of sight, another was over towards the east, and the fourth was way up north. Providing an inner defensive screen were the two battleships and six to eight cruisers or destroyers while the outer ring, 12 to 15 miles from the carriers, looked like light cruisers or destroyers. It was virtually impossible to identify ship types from nearly 20,000 feet with any great accuracy, but it didn't matter. The carriers stood out prominently, and they were McClusky's targets.

The CAG decided that if *Hornet*'s SBDs made contact they would probably take out two carriers, so he assigned VB-6 and VS-6 to the two nearest flattops. It seemed that any attempt to attack one carrier with less than a squadron would jeopardize the prospects of sinking the ship or at least knocking it out of the battle.

McClusky now broke radio silence and reported his find to *Enterprise*, then directed Scouting Six to follow him down on the nearest carrier while Bombing Six took the other. Radio communications failed at this important point, however, and Best did not hear McClusky's instructions, nor did the CAG hear Best's broadcast saying VB-6 would dive on the nearest ship. Standard dive-bomber doctrine was that the trailing squadron— Best's in this case—would dive on the closer target while the lead squadron proceeded to the next in line. But Wade McClusky was a fighter pilot by trade, relatively new to dive bombers. He prepared to dive on the nearest carrier, marvelling all the while at the total lack of opposition. Not a Zero rose to challenge the Dauntlesses, not a burst of AA fire marred the clear, cool upper air.

Neither the *Enterprise* nor *Yorktown* fliers were as yet aware of one another's presence over the enemy fleet, the former approaching from the south and the latter from the southeast. The 70 torpedo plane pilots and gunners who died attacking the Carrier Striking Force had concentrated the enemy's attention to low level. With the Zeros dancing just above the waves, the AA guns trained low to counter the obsolete Devastators, it was easy to forget about dive bombers. And above 10,000 feet the sky belonged to the Dauntlesses.

Max Leslie settled into his upwind dive, lined up the easternmost carrier in his sight, and ruefully remembered he had no bomb to drop on it. The best he could do was help suppress antiaircraft fire so he squeezed the trigger on his stick grip and kept firing for 6,000 feet, aiming at the carrier's bridge, until the twin .50s jammed. But Leslie persisted in his dive, the only one he would make on an enemy ship, leading the way for Bombing Three.

Above and behind the first Dauntless, 16 others had peeled off from 14,000 feet and were diving down the fore-and-aft axis of the carrier, which was caught by surprise and lay wide open to attack. Leslie remained in his descent until he was totally convinced there was nothing else he could do. Then he pulled in his flaps and started his recovery, noting there was no damage to the other two carriers in the immediate vicinity.

Leslie's wingman, Paul "Lefty" Holmberg, had ridden the skipper's tail all the way down. But not until Leslie pulled out did Holmberg have a really good view of the target. He centered the crosshairs of his three-power telescopic sight on the big red ball up forward and held his SBD steady as he dropped through 2,500 feet. Then Holmberg pushed the electric bomb release button top of his stick and, remaining in the dive, reached down to give a good tug on the manual release, just to make sure. Bombing Three's second aircraft had just pulled into level flight under a heavy G-load when Holmberg's 1,000-pounder hammered through the scarlet disk. His gunner, AMM2/c George LaPlant, gleefully shouted through the intercom, telling Holmberg he'd scored.

The shock of that blast flipped a plane overboard, and as the orange-yellow flames and dark gray smoke broiled up from the carrier's bow a lethal sequence of events began. Admiral Nagumo had delayed launching his second strike of the day so he could rearm his torpedo planes and also close the distance to the American carriers. In the haste of the operation, bombs and torpedoes were carelessly pushed aside, and all four carriers' flight decks were packed with fully armed and fueled aircraft. In short, they were attacked under conditions of maximum vulnerability.

The Dauntless pilots were now taking full advantage of the situation. Bombing Three was cool and deadly; every bomb looked to be a direct hit or a damaging near miss. By the time the eleventh SBD had dropped and pulled out, the carrier was gushing smoke and flame to such an extent that she looked worthless as a target. Ensigns Bob Elder and Randy Cooner changed course in their dives and went after a destroyer, while Lieutenant O. B. Wiseman and Ensign John Butler released over one of the two battleships. They came close, but scored no hits.

The thirteenth and seventeenth pilots, however, kept after the carrier. Lieutenant Dave Shumway intended to finish off this floating inferno. His bomb was the fourth direct hit, and Bud Merrill saw it explode. Now fully aroused, the Japanese AA gunners concentrated their fire on Merrill's plane, but they could have spared themselves the trouble: it was one of the four which had lost its bomb en route.

As Leslie made for the rendezvous spot to the southeast he was immensely proud of his pilots. The carrier was burning furiously, still being rocked by violent secondary explosions. Of the nine bombs dropped on the flattop, all had counted. Four were direct hits, three had exploded very close aboard the port beam, and two near-missed to starboard. This ship was definitely out of the battle.

Air opposition had turned up belatedly in the form of a Zero which jumped one of Bombing Three's SBDs as it dived, and a floatplane which made a pass at Ensign Roy Isaman low on the water. But Isaman's gunner scared it away. Amazingly, all 17 of Leslie's planes had attacked and escaped unharmed.

As Leslie orbited at the rendezvous, only one other Dauntless joined him. It was flown by Ensign Aldon Hanson, who had been the fifth to dive. The other planes had withdrawn to the northeast, joining in three-plane elements before setting course for home. The way back was slightly north of east, but before Leslie banked around he noticed two other ships, maybe 12 miles to the west, burning and exploding like his own target. It was hard to tell at first glance, but they could have been carriers.

Leading the second division of Scouting Six, Lieutenant Clarence Dickinson had four carriers in sight. The northernmost ship he correctly identified as *Hiryu*, and one of the nearer flattops he knew was *Soryu*. Commander McClusky's intended target, he thought, was *Kaga*. Dickinson had a good eye for recognition. Nagumo's Carrier Division One consisted of the 36,000-ton near-sisters *Akagi* and *Kaga*, while the smaller sisters *Hiryu* and *Soryu* formed CarDivTwo. But the identities of individual ships mattered little compared to the fact that at last, after six months, Japanese carriers were now at hand.

To the veterans of Scouting Six's ill-fated Sunday morning flight into Pearl Harbor, the four flattops represented the end of a six-month odyssey. There were only a few moments to study the elusive, hated enemy, then McClusky was on the air and Gallaher heard him say, "Earl, you follow me down."[9]

With that, McClusky abruptly pushed stick and rudder, felt the controls bite into the air, and drew a bead on the rectangular deck nearly four miles below.

Ensign Pittman, on McClusky's wing, was taken aback by his leader's sudden descent and hesitated slightly. His friend Dick Jaccard nosed over, taking Pittman's place, but accidentally pushed the selector lever marked W and extended his landing gear instead of his flaps. Pittman, with the squadron's camera in his wingroot, immediately followed Jaccard, who in turn was followed by Gallaher and the rest of Scouting Six.

Wade McClusky, out in front of everyone else, had a magnificent view of the big carrier. Her flight deck was spotted with dozens of planes, and she was now steaming placidly upwind preparing to launch her air group. The CAG was halfway down before he was spotted—an incredible development which insured the vessel's destruction. Some scattered bursts of AA fire were all to indicate the Japanese even knew the Dauntlesses were overhead.

In all, 25 of the bombers were slanting into their dives, flashing briefly in the sky as they tipped over one by one. To C. E. Dickinson it was the best dive he'd ever made—so many of the pilots later said the same thing—perhaps because this time everything had to be perfect. "The target was utterly satisfying," Dickinson would later recall, "this was the absolute."[10]

McClusky released at 1,800 feet and pulled in his flaps to recover as low as he dared. His bomb landed in the water barely ten yards from the carrier's bridge. Pittman and Jaccard also put their bombs close aboard, splashing water on her deck. It remained for Earl Gallaher to make the first score as his 500-pounder crashed into the tightly packed planes waiting to be launched. The destruction was widespread and immediate. Bombs, torpedoes, and high-octane aviation fuel erupted in a volcano of searing flames which turned the entire after flight deck into a holocaust.

Lieutenant (jg) Norman Kleiss of Gallaher's division was the seventh *Enterprise* pilot to push over. He decided to aim for the undamaged forward portion of the deck, and splintered the large red sun painted near the bow. Dickinson saw his 500-pounder explode abreast of the island. Though the conflagration continued unabated, each remaining Dauntless pressed the attack on the stricken carrier, which belatedly began to turn to starboard.

Lieutenant Dick Best, leading Bombing Six, had deployed his squadron for the attack and noted each section and division was correctly spaced. He'd just split his flaps prior to diving on the nearest carrier but was startled by a stream of blue gray streaks plunging vertically before him. McClusky's unorthodox tactic of taking the lead planes down on the closest target, plus the communications lapse, had confused the situation considerably.

The larger problem was that Best had only four other planes remaining with him—those of his first division. His entire second and third divisions had followed McClusky and Gallaher down on the right-hand carrier. There was nothing to do but pull in the flaps, rejoin formation and proceed to the other target. With only five planes Best knew he'd be hard pressed to put the port-hand carrier out of action.

Though her companion was burning and exploding spectacularly, this westernmost flattop unaccountably continued into the wind, giving not the slightest hint of danger. But Best didn't question the gift being presented him. He merely radioed to his four pilots, "Don't let this carrier escape."[11]

With his division spaced in preparation for the dive, Bombing Six's skipper checked the position of his wingmen, Ensigns Bud Kroeger and Fred Weber. All was ready; flaps coming open, throttle back, nose up slightly, than a half-roll and the attack was on. Best put his eye to the sight, taking his time. Starting at 15,000 feet, he had at least 13,000 to play with and he wasn't going to miss. The carrier looked big—*Kaga* or *Akagi* the pilots thought—and she made a fine target. A Zero was launched as Best went through 3,000 feet, but still no AA fire.

With the ship squarely in his sights Best pushed his dive right to the limit before toggling his bomb. Then he pulled out, wrapped his Dauntless into a tight bank and watched the 1,000-pounder smash through the flight deck directly abreast of the island. One pilot, possibly wondering if the C.O. would release in time to pull out, had dropped early and missed. But the other three emulated Best's determined tactics and two more heavy bombs hit among the parked planes. Best's division had recorded the highest percentage of the day, with three of five bombs being solid hits. For the third time that day, fire and explosions rocked another Japanese carrier.

Heading out of the immediate area, Best noted smoke and flames rising from the carrier he'd previously seen to the northeast. He realized the *Yorktown* SBDs had scored, too, though he had not been aware of Leslie's squadron at the time he attacked. "They must have struck from the east at almost exactly the same time I struck from the west," the VB-6 skipper recalled.[12]

Thirty-nine bombs had been dropped on three carriers within a three-to four-minute period, resulting in probably 11 direct hits. *Akagi*, *Kaga*, and *Soryu* were all mortally stricken. Only *Hiryu*, temporarily out of danger to the north, remained to carry on the battle.

Bombing Three's planes, scattered as they were, had a generally leisurely flight back to the task force. No Zeros showed up to avenge the destruction so recently wrought upon their roosts even though the *Yorktown* aviators kept a sharp lookout for them. In fact, they saw no enemy aircraft at all after clearing the scene of the attack. This despite some assertions that *Hiryu*'s strike which crippled *Yorktown* navigated by following some VB-3 Dauntlesses to the task force. Leslie flatly denies it, saying in part, "I am totally unaware of any Japanese planes following VB-3 back to *Yorktown* . . . it is a difficult assignment to follow small planes over vast expanses of ocean."[13] Furthermore, *Hiryu*'s strike group of 18 Vals and six Zeros didn't launch until nearly 1100—a full half-hour after

Bombing Three pushed over. It was nearly an hour's flight to the task force and no SBDs remained for long in the vicinity of the Japanese fleet. They had more than 30 minutes head start on the *Hiryu* strike.

The *Enterprise* fliers had a much rougher time of it. Wade McClusky was working at his navigation, trying to figure the most direct course home, when a series of tracers splashed the water around his wings. The CAG heard his gunner open fire and immediately realized some of the Zero CAP had found him. One of the fighters overshot, as if pulling out of a high-speed dive, but a quick glance back showed a second Zero 1,000 feet above, off the port quarter, initiating a gunnery pass. McClusky waited until the Japanese pilot was committed to his run and then whipped the Dauntless around to port to face his assailant. ARM1/c W. G. Chochalousek opened fire once more and the battle was joined.

McClusky stayed about 20 feet off the water to prevent attacks from below, and continually turned into each new attack. The Zeros were double-teaming the SBD, with one nearly always diving in to fire while the other regained altitude for another pass. The cat-and-mouse game continued for an agonizingly long five minutes until one Zero got in a solid burst. The port side of McClusky's cockpit was riddled and the CAG was painfully wounded in the shoulder. He was sure the next pass would dump the Dauntless into the sea.

McClusky vaguely heard more machine gun fire, then only the engine's steady beat. Wondering what had happened, he turned around to glimpse Chochalousek still grasping the twin .30s, alert to further attack. The gunner had knocked off one Zero, driving the other away. With three large 20-mm holes and over 50 smaller machine gun bullets in its fuselage and wings the battered Dauntless climbed to 1,000 feet and set course for *Enterprise*.

McClusky's wingman, Ensign Bill Pittman, also experienced a bit of high drama. Or more precisely, his gunner did. When Pittman pushed the plane over in a dive, the twin .30s somehow broke loose from their mount and nearly fell over the side. Machinist Mate Floyd Adkins grabbed at the guns and managed to hold them down until Pittman recovered from his dive. A Zero chose that moment to attack the Dauntless, but Adkins manhandled the 175-pound set onto the fuselage, held it steady and shot the Zero down in flames.

Later, when Pittman's Sail-18 landed, Adkins couldn't even lift the guns—two men were usually required to raise the weapons into the rear cockpit. Lieutenant Gallaher wrote out a citation for the Distinguished Flying Cross and a promotion for Floyd Adkins.

A destroyer gave Lieutenant Dickinson its undivided attention, firing wildly, but the shells were bursting 1,000 yards ahead. Glancing at his airspeed indicator, Dickinson knew why; he was making only 95 knots because the landing flaps were still down. The Japanese gunners had figured on their target doing twice that speed and allowed too much deflection. A few other scout pilots passing by at that moment later told Dickinson it seemed as if he were demonstrating his Dauntless to a prospective buyer. Landing and dive flaps were opening and closing, wheels going up and down. Finally he got everything sorted out.

But then a Zero passed to Dickinson's right and drew ahead, stalking another flight of SBDs. Dickinson moved in behind the enemy plane, took careful aim and triggered about 40 rounds from his twin .50s. The fighter fell off on its port wing and spun into the water. Dickinson continued on course towards *Enterprise* but ran out of fuel short of the task force. He ditched near a destroyer and was rescued with his gunner.

But a frightfully high number of other crews were unaccounted for. Lieutenant Charles Ware had led Scouting Six's third division down on McClusky's target, got his pilots clear of the enemy fleet, and mysteriously disappeared. Ensign John McCarthy, unable to find the "Big E," went down out of fuel. Lieutenant Penland of Bombing Six ditched with holes in his fuel tanks, barely 30 miles from the blazing, exploding carriers. Van Buren circled him and then departed in the direction of the task force but never arrived. Ensign Schneider was also missing; he'd run out of gas just before the attack. Of the 33 SBDs *Enterprise* had launched, ten bombers and eight scouts were missing. One of Best's planes which did return was badly shot up and would require major repair to wings, fuselage, and elevators.

More Dauntlesses probably would have returned if it had not been for a discrepancy in the position of Point Option. *Enterprise* was 60 miles from the briefed coordinates, and even with the new ZB homing beacon some pilots couldn't quite stretch their fuel supply. McClusky eventually homed in at 5,000 feet and dropped into the landing circle of the first carrier he saw. He was on the downwind leg when he realized the ship was *Yorktown* instead of her sister *Enterprise*. With his fuel gauge needle flicking dangerously around the five-gallon mark he made a straight-in approach on the "Big E," some five miles away. Another plane was in the pattern but McClusky good-naturedly thumbed his nose at the LSO's wave-off signal—normally a cardinal sin among carrier pilots— and landed his bullet-scarred plane with about three gallons remaining. He had been in the air almost five hours.

The CAG climbed stiffly out of his cockpit and rushed up the ladder to report to Admiral Spruance. Three enemy carriers had been hit and were last seen burning profusely, but the fourth ship was evidently intact. McClusky was then rushed to sick bay, where he was found to have five shrapnel splinters in his left arm and shoulder. His instrumental part in the Battle of Midway was over.

This Bombing Six SBD-3 has just landed safely aboard Enterprise *after the morning strike of 4 June 1942. Battle damage attests to the intensity of Japanese opposition. (U.S. Navy)*

Most of the "Big E's" dive bombers were back aboard by noon—those which were coming back. But casualties were worse among the torpedo planes. Of the 14 TBDs which launched with Gene Lindsey, only four returned to *Enterprise* and one of them was so badly shot up that it was pushed overboard. No other TBDs returned to a carrier.

As bad as things were for the *Enterprise* air group, they were worse for *Hornet.* Commander Ring led Scouting Eight back to the ship but only four Bombing Eight SBDs came with him. None of the ten Wildcats returned, and when the Dauntless pilots stepped into the wardroom they received a bigger jolt. The fliers sat by squadrons in the wardroom, with one squadron to a table. Nobody was sitting at Torpedo Eight's table.

Nearly 40 *Hornet* planes were missing—the equal of two squadrons gone at one crack. It wasn't known for several hours that most of Bombing Eight had followed Lieutenant Commander Ruff Johnson into Midway to refuel; a lengthy process with Midway's damaged facilities after the morning air raid.

Losses weren't quite so staggering among the *Yorktown* planes, but they were bad. None of Lieutenant Commander Lance Massey's 12 TBDs landed aboard, though two had ditched and three fliers were later rescued. One of Jimmy Thach's Wildcats had been shot down but the other five arrived back over the task force around 1145. The *Yorktown* strike was the only one which managed a somewhat coordinated attack and whose squadrons more or less returned as units, excepting VT-3. All 17 Bombing Three planes were told to circle overhead while the shorter-ranged Wildcats arrived and could be taken aboard.

None of Leslie's SBDs had to ditch on the way back because they'd been launched an hour and a half later than the *Enterprise* and *Hornet* planes. Consequently the *Yorktown* dive bombers had ample fuel remaining to wait for the fighters to be recovered.

While Leslie was still overhead, Admiral Fletcher was interviewing Jimmy Thach about the mission. The fighter skipper described VB-3's work as "the most beautiful dive bombing you ever saw"[14] and told of three carriers burning. But he had no information about the reported fourth carrier, which would have to be dealt with as soon as possible. Fletcher decided to release his reserve strike on the basis of incomplete information and dispatched ten of the 17 scouts still aboard. They were to search to the northwest, from 280 degrees through 020 degrees to a distance of two hundred miles.

At 1150 Max Leslie was finally given the go-ahead to enter the landing circle and come aboard. He hadn't been able to land before this because the CAP had to be reinforced and then the SBDs had to wait for their Wildcat escorts. It was about time, because after the scouts departed, VB-3's fuel was running low. Leslie settled into the groove, nicely approaching the deck, when he unaccountably got a wave-off. So did Holmberg, just as *Yorktown* radioed, "Get clear! We're being attacked!"[15] *Hiryu's* strike was 30 miles out and closing fast.

Bombing Three swung around to get out of the area lest some stray Zeros bother the unescorted SBDs. It was *Yorktown's* unfortunate luck to be the first carrier in view of the Japanese pilots, and though only seven Vals broke through to dive on her, they scored three direct hits.

By the time the surviving attackers retired, *Yorktown* was burning and dead in the water. *Enterprise* and *Hornet*, some 20 miles away, hadn't been attacked and consequently were able to recover their aircraft. Bombing Three was ordered to land aboard the "Big E" to await developments.

Leslie and Holmberg were en route to *Enterprise* when Gallagher in the back seat of Leslie's plane noticed a ditched TBD about ten miles away. The two SBDs circled the Devastator while Leslie called a destroyer to pick up the torpedo plane crew. Headed for the "Big E" once more, Leslie and Holmberg both seriously doubted they had enough fuel to get there. So they decided to put down next to the heavy cruiser they were passing over. She was *Astoria*, the same ship which had signaled "Good hunting and a safe return" some four hours previously.

A Dauntless splashes down out of fuel next to an American light cruiser following the eventful morning strike. More SBDs were lost to fuel starvation than to enemy action during the Battle of Midway. (National Archives)

Both SBDs splashed down safely within easy distance of the cruiser, Leslie about 50 yards to port. A whaleboat gathered in the four fliers and took them aboard the ship, where they would remain until 12 June. But Bombing Three's other 15 planes landed aboard *Enterprise* and prepared to carry on the battle.

Between 1400 and 1500 that afternoon several important developments occurred. First, *Yorktown's* determined damage control teams had extinguished her fires and by 1430 she was making 15 knots. Ten minutes later she was under attack again, for *Hiryu's* second strike of ten Kates and six Zeros found her apparently undamaged. Half the Kates were shot down but they put two torpedoes into *Yorktown* and once more she lay helpless, motionless in the water.

Just as *Yorktown* was coming under attack for the second time that day, Lieutenant Sam Adams of Scouting Five was trying to find the elusive fourth Japanese carrier. His flight had been uneventful until halfway back, when he caught sight of the telltale white wakes. Leading his wingman over for a closer look, Adams made out ten ships all headed north. Fifteen minutes after the first sighting he radioed his contact report: "One CV, two BB, three CA, four DD, 31-15 North, 179-05 West, course 000, speed 15."[16] It was *Hiryu*, 110 miles northwest of *Yorktown*.

Adams told his rear-seat man, Radioman J. J. Karrol, to transmit the same report by code key but Karrol was occupied at that moment. A Zero had sneaked up on the two SBDs but was driven away, and moments later Adams was headed back to the task force.

The contact report was delivered to Admiral Spruance about 1500, and the air staff went to work organizing a strike for immediate launch. It would have to be composed entirely of dive bombers since there were only three torpedo planes left and the fighters were needed to defend the task force. Scouting Six and Bombing Six had only 11 planes ready to go between them, but VB-3's Dauntlesses were available and spotted for launch. That made 25 SBDs, 11 armed with 1,000-pounders, the rest with 500-pound GPs.

With McClusky in sick bay and Leslie aboard *Astoria* it fell to Earl Gallaher to lead the strike. Best would take his small VB-6 contingent which included his wingmen from the morning mission, Weber and Kroeger. Bombing Three's executive officer, Lieutenant Dave Shumway, headed up the *Yorktown* formation and would fill in for Leslie. In all, 24 of the 25 pilots assigned to the mission had also flown on the morning strike.

But just as in the morning, engine trouble cropped up and one scout had to abort. It left ten *Enterprise* planes—six scouts and four bombers—plus Shumway's 14. The plan was for Gallaher to eliminate the remaining carrier as soon as the target was reached, then Best and Shumway would hopefully be able to knock off a battleship or one of the cruisers.

Launch commenced at 1530 and the two dozen Dauntlesses climbed to 13,000 feet for the 90-minute flight, heading into the reddening western sky.

Meanwhile, eleven VB-8 planes from Midway started landing aboard *Hornet* at the same time *Enterprise* began launching her strike. *Hornet's* deck crews worked fast, and 16 Dauntlesses were launched at 1603, just half an hour behind Gallaher. They were led by Lieutenant Edgar Stebbins of Bombing Eight, a reservist like so many of the pilots on the mission.

At 1650 Earl Gallaher had *Hiryu* in sight, 30 miles ahead. It seemed highly unlikely that the Dauntlesses could catch so experienced an enemy unawares for a second time in one day, and Gallaher led his wedge-shaped sections into a climbing port turn, working his way around to the other side of the Japanese formation. Surely a CAP must be airborne, but for the moment the SBDs had the sky to themselves as the shadows lengthened 19,000 feet below.

Japanese air strength had dwindled to almost nothing in the two strikes *Hiryu* had flung at *Yorktown*. Ranged on her deck were five Vals, four Kates and *Soryu*'s new Aichi reconnaissance plane. The six remaining Zeros were orbiting the force.

Gallaher looked back over his shoulder to check dispositions for the final time. Everything appeared orderly; the formations were tucked in close and solid, stepped down by threes and sixes. The Scouting Six skipper nosed down towards the pushover point, away from the sun, and made his dispersal order: *Enterprise* planes would dive on *Hiryu* while *Yorktown*'s went for the nearer of the two battleships. With that, Gallaher pulled up and over—to find himself nose to nose with a Zero.

A sudden belated warning of fighters overhead crackled in Gallaher's earphones but then he was in his 70 degree dive, playing with stick and rudder to set up the attack. Behind and above him the fighters were clawing savagely at the formation, and making their presence felt. Ensign Fred Weber, trailing slightly behind Dick Best, was shot off his leader's wing and fell out of formation.

At 1701 Gallaher was diving out of the southwest, sun to his back, achieving temporary surprise. The SBDs' attack warning was now becoming familiar to the Japanese: a flash of sunlight on polished canopies as wings tipped over in a dive.

As Gallaher's altimeter rapidly unwound, *Hiryu* finally took notice and heeled hard over in an evasive turn to starboard. As a result, Gallaher's bomb missed, and though Scouting Six claimed a possible hit the carrier showed no visible damage. *Hiryu*'s chances of survival had just improved considerably.

Heading for the battleship, Dave Shumway astutely evaluated the situation and decided to shift targets. He swung his 14 VB-3 planes around to dive on *Hiryu*, for in a carrier duel even a depleted enemy air group was more dangerous than the most formidable battleship. *Hiryu*'s turn and thick flak had spoiled the aim of Gallaher's pilots but as Shumway came around, slanting down out of the sun, he had the advantage of extra seconds to size up the problem. The Zeros had time, too, and they aggressively followed the Dauntlesses down, attacking six VB-3 planes in their dives.

Black bursts of heavy AA fire were dotting the sky by this time, jarring the *Yorktown* pilots' aim, for the first bombs were misses. Shumway was forced to release at 4,000 feet and, heavily pursued by fighters, dropped into the cloud layer between 2,000 and 3,000 as his plane was hit repeatedly. He finally evaded by feinting destruction. The other pilots of Shumway's flight released at an average of 2,000 feet but still without luck. Only a few SBDs were still in their dives.

Then *Hiryu*'s flight deck was smothered in rapid succession by three direct hits.

Shumway's decision to attack the carrier instead of the battleship was plainly the correct one, but it unintentionally cut out his old Naval Academy classmate, Dick Best. For the second time that day another squadron had pushed over above Best's formation and hurtled down in front of him. Undaunted, the Bombing Six skipper took his two remaining pilots down with the *Yorktown* bunch and laid another bomb on *Hiryu*'s flight deck ,the fourth solid hit. Shumway's two tail-end pilots, Ensigns R. K. Campbell and R. H. Benson, saw the carrier was finished and returned to their original target, near-missing the battleship.

Pulling out of the area still under persistent fighter attack, various pilots estimated "at least a dozen" Zeros and Messerschmitt 109s.[17] There were no Messerschmitts, of course, but the remaining Zeros doggedly pursued the SBDs. Lieutenant (jg) Wiseman and Ensign Butler, both of Bombing Three, failed to return and were presumed shot down after dropping their bombs. Lieutenant (jg) Sherwood was chased for about eight minutes, and AOM2/c C. R. Bassett in Ensign Cooner's plane was badly wounded in one leg. But Bassett turned the tables by shooting down one Zero.

Clear of the fighters, the SBD crews saw that *Hiryu* was a smoking, shattered wreck. Her entire forward flight deck was laid wide open and a large part of her forward elevator was jammed up against the bridge. Gallaher, Best, and Shumway led their planes back towards *Enterprise*.

Lieutenant Stebbins and his 16 *Hornet* SBDs arrived on the scene at 1730, attacking two cruisers and the battleship *Haruna*. But no hits were obtained, and shortly thereafter they too were headed east for home and the end of a long, long day.

Not for two more years would four aircraft carriers be sunk in a single day. Japan's veteran flattops went down in 350 fathoms, and with them went the best and most experienced naval aviators Japan possessed.

In return for the four carriers destroyed and the air groups which vanished with them, the seven Dauntless squadrons engaged during the day (six Navy and one Marine) lost some 35 aircraft and about 40 aviators. Several other SBDs were badly shot up, such as the plane in which Dave Shumway staggered home. His Baker-13 was holed in the starboard dive and landing flaps, horizontal stabilizer, rudder, fuselage, starboard main fuel tank and even the engine. But it got him back. Shumway's battle had been won as much at the Douglas assembly line at El Segundo as at Midway.

The question remained—and remains today—as to which squadron hit which carrier in the incredible four or five minutes which saw McClusky and Leslie's planes cripple *Akagi*, *Kaga*, and *Soryu*. The *Yorktown* pilots hold steadfast to the opinion that they hit a large carrier, and not the smaller *Soryu* which is generally attributed to them. The VB-3 and VS-6 action reports both list *Akagi* or *Kaga* as their victims, while VB-6 claimed only "enemy carriers."

Two divergent points of view are clearly illustrated in the postwar opinions of two squadron commanders, Max Leslie and Dick Best. Leslie said in 1972, "It is my opinion that Bombing Three attacked *Kaga* in the morning strike of 4 June. Dave Shumway called it *Akagi*, I believe, because he knew it was a big one compared to the smaller *Soryu* and *Hiryu*. A conflict of opinion developed in this identification but it was resolved quite authentically as far as I was concerned when Thaddeus V. Tuleja, the author of *Climax At Midway*, wrote me to say he had decided it was *Kaga* vice *Akagi* . . ."[18]

Dick Best pulled no punches when he stated 30 years after the event, "I don't think any pilot's opinion of what carrier he dived on that day is worth the paper it's written on. I believe that subsequent analysis combined with Japanese information has given a far better account of which groups attacked which Japanese carriers than any one person can give."[19]

The controversy did not even arise until well after the battle, and must of necessity remain academic. On the night of 4 June nobody really cared whether he'd hit a big carrier or a smaller one—it simply didn't matter. The *Yorktown* pilots were bedded down aboard the "Big E," and it wasn't too difficult finding sleeping space for them. Wally Short's crews, for instance, just moved into the Torpedo Six quarters. Nearly all the fliers had been awake 16 hours at the time of the attack on *Hiryu*, and many were at the point of exhaustion. But the battle was not yet over.

Activities resumed early on the fifth, with a patrol plane report that a carrier was still afloat. She was *Hiryu*, drifting and abandoned during the night. She sank at 0830 that morning, unknown to either side, and caused a good deal of confusion throughout the rest of the day. Also reported were two enemy "battleships" in the same general area. A dozen Marine dive bombers were dispatched from Midway—six SBDs and six SB2Us—which found the heavy cruisers *Mogami* and *Mikuma*. The Marines attacked through thick AA fire, losing one Vindicator, but no other damage was done.

At 1500 that afternoon Admiral Spruance acted on the erroneous report that one and possibly two Japanese carriers were still afloat. Two strikes were flown off at maximum range, an estimated 230 miles, to contact and sink any surviving carriers. The two attack groups totaled 58 Dauntlesses: 32 from *Enterprise* and 26 from *Hornet*. All they found was a lone destroyer, *Tanikaze*, which was on essentially the same mission as the SBDs: to discover if one of the carriers were still afloat. All 58 Dauntlesses dived on her at 1830, and pilots claimed one possible hit on the "light cruiser," but *Tanikaze* escaped unharmed. Not so the SBDs—Lieutenant Sam Adams, a veteran of Coral Sea and the pilot who had located *Hiryu* for Spruance, was shot down by the destroyer's AA battery. The other Dauntlesses were recovered in darkness.

At dawn on the sixth Spruance launched 18 scouts to relocate the two heavy cruisers. He'd steamed at low speed during the night so as not to be drawn too far from Midway. Contact was made at 0645 and *Hornet* launched 26 SBDs with two divisions of F4Fs to initiate the first of three strikes. They went in a little before 1000, to be followed by Wally Short leading 31 *Enterprise* and *Yorktown* Dauntlesses at 1230. In all, 112 sorties were flown against *Mogami* and *Mikuma* of which 81 were by SBDs.

One Dauntless was shot down by the heavy AA fire, but the pilots were at last free from worry of fighter interception or the combined firepower of the entire Carrier Striking Force. The claim for over 20 hits on the two cruisers was exaggerated, but the damage was real enough. *Mogami* took five bombs and barely limped into Truk, the big Japanese fleet anchorage in the Carolines. She would be out of action for two years. But her sister *Mikuma* was unable to withstand the massed attacks. She sank that night, taking a thousand of her crew with her.

Yorktown sank on 7 June, finally done in by a prowling Japanese submarine, *I-168*. When she slid under at 1701, the Battle of Midway was over. Spruance turned eastward to link up with the tankers, and also received 34 replacement aircraft from *Saratoga*, which had sailed from San Diego just in time to miss the action. The replacements were badly needed, for the *Enterprise* and *Yorktown* SBD squadrons were down to about half strength. Scouting Five, for instance, had lost nine aircraft when *Yorktown* sank and Adams' plane was shot down by the destroyer *Tanikaze*. Of the remainder, six stayed with *Enterprise*, two went to *Hornet*, and one was returned to Pearl for repair.

Overall, Midway tended to reinforce the lesson of Coral Sea—that carrier versus carrier battles would inevitably result in very high losses. Nearly 110 U.S. carrier aircraft were lost to all causes in the three-day engagement, or about half the total number which departed Pearl Harbor. Potentially severe personnel losses were reduced in the ten days after the battle as PBYs ranged the expanse of the mid-Pacific, rescuing 27 downed fliers. Among them was Ensign Schneider of Bombing Six. Others, like Lieutenant Penland, were picked up by destroyers.

For the aviators, the dominant feeling after three days of constant strikes, searches and patrols was one of numbness. Wally Short's case

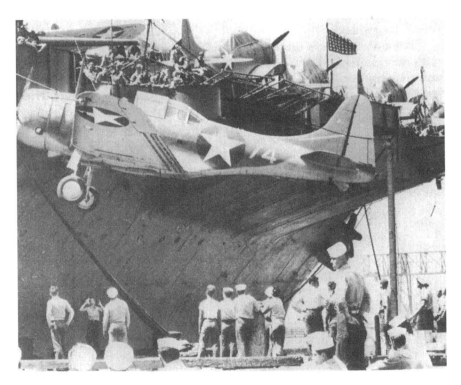

An SBD-3 is hoisted aboard Saratoga *at Pearl Harbor on 6 June 1942. Arriving from the West Coast too late to participate in the Battle of Midway, "Sara" delivered replacement aircraft to* Enterprise *and* Hornet. *(National Archives)*

was typical; he'd flown nearly 13 hours in three days. But if Midway inflicted hardship and loss upon the American air groups, certainly there were exceptional results. The Japanese had lost all of their carriers which were directly engaged; the Americans lost one-third of theirs. Nagumo lost all of his available air strength; Spruance and Fletcher retained half of theirs. By sinking four flattops the SBD squadrons had deprived the Imperial Navy of 47 percent of its front-line carrier tonnage—a staggering blow.

Midway has been called the most important naval battle since Trafalgar. Certainly it was the most important of the twentieth century, and it vindicated the early carrier advocates as the battle was decided entirely by seaborne air power. But though it lasted for over three days the heart of the struggle occurred during the morning of June 4 when fewer than four dozen SBDs arrived over the greatly superior enemy force at its single most vulnerable moment, then struck with inspired dive bombing and cleared out, all in six minutes. Probably no one has better conveyed the essence of that moment than Commander Edward P. Stafford, *Enterprise*'s biographer:

"In a dive bomber's dream of perfection, the clean blue Dauntlesses— with their perforated dive flaps open at the trailing edges of their wings and their big bombs tucked close and pointing home, the pilots straining forward, rudder-feet and stick-hands light and delicate, getting it just right as the yellow decks came up, left hands that would reach down and forward to release now resting on the cockpit edge, gunners lying on their backs behind the cocked twin barrels searching for the fighters that did not come—carved a moment out of eternity for man to remember forever."[20]

In the South Pacific there is an island, dark
and brooding. It is not large as islands go,
nor yet so small as to be forgotten when
one has seen it.

James Michener
Return to Paradise

The first American offensive of World War II opened shortly after dawn on Friday, 7 August 1942 at Guadalcanal in the southern Solomons. Eight months after Pearl Harbor, two months after Midway, the U.S. Navy had overcome the seemingly insurmountable advantage held by the Japanese. The SBD had been instrumental in achieving a new and approximately equal balance of naval power in the Pacific, and now SBDs flew ground support missions for General Alexander Vandegrift's 19,000 Marines as they waded ashore.

Admiral Nimitz had allotted the bulk of his carrier strength to cover the Guadalcanal landings while holding *Hornet* in Hawaiian waters. Three flattops—*Saratoga, Enterprise*, and *Wasp*—were under the direction of Nimitz' most experienced carrier commander, Rear Admiral Frank Jack Fletcher. The "Big E" and "Sara" were veterans of the Pacific, but *Wasp* was a newcomer, having just transited the Panama Canal on 10 July. She carried 30 SBDs of Scouting Squadrons 71 and 72 which, combined with the 37 aboard *Saratoga* and 36 in *Enterprise*, gave Fletcher's three carriers a total of 103 scout-bombers, 99 Wildcats, and 41 new Grumman Avenger torpedo planes.

Wasp's Dauntlesses first got into action when 15 of them worked over the enemy seaplane base at Tulagi early on the seventh, sharing with F4Fs the destruction of 21 moored floatplanes and seaplanes. But in the coming days *Wasp's* SBDs would even outdo her Wildcats, as VS-71 and VS-72 shot down seven Japanese aircraft before the ship's fighters could score a single victory.

Standing air patrols were maintained throughout the morning of 7 August, with Commander Harry Don Felt of the *Saratoga* air group directing most of the sorties from his SBD. There was little ground opposition, and elements of the First Marine Division soon occupied the partially completed Japanese airfield which was the main objective of the invasion. But the Japanese lost little time in reacting to the U.S. foray.

At 1315, 27 Betty bombers and 18 Zeros from Rabaul, 640 miles to the north, were picked up on American radar. Throughout the two enemy air attacks of the day Fletcher's F4Fs lost 11 of their number for 14 of the attackers. The only other U.S. aircraft loss during the seventh was an SBD which jumped four Zeros single-handed, taking them by surprise. The Dauntless pilot opened fire from above and behind, hitting the lead fighter, and quickly banked around heading for the cloud cover.

Flying that lead Zero was Flight Petty Officer Saburo Sakai, an outstanding pilot, who had shot down an F4F earlier in the mission for his fifty-ninth victory. The Japanese ace pursued his assailant through a cloud and shot it down. The SBD pilot—Lieutenant (jg) D. H. Adams of the Wasp's VS-71—bailed out, and was rescued by a U.S. destroyer.

Fletcher's three carriers remained in the area during the eighth but he declined to stay any longer, claiming his fuel situation was approaching the critical point and that his 78 operational fighters were insufficient to protect the task force.

Following Fletcher's controversial decision to withdraw, the Japanese had exclusive use of the sky over all the Solomons, making land-based airpower essential for General Vandegrift's Marines. Rear Admiral John S. McCain, newly appointed commander of all air forces in the South Pacific, stated the requisite course of action to Vandegrift in one succinct message: "The best and proper solution is to get fighters and SBDs onto your field."[1]

The field in question was named for Major Lofton Henderson, the Marine dive bomber leader who died at Midway. By the twelfth the Marines and some Navy personnel had improved upon the work done by the Japanese to the point where the runway was 2,600 feet long and 160 feet wide. A week later, using captured Japanese heavy equipment, the field was over 3,700 feet and covered with gravel.

Henderson Field was about a mile and a half south of Lunga Point, on a grassy plain just off the east bank of the Lunga River. It ran nearly east and west and was only a quarter-mile from the northern base of a mile-long piece of high ground which will always be known in Marine Corps history as Bloody Ridge. The First Division held only a small pocket between Point Cruz on the west and the Ilu River to the east, but it was the defensive perimeter for Henderson Field. A second airstrip, slightly south and east of Henderson, would be designated for fighter use.

The unit chosen to spearhead the air defense of Guadalcanal was Marine Air Group 23. The group had been formed in May at Ewa Field in Hawaii and was training pilots for operational flying in second-line aircraft. The two fighter squadrons were using antiquated Brewster Buffaloes while the two scout-bomber units, VMSB-231 and 232, had cast-off SBD-2s. The Dauntless squadrons were the same ones which had been clobbered on the ground at Pearl Harbor.

The skipper of VMSB-232 was Lieutenant Colonel Richard C. Mangrum, an old hand around Marine aviation. He had joined the Corps out of college in 1928 and had flown fighters as well as dive bombers, in addition to a stint at instructing in the reserves. Mangrum had been at Pearl Harbor all through 1941 with MAG-21 and his session with the Sunday paper had been interrupted by the sound of exploding Japanese bombs on 7 December. He had assumed command of VMSB-232 in January 1942, and spent the next six months trying to keep the squadron all together long enough to make it operational.

It was no easy job, as Mangrum recalled, "New pilots trickled in slowly, as did new enlisted personnel, and squadrons subdivided like amoeba forming new units. With five officers of varying experience, I acquired around 1 July ten new second lieutenants fresh from accelerated flight training and their average flight time was some 250 hours, mostly in various training aircraft and none of it in SBDs."[2]

Mangrum had some 3,000 hours flying time, nearly all in various single-engine types, and began a rigorous training program intended to impart as much of his knowledge to the youngsters as possible. His operations officer was Captain Bruce Prosser who in mid-1942 had the priceless asset of some combat experience, having flown an SB2U at Midway. With nearly 700 hours of military flying, Prosser was a big help in Mangrum's stepped-up training program. Mangrum characterized Prosser as "literally the backbone of 232, a superb pilot beloved by the younger pilots."[3]

In early July, MAG-23 became the unexpected recipient of top-line combat aircraft, meaning F4F-4s for VMF-223 and 224, and SBD-3s for VMSB-231 and 232. The forward echelon of the group would be VMF-223 and VMSB-232, with the other squadrons to follow two weeks later. It gave the first two units less than a month to be combat-ready before shipping out. Mangrum's squadron was officially alerted on 5 July for the South Pacific—destination unknown—and obtained the last 12 SBD-3s in the Fleet Aircraft pool. There weren't any more available, leaving VMSB-232 under strength by one-third.

The squadron's enlisted personnel were also under half strength but Mangrum and Prosser did what they could to get ready. Mangrum recalled, "The next 30 days was a period of frantic shakedown of pilots, planes and rear-seat gunners; dive bombing practice day and night, and carrier qualification for the new pilots. For aircraft maintenance, tools and spare parts were practically nonexistent and we had to make do with what little we could collect and improvise. Under the circumstances and in light of later experience, it was rather remarkable that our contribution was effective."[4]

On 2 August, the 12 SBDs of VMSB-232 and 19 Wildcats of VMF-223 were loaded onto the escort carrier *Long Island*, while the ground crews and their equipment went aboard a transport and slipped out of Pearl Harbor. The plan was to put the two squadrons ashore just as soon after the Guadalcanal landings as possible, but the loss of allied cruisers *Astoria, Quincy*, and *Vincennes* in the Battle of Savo Islands on the ninth forced a delay. *Long Island* put into the Fijis on the thirteenth, awaiting further developments.

A few days later the situation had stabilized enough for *Long Island* to proceed with her mission. In the meantime, Mangrum had received orders to hang a 500-pound bomb on each SBD to help supplement the meager supply on hand at Guadalcanal. He remembers the reaction as:

"Consternation! We could see ourselves flopping into the water off the bow."[5]

Long Island was a converted merchant vessel with a 400-foot flight deck, only half the length of a regular flattop and not much more than half the speed. It would be a tricky matter getting off that short space in even a lightly loaded aircraft. Bruce Prosser noted with something less than enthusiasm that, in addition to the bombs, the crew chiefs and rear-seat men had stowed away as much baggage and bulky material in the planes as room allowed. Tool chests and spare parts had been stashed in many SBDs in anticipation of limited supplies on Guadalcanal. All in all, it appeared that getting off *Long Island's* short deck would involve more luck than skill.

There was a bit of light shining through the gloom, however, in the form of the ship's catapult—a not altogether trustworthy device. But the "cat" would have to be used, because with 31 planes on deck there was absolutely no room to spare for a deck run.

By the early afternoon of 20 August the little carrier arrived at a point nearly two hundred miles southeast of Guadalcanal. Fortunately the Pacific remained perfectly calm, a stiff breeze conveniently picked up, and the pilots had all the wind they needed for a safe launch. It was a tedious process, though, because owing to insufficient space on deck and the single catapult, all 31 planes had to be fired off one at a time. *Long Island* plowed into the steady southeast trade wind for over an

The escort carrier Long Island, *which delivered the first two Marine squadrons to Guadalcanal on 20 August 1942. Twelve SBDs and 19 Wildcat fighters were catapulted off her short deck. (U.S. Navy)*

hour until the last plane was flung off the deck. Though many of the pilots were brand new to carrier operations, the dozen SBDs and 19 F4Fs all got off without a hitch. After one last circle over the ship the Marines set course for Guadalcanal.

It was getting on towards 1600 when the "Mud Marines" detected the sound of many aircraft approaching the island. From force of habit developed since the initial landings they assumed it was another Japanese raid. This time, however, the planes sported the white star instead of the red sun and a crowd quickly gathered to watch Guadalcanal's air force arrive.

The Marines who had been on the receiving end of so many Japanese bombs were delighted to see the Grumman Wildcats, but General Vandegrift was particularly glad to have the dozen SBDs. They were a small but very real threat to Japanese shipping in the lower Solomons and once arrived at CACTUS (code name for Guadalcanal) immediately became a more prominent threat. Lieutenant Colonel Mangrum was the first to land and was warmly greeted by Vandegrift.

Mangrum at once began scrutinizing the setup, and it was something of an enlightenment, to understate the situation. The fliers had absolutely no previous knowledge of the conditions under which they would live and work but, as Mangrum said, "The general concept of Marine Corps operations and training and planning envisions rough field conditions, but just how rough is sometimes a bit shocking even to Marines!"

To begin with, there were no vehicles for refueling or arming the aircraft so nearly all heavy work had to be done manually. This was a tedious and time-consuming task, performed largely by a Navy service unit. Bombs, ammunition, and fuel drums had to be manhandled, and there wasn't much manpower. Fuel was hand-pumped from 55-gallon drums, but the overworked pumps soon wore out.

The field itself was troublesome. It had been covered with gravel but the parking areas were dirt—"either mud or dust, or both at once," Mangrum said.[6] It was widely held that Guadalcanal was the only place on earth where you could stand up to your knees in mud and still have dust blow in your eye. The loose gravel, blasted by prop wash, turned the SBDs' undersides into battered, twisted metal. After awhile landing flaps were pitted from the gravel kicked up during takeoff because the pilots had to partially lower their flaps to help get heavily loaded aircraft off the relatively short field.

Maintenance on the aircraft was virtually impossible for all but the barest essentials because of the chronic shortage of mechanics and tools. The climate and working conditions were far from conducive to sanitary repairs, but the few mechanics and crew chiefs who were on hand did a bang-up job. Mangrum observed that, "Fortunately the handful of squadron mechanics who were brought up from Efate by destroyer, and who had to carry the whole load for the first two weeks, were experienced oldtimers and they were absolutely magnificent."[7]

But Mangrum also placed a good deal of credit on the aircraft itself. "The ruggedness of the SBD kept us in business," he said. "The Dauntless never let us down."[8]

Though loose gravel caused trouble with landing flaps and propellers, it was strangely not much worse on planes maintenance-wise than the pierced steel planking (PSP) which was laid down to improve the field. PSP was a big improvement in that it reduced rock and gravel damage and made the field more usable in muddy conditions. But a bomb hit on the planks resulted in a twisted, jagged rip in the steel which easily cut a tire to shreds, and a blowout on takeoff could be calamitous. The SBDs' small, hard rubber carrier-type tailwheel tires were also unsuitable for land-based operations, but the larger pneumatic tires were slow in coming.

A little more equipment was unloaded from transports in the next couple of weeks but the strain of heavy work never eased. Only a couple of small tractors were available to haul planes, but bomb lorries and hoists were nonexistent most of the time and even 1,000-pound bombs had to be manhandled into place. But Bruce Prosser observed that Yankee ingenuity made up for the lack of certain equipment: "One thing that struck me on Guadalcanal was the dedication and long hours the men put in, plus the ingenuity that Americans have. If something broke down or we didn't have it, there always seemed to be some kid who was raised on a farm who could rig up something which would do the job."[9] Thus by a blending of dedication, skill, and inventiveness did the small air force on CACTUS stay in the air.

There was no breaking-in period for the newly arrived fliers. The schedule devised for VMSB-232 called for morning and evening searches to provide advance warning of Japanese bombardment missions or new attempts to land more troops. The Marines flew the same style of search missions as their Navy counterparts—two-plane sections, each SBD armed with a 500-pound, general-purpose bomb.

Mangrum's dive bombers had been largely intended for use against enemy shipping but in no time at all they were flying every possible type of mission: searches, patrols, strikes, infantry support, message drops and even antisubmarine work. Flying in the Solomons took some getting used to, because Guadalcanal is ten degrees below the equator. The sun rises with astonishing abruptness in those latitudes; Bruce Prosser recalled his first night patrol: "I was flying around not really sure where I was. Then the sun came up so fast that it kind of hurt my eyes, and I saw I was over all kinds of islands I hadn't even known were there."[10]

Night flying was done by aid of lanterns put at both ends of the runway; none were needed along the sides. The SBD, being a stable aircraft, helped simplify the potentially risky business of landing on a darkened and not entirely familiar field at night with tall palm trees all around.

In the uncertain days VMSB-232 spent on Guadalcanal the pilots often wondered when they took off who would be in possession of Henderson Field when they returned. Many of the searches were flown "to see if we or the Japanese were getting supplies that day." More often than not it was the Japanese in the early period following the squadron's arrival, but the enemy soon became wary of operating their ships within SBD range during daylight. After that, American transports would unload off the beach by day while Japanese ships, usually fast destroyer-transports dubbed the "Tokyo Express," performed a similar function by night.

The Tokyo Express became a familiar feature of life at Guadalcanal. It was impossible to get enough sleep between frequent naval bombardments by Japanese warships and low-flying enemy aircraft known as "Washing Machine Charlies." And living conditions were just about as basic as were those for aircraft maintenance. Everybody lived in tents with dirt floors. Food was bland and unappealing, consisting largely of Spam and captured Japanese rice.

Despite the rugged conditions, the pace of operations picked up almost immediately and the first major Japanese thrust developed on the afternoon of 23 August. A PBY detected an enemy transport force heading south, obviously for Guadalcanal. It posed a serious threat to Vandegrift's tenuous hold on his little part of the island, and he made a tough decision which, for all he knew, would cost him most of his tiny air force. The general ordered what amounted to a maximum effort strike—nine SBDs and a dozen F4Fs. Mangrum led the formation off at 1630 and headed out to attack the transports.

Unknown to Vandegrift or Admiral Fletcher, who was back in the area with his three carriers, the transports reversed course to avoid being caught without air support and were never attacked. They were part of a typically complex Japanese naval plan which included carriers, battleships, and cruisers spread over a wide expanse of ocean with the aim of eliminating whatever air cover might be available to the Marines. Once Henderson Field was delt with and the U.S. carriers were sunk or driven off, it would be much easier to recapture Guadalcanal.

In pilots' slang the weather was dirty, with low clouds and heavy rain squalls. Not an hour away from Henderson, Mangrum's formation ran smack into torrents of rain and near-zero visibility. There was no point in proceeding under such conditions so the 21 pilots reluctantly turned back. It was highly distressing to all concerned, for the Japanese transports would presumably land their troops during the night. Not until much later did a belated PBY contact report inform those on CACTUS that the transports were withdrawing to the north.

Fletcher also knew about the transports, and launched a much larger strike from *Saratoga*. The 31 SBDs and six TBFs led by Commander Don Felt encountered the same squall line as Mangrum, but from the opposite, seaward side. The carrier pilots flew through the storm on instruments and, not finding their target, set course for Henderson Field to spend the night. They might not have found *Saratoga* in the dark.

Felt arrived with his planes at dusk, about 1830, and all were safely down by 1900 thanks to an improvised lighting system composed mainly of jeep headlights. The Navy fliers drew some scattered tracer fire, either from nearby Japanese or trigger-happy Marines, but there was no damage. Mangrum made his guests at home, as much as the limited facilities allowed, and found temporary berths for them in the tents situated around the field. Felt's crews dug into the emergency rations carried in their planes, preferring them to the meager fare the Marines had to offer. The little group of Navy servicing personnel worked through the night to have all 37 *Saratoga* aircraft fueled by dawn.

During the evening Felt was in contact with his ship and received orders to take the air group back aboard at 1100 next morning. The hard-working, sweating ordnance and maintenance men detached nearly thirty 1,000-pound bombs from the SBDs, to be left on Guadalcanal since none of the heavy bombs were currently on hand. Felt then took off with his carrier planes and headed out to sea. They had a date with a Japanese carrier later that day in the engagement which became known as the Battle of the Eastern Solomons.

Late that night, the twenty-fourth, another formation of Navy SBDs was overhead. They belonged to the *Enterprise* air group, having flown a lengthy search-strike mission. Not finding any Japanese ships, the formation leader, Lieutenant Turner F. Caldwell, elected to head for Guadalcanal with his 11-plane unit (eight from VS-5 and three of VB-6) known as *Enterprise* Flight 300. Despite a dark night and restricted visibility owing to low clouds all 11 SBDs made it to Henderson Field but the crews arrived "without even so much as a toothbrush."

Flight 300 would become an integral part of the defense at Guadalcanal, and its arrival doubled the offensive capability of Vandegrift's airpower. Caldwell and his ten pilots would live, eat and fly with Mangrum's crews, often in the same formations, because between the Marine and Navy dive bombers there was barely a whole squadron.

Flight 300 received a rude welcome to "the Canal" shortly after midnight as five Japanese destroyers shelled the area for two hours. Mangrum took two of his pilots, Captain Iverson and Lieutenant Baldinus, aloft at 0230 to exact some sort of revenge upon the offending vessels, but no hits were obtained. "I doubt we accomplished much more than astonish the hell out of them," Mangrum said.

The fliers wouldn't give up, though, and about an hour before dawn three *Enterprise* pilots took a shot at the destroyers that were clearing out through Indispensable Strait. The Navy SBDs were led by Lieutenant Roger Woodhull, a Coral Sea veteran and executive officer of Scouting Five, with Ensigns Walter Coolbaugh and Walter Brown on his wing. The Japanese ships proved as slippery as before and evaded damage, but Brown became disoriented in the dark and ran out of fuel. He ditched his SBD safely off Malaita, northeast of Guadalcanal. Flight 300 had lost its first plane barely six hours after arriving.

The sun had been over the horizon little more than an hour when the third strike took off. Eight SBDs—Mangrum with four Marines and Caldwell with two more Navy planes—were designated to go after the same transport group which had caused so much concern the day before. The three transports were accompanied by four elderly destroyers and the light cruiser *Jintsu*, plus the troublesome quintuplet of destroyers the Dauntlesses had attacked in the small hours of the morning. Flying above the clouds the eight SBDs were able to initiate a surprise attack on the ships with Mangrum's division drawing a bead on *Jintsu* while Caldwell took his section down on the largest transport. There was no opposition but Mangrum's bomb didn't release, so he pulled out with it still in place. But his fledgling dive bombers gave the old cruiser a working-over. Second Lieutenants Hise, Thomas and McAllister each obtained near misses and the last man down, Lieutenant Larry Baldinus, planted his bomb on the forecastle between the two forward 5.5-inch gun mounts.

Turner Caldwell missed his target, the transport *Kinryu Maru*, but Ensign Christian Fink was right behind him and got a direct hit amidships, starting a fair-sized fire. The flames spead to the ammunition and secondary explosions stopped the ship dead in the water, in sinking condition. *Jintsu* too was in bad shape and had already turned north for Truk when, after reforming his eight planes, Mangrum turned command of the formation over to Caldwell and went back to put his bomb where it would do some good.

Two-Thirty-Two's SBD-3s didn't have the electrical bomb releases which most later models featured, and the manual mechanisms sometimes didn't work. It could have been anything; "dirt in the works or maybe I simply didn't yank hard enough," Mangrum speculated. At any rate, he dived on one of the transports and dropped his bomb close in the water. After pull-out he suddenly found himself face to face with a Japanese single-engine floatplane which presented a good target for the

SBD's forward-firing .50 calibers. But Mangrum's guns wouldn't fire and, "We both sought the interior of friendly clouds and I never saw him again."[11]

It was the Marines' first introduction to enemy aircraft in general and to the various types of floatplanes which abounded in the Solomons. These particular aircraft, which included a float-equipped version of the notorious Zero, were also encountered by the rest of the Dauntlesses on the trip back to Henderson. Marine gunners claimed two shot down, but it is unknown if they were actually destroyed.

This mission of 25 August was one of the very few times VMSB-232 tangled with enemy aircraft. Inexperienced as most of his crews were, Mangrum realized that air combat would have been a futile affair and recommended that if faced with another scrap, the pilots should resort to evasion. Fighter escort, owing to the restricted number of available Wildcats, was impossible. "We thought it would be nice to have fighter escort when we went somewhere," Mangrum said, "but the essential task of our fighters was to protect the beachhead against air attack and they were superb in the job. Conversely, the primary task of Japanese fighters was to protect their bombers and Guadalcanal was then at about their maximum radius of action. Thus they had no time to get after us, and we could usually keep out of their way."[12]

The eight Dauntlesses returned from the first effective Henderson-launched shipping strike to be refueled and rearmed, but the sorely undermanned ground staff took two hours to get nine planes ready to go. The exhausted pilots and gunners tried to catch up on the sleep they'd missed during the night but were back in the air before noon. All serviceable planes were scrambled to avoid an incoming Japanese raid which did little damage. The few holes in the gravel runway were filled before the CACTUS airplanes returned, while Bruce Prosser led a small attack on enemy troops. The night of the twenty-fifth was blissfully unexciting, allowing the pilots of VMSB-232 to get the first decent sleep they had since landing five days before.

When General Vandegrift took time to total up the state of his air force that evening the picture was grim. Eleven of the 31 F4Fs and SBDs that had landed on the twentieth were either lost or down for maintenance. In statistical terms it meant that five days after air operations began on Guadalcanal the original air strength had been reduced by a third. Nine of 232's SBDs remained operational, two were grounded pending arrival of spare parts, and one had crashed. As Mangrum noted, "For about two days there was practically no maintenance done—we just flew 'em as they were."[13]

Turner Caldwell's ten remaining SBDs made up for a lot. An Army fighter squadron had landed a few days before but its Bell P-39s were almost useless for attacks on warships. Vandegrift sent an urgent message to the Commander, South Pacific Forces which ended, "Recommend rear echelon MAG-23 arriving Samoa late August be sent CACTUS with spare aircraft, earliest practicable date."[14]

The long, seemingly endless trail had begun. The aviators lived in a perpetual state of chaos, going from one crisis to another in their determined efforts to keep the Japanese from reinforcing the island. The pace was rigorous—Bruce Prosser, for instance, would fly 28 missions of various natures in 29 days.

Dauntlesses got another crack at enemy warships late in the afternoon of 28 August. A pair of scouting SBDs dived on four troop-carrying destroyers just 70 miles north of Guadalcanal at 1700. Though they got no hits, they radioed a warning which brought 11 dive bombers down on the Japanese ships within 30 minutes. Turner Caldwell, whose Flight 300 was by now virtually an integral part of Mangrum's squadron, led his five planes in first. Ensign Chris Fink boresighted the leading destroyer, *Asagiri*, and drilled her through the middle with his 1,000-pounder. She blew up and sank on the spot. The quietly efficient Caldwell put his heavy bomb on another destroyer, *Shirakumo*, which was so heavily damaged she had to be towed from the area by the only undamaged ship remaining. The other destroyer was *Yugiri*, which suffered extensive damage at the hands of Mangrum's half-dozen planes.

Antiaircraft fire from the undamaged *Amagiri* accounted for the only loss on this mission as Lieutenant Oliver Mitchell's SBD crashed in the water. Mitchell and his gunner were the only VMSB-232 personnel lost in the air to enemy action during the squadron's eight weeks in combat. But the mission proved conclusively for the second consecutive occasion that it was futile to attempt daylight reinforcement of Guadalcanal as long as offensive aircraft remained on Henderson Field. The "Cactus Patch" was growing thorns.

Henderson's offensive capability was increased on the twenty-ninth with the arrival of VMSB-232's ground personnel by transport. It had been nine days since the Dauntlesses had received more than cursory maintenance. Since Caldwell's flight was also operating with Mangrum's unit the maintenance program was larger than envisioned. But all concerned were much relieved to have an adequate ground staff on hand.

The mechanics and weapons specialists arrived none too soon, for the SBDs were airborne that night in search of a Japanese destroyer force which had been reported south of the Shortland Islands, off Bougainville. The operational Dauntlesses took off at midnight, with a full moon and few clouds, on a search-strike mission which held some promise, but the destroyer-transports escaped detection. If the mission accomplished nothing else, at least it served notice to the Japanese that not

Lack of proper maintenance facilities was a constant problem during the Guadalcanal Campaign. Note the rough patches on the tail of this Marine SBD-3. (U.S. Marine Corps)

even the fabled nocturnal runs of the Tokyo Express could go completely unchallenged.

The next day, 30 August, was an auspicious one for the infantry and aviators alike. It saw the first aerial reinforcements touch down at Henderson: a dozen SBDs of Major Leo Smith's VMSB-231 and 19 Wildcats led by Major Robert E. Galer of VMF-224. These two units completed MAG-23 and more or less—mostly less—brought the group up to strength. It now numbered 30 SBDs and 26 F4Fs. Smith's executive officer was Captain Elmer Glidden who had flown at Midway.

Henderson Field's air strength would be augmented further by a curious twist of fate which was the Navy's misfortune and the Marines' windfall. Cruising southeast of San Cristobal on the last day of August the unlucky *Saratoga* caught a submarine torpedo, her second of the war. She was in no danger of sinking but required extensive repairs. Except for a minimum force of antisub and CAP aircraft the "Sara's" air group flew to Espiritu Santo. Admiral John McCain, ComAirSoPac, directed all available carrier squadrons to proceed to Guadalcanal at the earliest possible date. But it would be many days before any new planes arrived.

Other means of assistance were also headed for Guadalcanal, not the least of which was an overall air commander for the CACTUS air force. He was Brigadier General Roy S. Geiger, who landed in an R4D on the evening of 3 September. Imbued with a highly aggressive spirit, Geiger had been a Marine aviator since 1917.

Under Geiger's direction the aircraft began new operations almost immediately. On the sixth, rather soupy weather prevented Japanese air attacks on Henderson so he sent 11 SBDs up the island chain to work over ships and whatever targets might be found ashore at Gizo Bay in the New Georgia group. Two Dauntlesses of VMSB-232 became lost in the storms which built up that afternoon, as Major F. L. Brown and Lieutenant C. B. McAllister never returned.

Replacements arrived the same day, however, as the first *Saratoga* SBDs landed at Henderson Field. Six VS-3 aircraft, preceding the main group by a week, immediately took over scouting duties, thereby relieving the Marine squadrons for more strike missions. Heavy and persistent rain on the seventh didn't prevent one of the *Saratoga* pilots from discovering several Japanese troop barges and shooting them up. Air operations could have been cancelled the next day because of more rain, but they weren't. Henderson Field was as yet only partly covered with pierced steel matting, leaving most of its length in a six-inch-deep morass of sticky mud. The accident rate was accordingly high—six Wildcats piled up—but SBDs with their wide landing gear didn't have as much trouble.

Two days later, 9 September, the fighters moved over to their own field, helping relieve some of the congestion which characterized life at Henderson.

On the evening of 12 September, Scouting Three reported three different groups of Japanese warships proceeding down The Slot—the open stretch of water between New Georgia and Santa Isabel. The most threatening of these was that built around the cruiser *Tenryu* and three destroyers. Obviously their mission was a bombardment of the Marine positions, but as darkness fell it was impossible to maintain contact. The only thing to do was dig in and wait.

It wasn't as long a wait as the Marines were accustomed to. The Japanese ships shelled American positions twice but Henderson Field was not the primary target. When the first bombardment opened up at 2200, the shells began exploding on Bloody Ridge, just south of the airfield. It was part of a large plan to capture Henderson, as the Japanese had learned through painful experience that the ridge was the key to the area. Vandegrift's infantry held on, though, and remained in position. But Henderson's proximity to the front lines—the runway was barely 2,000 yards to the north—served to bring the fliers under fire anyway. Several shells evidently fell short of their mark and exploded near the encamped aviators, killing three and wounding two. Two of the dead and one of the wounded were from Lieutenant Colonel Mangrum's veteran VMSB-232, which now had only half its original pilots left.

Sunday the thirteenth was another important day in the history of the CACTUS air force. The Wildcats fought a day-long series of running battles with numerous enemy aircraft but nobody saw two Rufe float-plane fighters which darted in low and fast across Henderson at 1730. Lieutenant O. D. Johnson of VMSB-231 was in the landing pattern at that moment and was caught completely helpless at 500 feet. The two Rufes shot the SBD down directly over the field and were gone almost before anyone knew it. The Dauntless exploded on impact.

Ten minutes later 18 planes were overhead and the jumpy antiaircraft gunners immediately opened fire. It was an ungrateful way to greet the largest contingent yet assigned to Geiger's air force, as the newcomers were reinforcements from Espiritu Santo. Actually they weren't strangers to Guadalcanal at all, because most of them had stayed the night of 23 August when Commander Don Felt's *Saratoga* formation dropped in. The new arrivals, happily undamaged, were the remainder of Scouting Three plus six Avengers. The dozen SBDs were led by Lieutenant Commander Louis J. Kirn, skipper of VS-3.

They arrived just in time to fill the gap left by the first dive-bomber unit on the island, VMSB-232. Though the remaining personnel wouldn't depart for about another month, 232's contribution was nearly at an end. Lieutenant L. E. Thomas was tragically killed on the eighteenth when his SBD was hit by AA fire from an American ship, and though two or three VMSB-232 pilots did some flying after mid-September, the fresher new units took over the load.

The load was a tremendous one for the new units to carry, and their task was in no way eased by the rain and low ceilings which clamped right down again during the latter part of the month. Even the more recent arrivals were affected by the adverse climate, weather and living conditions—so much so, in fact, that no enemy ship was hit by a bomb all during September. Lack of sleep, which was often the virtual absence of it, plus the unrelenting strain of operations made itself felt. Pilots and gunners were approaching the point where they were bone-weary all the time. The tireless Roy Geiger, possibly recalling the adage that if you want anything done you have to do it yourself, decided to do just that.

Before noon on the twenty-second the 57-year-old air commander climbed into a Dauntless, started the engine, and gunned the airplane down the runway with a 1,000-pound bomb tucked under its belly. It was the second time Geiger had flown into combat during a world war, as 24 years before he led one of the Marine squadrons in France. The flying general headed west to Cape Esperance and dropped his bomb on an enemy camp. Marines have always led by example but surely Geiger's exploit was one for the books.

Almost as if in response to Geiger's colorful action, the advance section of another SBD squadron landed at Henderson the next day. These were five planes of VMSB-141, the balance of the unit arriving over the next two weeks. Major Gordon A. Bell took the largest portion of 141 to The Canal on October 5 when he and 20 other pilots landed. This was the largest unit to operate from Henderson Field during the campaign, with a total strength of 39 crews.

On 27 September, nearly 20 Bettys with strong Zero escort battled past the defending F4Fs to inflict heavy damage on Henderson. Only one SBD was destroyed, but four more Dauntlesses and three TBFs sustained damage serious enough to ground them indefinitely. That evening Geiger could count on just 18 SBDs and a pair of Avengers as operational strike aircraft. At the same time Turner Caldwell and the last four of his *Enterprise* pilots departed Guadalcanal. For over a month they had learned how their Marine counterparts lived, firsthand. The carrier pilots had made their presence felt during their tenure with Mangrum's squadron; they sank a transport and a destroyer and damaged at least one other destroyer.

As was fortuitously so often the case on Guadalcanal, more pilots and gunners arrived to take the place of those who were leaving. Six SBDs and four Avengers flew in from Espiritu Santo late on the twenty-eighth to help bring Geiger's forces up to strength. Three of the Dauntlesses were late additions to Scouting Three and the rest were Scouting 71 planes, lately of the *Wasp* Air Group. Their leader, Lieutenant Commander John Eldridge, would join Turner Caldwell as one of the outstanding Navy pilots to fly from Henderson Field. Eight more of Eldridge's planes joined him five days later, on 3 October.

One of the VS-71 pilots, Lieutenant (jg) R. H. Perritte, mysteriously disappeared during a patrol on 2 October. Then the mid-afternoon search the next day turned up more big news, predictably bad. Around 1530, a pair of scouts located the Japanese seaplane tender *Nisshin* escorted by six destroyers about two hundred miles northwest of Guadalcanal. *Nisshin* was carrying tanks and other heavy equipment destined for delivery late that night. The two SBDs were jumped by ten Zeros and barely succeeded in getting away. At 1600 in the western search sector three more destroyers were spotted en route to the island. It was a heavier than usual reinforcement, which meant the ships had to be dealt with immediately.

A strike force of eight SBDs and three TBFs was thrown together and departed 15 minutes after the second contact was radioed in, one Dauntless aborting with engine trouble. The remaining planes headed up The Slot to handle the *Nisshin* force, making contact a little before 1730. The attack was led by Lieutenant (jg) A. S. Frank of Scouting Three but stiff resistance in the form of thick AA fire and wild maneuvering prevented any hits from being made. The Tokyo Express continued on course, arriving at Cape Esperance some five hours later.

In a pot-luck type of mission which would become the norm at Henderson, four Dauntlesses representing four squadrons took off at 2230 with Lieutenant Commander Eldridge of VS-71 in the lead. The strike was almost defeated before it departed, however, as the ex-*Wasp* planes couldn't receive or transmit on the same radio frequency as the other aircraft and Eldridge's flight became separated in the dark. In the end, just Eldridge and his Scouting Three wingman found the vaguely defined shapes below on the dark water, dropped their bombs "by guess and by gosh," and missed the target altogether. The Japanese continued their unloading operation and departed unharmed that night.

The month-long dearth of bomb hits on enemy ships ended 5 October when half a dozen destroyers were located 170 miles west of Guadalcanal during the afternoon search. Considering the large number of troops and equipment landed two nights before, there was no question of the absolute necessity of stopping the next installment of the Tokyo Express. The Marines were barely killing off enemy troops at a rate sufficient to maintain the status quo. If the Japanese obtained a significant advantage for any length of time it could prove decisive to the entire campaign. Lieutenant Commander Kirn of Scouting Three took nine SBDs to try and put a good-sized crimp in the schedule of the Tokyo Express.

Kirn's squadron hadn't had much luck during the Battle of the Eastern Solomons back in August when only near-misses had been scored on the light carrier *Ryujo*. The "Sara's" pilots made a little progress towards redressing that deficiency as Kirn pushed over and lined up the destroyer *Minegumo*. Kirn's bomb and one other exploded very close aboard, one on each bow, rattling the five-year-old destroyer viciously. The VS-3 skipper had reason to believe he'd sunk his target; at least it looked that way from above with two "hits." The damage wasn't quite that severe, however, and *Minegumo* survived to limp back north at less than half her top speed. Three other Dauntlesses plunged down on *Murasame* and laid their bombs close to her port bow. Holed innumerable times by large and small fragments, *Murasame* turned around and followed *Mine-gumo* to the Shortlands.

The remaining four destroyers proceeded with their mission, despite an attack by more SBDs which obtained no hits. Supplies were unloaded west of Lunga Point, just a few miles from Henderson Field, after dark. Dauntlesses with flares to illuminate the area for bomb-toting Avengers were airborne in the night hours, hoping to destroy at least some of the equipment and provisions which got ashore. As was so often the case, results were either negative or unobserved.

Results were observed, however, when VMSB-141 aircraft caught a Japanese force of two light cruisers and four destroyers north of New Georgia. Lieutenant W. H. Fuller claimed a direct hit on a cruiser and the other pilots reported damaging a destroyer, but it is not known how accurate their claims may have been. But three of the ubiquitous enemy floatplanes which intercepted were shot down.

On the evening of 11–12 October, SBDs shadowed various enemy surface units until well after dark. Sufficiently forewarned, the Navy organized a cruiser-destroyer task force which intercepted the Japanese and prevented another bombardment of Henderson Field and the Marine perimeter. The result was a full-scale surface engagement in classic Solomons fashion: nocturnal, brief and bloody. It was called the Battle of Cape Esperance and resulted in the sinking of one American and two Japanese destroyers with heavy damage to cruisers on both sides.

Sixteen SBDs were airborne shortly after dawn on the twelfth to look for targets of opportunity—any Japanese ships which might be left immobile from the night's battle. For one of the very first times in the campaign the dive bombers had heavy fighter cover. North of Russell Island, roughly 30 miles from where the ships had slugged it out, John Eldridge found three enemy destroyers. Two undamaged "cans" were attending to one which had been pummelled during the night's gun duel. Eldridge took his five Scouting 71 planes down on the vulnerable vessels, but all the *Wasp* pilots missed. One of the other three pilots got a near miss on *Murakumo*, holing an oil tank.

At 0800 six SBDs, six TBFs, and 14 Wildcats conducted what was quite possibly the best coordinated air attack of the campaign. The redoubtable Lou Kirn led a mixed group of dive bombers from VS-71, VMSB-141, and his own VS-3 which waited for the Wildcats to strafe the destroyers and suppress AA fire. The Dauntlesses then pounced on *Murakumo* and did some of the best bombing seen in the Solomons for almost a month and a half. Three of the six got near misses which set up the destroyer for the Avengers. One of the Torpedo Eight pilots slipped his fish into *Murakumo*'s side, bringing her to a stop. She went down that afternoon, the first enemy ship sunk by aircraft from Henderson Field since Turner Caldwell's Flight 300 did away with the destroyer *Asagiri* on 28 August.

The SBDs didn't have to share the next kill with anyone. Eldridge was out again an hour before dusk with a ten-plane strike which caught up with the last two undamaged destroyers. The VS-71 skipper led pilots from three squadrons in the dive on *Natsugumo* and expertly put his bomb slightly aft of amidships. Two other pilots scored near misses which put a finish to the thin-hulled ship. She exploded, turned on one side and slowly settled.

Retribution for the unqualified drubbing the CACTUS air force had inflicted on the destroyers was not long in coming. Two heavy air raids disrupted Henderson during the thirteenth, the date VMSB-232 officially left Guadalcanal, but were ineffectual by comparison with what happened beginning at 0140 on the fourteenth. The dense tropical darkness was suddenly split open in three places by garish splotches of red, white and green lights as an enemy floatplane dropped parachute flares from east to west directly above Henderson's runway; they were gunnery markers.

As the Marines scrambled for their dugouts and foxholes they detected a growing rumble in the air which increased in intensity and terminated in incredibly huge explosions and concussions which literally shook the ground. Two Japanese battleships hurled over nine hundred 14-inch shells at Henderson Field in less than an hour. They ceased firing at 0230 but were replaced by night-flying Betty bombers which ensured that the Americans on Guadalcanal spent a thoroughly miserable six hours.

At dawn the shaken, stunned defenders dug themselves out of the incredible wreckage and began to take inventory. Over 40 personnel had been killed during the terrible shelling, which forever after would be known as The Bombardment. It had left VMSB-141 virtually leaderless as Major Bell, his executive officer, a flight commander and two pilots had been killed; in short, every officer above the rank of second lieutenant. Scouting 71 also lost a senior pilot, Lieutenant W. P. Kephart.

Radio communications were out for hours and almost the entire supply of high-octane aviation gas was gone, burned up. It was just as bad among the strike aircraft: only seven Dauntlesses remained airworthy of the 39 which had been available the day before, and no Avengers were fit for service. The one redeeming feature was that thanks to the movement of all fighters to the "Cow Pasture," nearly 30 F4Fs were serviceable.

But whatever satisfaction existed about the island's fighter force disappeared when the morning scouts reported two groups of enemy ships bearing down on Guadalcanal—six transports with destroyer escorts, and two heavy cruisers with a pair of destroyers. There was never a gloomier or more dismal outlook for the prospects of holding Guadalcanal than on the morning of 14 October. Major elements of the Imperial Navy were obviously bent on shelling the rubble left by the two battleships while tremendous troop reinforcements were put ashore. It didn't require a pessimist to deduce the situation was approaching the irretrievable.

Meanwhile, the mechanics worked with dogged perseverance patching up just a few more dive bombers to help meet the new threat. Under the direction of Lieutenant William Woodruff the Navy servicing unit had four SBDs adequately repaired to make an attack upon the rapidly approaching transports by 1500. The troopships were well defended, however, and no hits were made. Lou Kirn led nine of his Scouting Three planes out in hopes of hitting the ships in the dark, flying on gas drained from wrecked B-17s. This attack too was ineffective, even though supported by Marine and Army fighters. Kirn's pilots had to land after dark on the cratered runway, risking further aircraft losses at a time when Geiger could least afford it. He clamped down and flatly refused to authorize more night flying. There were precisely five flyable Dauntlesses left on Guadalcanal at the end of the day.

The only land-based dive bombers in the South Pacific which were not on Guadalcanal were eight ex-*Enterprise* SBDs and nine spares, all at Espiritu Santo, thus the total reserves available to the Navy and Marines were 17 Dauntlesses with eight crews to fly them. The eight VB-6 planes had gone south with Lieutenant Commander Ray Davis after the

A Dauntless is pulled ashore from a ferry barge at Espiritu Santo in the New Hebrides, a staging base for Guadalcanal. (U.S. Navy)

Eastern Solomons battle. Now they were ordered immediately up to Guadalcanal and a transport plane was sent to fetch nine fighter pilots back to Espiritu so they could fly the spare SBDs to Henderson. The Pacific Fleet's two remaining carriers were in no position to lend a hand at the time, since *Enterprise* was still at Pearl Harbor and *Hornet* was well out to sea.

Top priority was given to shipment of aviation fuel by sea and air but Henderson Field was chronically short of gas and there had been no way to build up any kind of appreciable reserve in anticipation of a catastrophe like The Bombardment. The fuel en route to Guadalcanal was only enough to maintain the supply at the minimum level. Complete replenishment would take longer, but at least ComSoPac appreciated the problem and moved to deal with it.

Almost lost in the confusing maze of the day's events was the departure of Lieutenant Colonel Richard Mangrum, the first CACTUS pilot to touch down on Henderson Field and the last of the original group to leave. Six of his 12 pilots had been killed or were missing and the remaining five had departed by 2 October. Mangrum flew to Efate to round up some of his wounded personnel and proceeded to Noumea to rejoin the other survivors. He had spent 55 days on Guadalcanal, and in the estimation of his associates had done as much as any individual to defend the island.

Henderson Field took another beating that night, and while it wasn't as vicious as the one before, it was bad enough. Two heavy cruisers did quite a thorough wrecking job while another 4,000 enemy troops went ashore. In the morning's first light the Marines could see five Japanese transports discharging their cargo, confident that no effective air force remained ashore.

They weren't far wrong. Only three Dauntlesses remained operational and Henderson's runway was spotted with 19 large-caliber shell holes. By scrounging fuel from wrecked aircraft—of which there were plenty—it was possible to prepare the trio of dive bombers for action. The air operations officer, Major Joe Renner, laid out a winding, crooked path through the craters with a series of flare pots. Fortunately the fighter strip was more or less intact and Renner led two of the SBDs to a position at the end of the fighter runway, the pilots using the flares to find their way in the dim light. Half of this miniature strike force was wiped out when one SBD ran into an unseen shell hole near the middle of the runway.

Renner decided more of a detailed briefing was needed so he collected the second pilot, Lieutenant Robert M. Patterson of VMSB-141, and drove him the length of the fighter strip in a jeep, shining a flashlight at the more notable features. It was still before 0500 when Patterson stood on the brakes, ran his engine up to full power and started down the field. But he fell afoul of the same hazard as the first pilot when one wheel ran over the edge of a large shellhole. Both Patterson and his gunner emerged unharmed from the wreck gamely asking to try again with the last remaining SBD. By this time there wasn't much difference between one operational dive bomber and none at all, so permission was granted.

The intrepid Patterson took off successfully at dawn but immediately discovered he had all kinds of problems. The landing gear wouldn't retract and the dive flaps wouldn't work either. Shell fragments had punctured the plane's hydraulic system during the shelling and nobody had noticed it in the darkness. No one would have blamed him for turning around and trying to land but Patterson elected to continue. He began climbing as fast as he could to gain altitude for a lone attack on the transports just ten miles west of Henderson Field. With his wheels down and dive flaps still frozen shut, Patterson went down through a heavy AA barrage, all the time trying to get his sights steadied on target as the SBD bucked and jerked in protest to the odd diving configuration. But Patterson was master of the situation and had the pleasure of seeing his bomb strike one of the transports.

Meanwhile the ground staff had accomplished two not-so-minor miracles. Over 350 half-forgotten drums of gasoline had been rediscovered, and Lieutenant Woodruff's maintenance people were repairing SBDs sufficiently to fly. Several pilots made solo attacks until Geiger stopped individual sorties in order to organize a maximum-effort strike of 21 aircraft composed of five different types. The mechanics had a dozen SBDs ready to go by mid-morning, probably the third little miracle of the day, and they would coordinate with four Wildcats, four Army P-39s, and General Geiger's personal PBY which was armed with two torpedoes.

The mismatched formation went in to the attack at 1000, with the Dauntlesses diving on the transports from 9,000 feet while the PBY went in low and got one hit. The strike was more successful than anyone expected, and as more missions proceeded throughout the day three transports were beached while the fires raging aboard gradually burned themselves out. Zeroes were overhead most of the time, shooting up several planes, but the transports took a beating. The two not sunk were both damaged in a final mission by three Bombing Six planes.

On the debit side of the ledger was the fact that all the enemy troops and most of their supplies had been put ashore and six of the CACTUS planes had been lost. Three were SBDs, the crews missing in action. At the end of the day Geiger's maintenance and ordnance crews slumped in exhaustion after 48 hours on the job.

Another fearsome bombardment began early on 16 October but damage to aircraft was slight. Partially it was due to the fact that so few planes remained intact; the SBDs were down to ten effectives at daybreak. But together with seven P-39s they carried out bombing and strafing missions against the newly landed Japanese forces. The Army and Marine planes flew as often as possible, many times only in sections of two, which made the absence of Japanese fighters fortunate indeed. The only loss was yet another SBD of VMSB-141, a victim of ground fire.

The sixteenth saw the departure of the last elements of MAG-23, the first air group to operate on Guadalcanal. The first two squadrons had already gone, and now the pilots of VMF-224 and VMSB-231—what was left of them—were flown out by R4D. The last four active pilots of 231 were Captain Elmer "Iron Man" Glidden, Lieutenant G. B. Loeffel and two flying staff sergeants, L. F. Blass and W. W. Witherspoon. Upon their departure Marine Air Group 14 took control of air operations from MAG-23. Next day saw Lieutenant Commander Lou Kirn and the seven remaining VS-3 pilots depart after six weeks in combat, away from the luxury and comfort of Saratoga's easy way of living.

During the afternoon search of the seventeenth Lieutenant (jg) C. H. Mester of VS-71 found himself over Rekata Bay, well known as home of the enemy floatplanes. Mester came upon a Pete biplane taking off from the bay and shot it down, but was jumped in turn by four more Petes and a Rufe. The Dauntless pilot tried to outrun the Mitsubishis but splashed down off Santa Isabel, eventually getting his wounded gunner to safety with an Australian coastwatcher.

That same day SBDs did a turnabout where bombardments were concerned, as three Dauntlesses served as aerial spotters for two U.S. destroyers which shelled Japanese positions at Kokumbona, west of Lunga Point.

Late October saw the largest and most ambitious Japanese effort to capture the most important military position in the South Pacific. A combined offensive with the Imperial Navy and Army working more or less in unison was opened on the twenty-fifth with concentrated attacks on Henderson Field and the fighter strip by air, naval bombardment, land-based artillery and furious infantry charges south of the airfields along Bloody Ridge. The carrier battle of Santa Cruz was a part of this effort.

The weather, ever capricious in the Solomons, favored the Japanese this time. Intense rains again virtually turned the fighter strip into a swamp while enemy field pieces lobbed shells into Henderson every few minutes. The sun was still low on the horizon when six pilots of VMSB-141 risked takeoff under these hazardous conditions for the morning search. Somehow they all made it, and one Dauntless pilot reported three Japanese destroyers less than 40 miles away, heading for The Canal at high speed. Another scout sighted a larger and more potent force a little later about a hundred miles from the field. It was the light cruiser *Yura* and five more destroyers. Things were bad enough without a combined force of eight destroyers and a cruiser shelling Henderson, so a five-plane strike group was formed under the tireless VS-71 skipper, Lieutenant Commander John Eldridge. That left seven SBDs to deal with any other ships which might turn up, but owing to the poor condition of the runway it wasn't until after mid-day that Eldridge led his little group away.

The *Yura* force was picked up within 50 miles of Henderson Field at 1300. Eldridge circled the six ships, evaluating the situation and directing his planes to their targets. He was the first to attack as he rolled his Dauntless into a dive over the hard-turning cruiser. Straining forward against his shoulder harness, Eldridge had the ship firmly in his sights and released at twice the usual altitude. But he was a professional dive-bomber pilot and he did a very professional job as his 1,000-pounder hammered through *Yura*'s deck from 3,000 feet. Eldridge's wingman got a near miss. Then another pilot near-missed the light cruiser with a 500-pound GP, and the battered 20-year-old ship slowly came to a stop.

Following an attack by bomb-carrying P-39s, the SBDs were back again by 1500 as Lieutenant Commander Ray Davis, skipper of Bombing Six, led two Scouting 71 pilots to the crippled *Yura*. Davis went after the destroyer *Akizuki*, the other two after *Yura*. Near misses were scored on both vessels, causing flooding in each. Eldridge was back on the scene 90 minutes later with four SBDs, four P-39s and three F4Fs. An Army pilot put his light bomb on *Yura*, and *Akizuki* took a third near miss. As if that weren't enough, half a dozen B-17s came along and claimed to have hit the cruiser, which was burning by this time. The old *Yura* was sunk by torpedoes from her escorting destroyers off Santa Isabel, and *Akizuki* crawled back north at reduced speed. No naval gunfire was directed at Henderson Field that night.

With the conclusion of the carrier battle off the Santa Cruz islands on the twenty-sixth, a feverish period of operations closed out for the men at Henderson. It was not the last time they would work round the clock in the face of a potentially ruinous situation, but it was the next-to-last time. The aircrews and ground personnel had literally worked themselves into exhaustion during the past two weeks, and while the next several days were by no means inactive, they at least afforded time to recuperate, to bid farewell to many of the old hands and to greet the replacements.

VMSB-141, with Lt. W. S. Ashcroft in command, would stay on for awhile longer but the two Navy contingents, Scouting 71 and Bombing Six, said good-bye to their Marine friends during the first week in November. Arriving at the same time was VMSB-132 under Major Joseph Sailer as the advance element of MAG-11. When he landed on 1 November, Sailer had 37 days in which to fulfill his destiny as a dive-bomber leader.

Sailer's squadron, like nearly all units which flew from Henderson Field between August and November, was in action within 24 hours of its arrival. And it also suffered its first losses in the same period. A large Japanese destroyer force was landing troops on the night of 2 November under cover of low clouds which presumably would keep the dive bombers grounded. But John Eldridge, whose squadron would leave in five days, took off with two of the new Marine pilots to see if the enemy ships could be attacked. General Geiger had recently told Eldridge that he shouldn't do any more flying, as he had already led 14 shipping strikes in addition to numerous other missions in the past five weeks.

It is not known if Eldridge and his two Marine wingmen ever found the destroyers they were looking for, but two of the Dauntlesses were discovered crashed on Santa Isabel. They belonged to Eldridge and Lieutenant Melvin Newman, victims of the intense thunderstorms that had brewed up during the night. The third plane, flown by Lieutenant Wayne Gentry, simply disappeared. Seven of Eldridge's ten pilots finally left Guadalcanal.

The CACTUS air force's last command change came that same week when General Roy Geiger was relieved by Brigadier General Louis Woods.

Prelude to the last of three successive mid-month crises began on Saturday, 7 November when General Woods dispatched a strike of seven SBDs under Major Sailer and three torpedo-packing Avengers to handle a force of 11 destroyers bearing 1,300 enemy troops. One ship was incorrectly identified as a cruiser and received a disproportionate share of the fliers' attention, with claims for two torpedoes and one heavy bomb hit. Pilots said another destroyer took a torpedo and two bombs. Regardless of the relative accuracy of these claims, the destroyers *Takanami* and *Naganami* received some rough handling and were forced to turn back. But despite such reverses the tenacious Japanese continued their supply runs, and landed 65 destroyer loads and two cruiser loads of troops in the first ten days of November.

The CACTUS air force was also receiving reinforcements during this period, and 12 November saw the last Marine SBD squadron to arrive until December. This was VMSB-142 under Major R. H. Richard which accompanied the first Marine TBF squadron to enter combat, VMSB-131. Only ten SBDs arrived with 142's advance echelon, the rest of the squadron coming north the next month. But another six Dauntlesses of Joe Sailer's 132 had landed on the seventh, so while there was no surplus of dive bombers, at least the number was adequate.

But the wily Japanese now had a way of countering the buildup of air power on Guadalcanal. By skillful timing the Tokyo Express could arrive within air scouting range of the island just late enough to make a dusk air attack impossible. The CACTUS air force then had no choice but to attempt a strike in the dark, and nocturnal air attacks had never been very effective since the campaign began.

Henderson's air strength had stabilized on the twelfth at 45 operational aircraft, 24 of which were potentially effective against ships. These were 16 Dauntlesses and eight Avengers, the remainder being Marine, Navy and Army fighters. General Woods was not at all certain this force was substantial enough to handle a large concentration of capital ships such as was expected during the night of the twelfth and thirteenth.

It had been one month since the two battleships had clobbered Henderson Field and the perimeter, and there were plenty of Marines still on Guadalcanal who remembered that bombardment all too well. They fully expected a repeat performance, and when a cruiser floatplane was heard circling overhead at 0130 on Friday the thirteenth, the take-cover warning sounded. Green flares very much like the ones dropped a month before started floating down over Henderson as fliers, mechanics, and staff alike scrambled for cover.

But the only naval gunfire came from the northwest, out towards Savo Island. The fliers realized that American ships were imposing themselves upon the powerful Japanese bombardment force of two battleships, a cruiser and 11 destroyers. Rear Admiral Daniel Callaghan's task force of five cruisers and eight destroyers slugged it out with the Japanese heavyweights, losing two cruisers, *Atlanta* and *Juneau*, and four destroyers, *Cushing*, *Monsson*, *Laffey*, and *Barton*. But the enemy was too occupied to shell the airfield, and the main portion of the naval action was over in half an hour.

The morning scouts were up before dawn, picking their way around scattered squall lines under the low cloud ceiling. On the outbound leg of the Santa Isabel search sector an SBD pilot found a battleship just north of Savo Island. He knew it couldn't be friendly, and upon closer examination saw a light cruiser alongside. The battleship was apparently damaged, and the Dauntless attacked, but its 500-pounder missed.

Three more SBDs were looking for stragglers from the night's battle, and only when they reported back did it become apparent how bloody the surface engagement must have been. Between Savo Island and Lunga Point, a distance of less than 20 miles, were the burning or drifting remains of five American ships and two Japanese. The scout pilots saw the damaged cruiser *Portland* sink the lone Japanese destroyer with a few salvoes. Then they turned their attention further north and sighted the battleship *Hiei*. The 31,000-ton dreadnaught was in a most unenviable position; powerless to move out of air range and unable to maneuver adequately to avoid bombs or torpedoes.

Hiei's plight provided the Marines with an exceptional chance to exact vengeance upon one of the hated ships which had pummeled them so terribly for so many sleepless, terror-filled nights. As quickly as SBDs and TBFs could be armed and fueled they were sent out to work over the 30-year-old battleship. Five Dauntlesses of VMSB-142, serving its first full day on Guadalcanal, took off at 0600 led by Major Robert Richard. They formed up, flew over to Savo Island and 15 minutes after departing the field were diving on their first target. They got a direct hit and a near miss with their 1,000-pounders. It was the first in a day-long series of bomb and torpedo attacks which would become a main feature of the busiest single 48 hours in the history of the Guadalcanal air force.

While Dauntlesses and Avengers concentrated on *Hiei* during the early morning, an important scouting flight was dispatched. A frightening but fortunately inaccurate report of an enemy carrier force in the area occupied ten SBDs and eight escorting F4Fs until they reached the limit of their search about 0720. They radioed back that no Japanese ships had been located, thus setting the stage for the arrival of yet another carrier air group on Guadalcanal.

Enterprise, repaired after damage incurred during the Battle of Santa Cruz in late October, was the only fleet carrier remaining to the U.S. Navy in the Solomons. Her Air Group 10 was waiting to launch aircraft for Henderson Field when and if it was determined there were no Japanese flattops operating nearby. Once that was confirmed, the "Big E" began launching TBFs which detoured to attack *Hiei* before landing on Guadalcanal. The Avengers were on their way by 0830 and spent the rest of the day attacking the crippled battleship with Marine SBDs and TBFs. *Enterprise* kept her SBDs aboard in case they were needed to handle an unexpected threat.

Major Joe Sailer led most of the dive-bomber flights against *Hiei*, his second trip of the day being in company with five VMSB-132 planes. The six pilots made three direct hits at 1120, just before Torpedo Eight launched its last attack before going south to Espiritu. Two torpedoes hit. The *Enterprise* TBFs made another three hits a couple of hours later, and Sailer was back again for the last strike at dusk. He had seven SBDs from 132 and 141 but in the thick weather and gathering darkness the formation became scattered. Sailer was the only pilot to find the target, but his bomb was a near miss on one of the attendant destroyers. Sailer got back to Henderson, safely, as did four others, but Lieutenants Knapp and Sandretto of 141 were downed by the treacherous Solomons weather. Their two SBDs were Henderson Field's only losses that day.

Hiei was still afloat at sunset but she was beyond all help. In addition to 85 shells from Admiral Callaghan's ships, she was battered by ten torpedoes and five direct bomb hits. The survivors of her crew scuttled her that night, according *Hiei* the dubious historical distinction of being the first battleship sunk by American airpower. The Navy and Marine pilots toasted their accomplishment with mixed drinks—grapefruit juice and torpedo alcohol—and celebrated until nearly midnight. Less than two hours later the celebrants were decidedly less joyful as a pair of Japanese cruisers conducted another bombardment. There were no U.S. ships around to stop them this time, but either their aim was bad or their target ill-defined, because Henderson Field was not touched. But the air staff now had positive knowledge of 12 transports with heavy destroyer escort bearing down from the north. The climax was at hand for the air force on Guadalcanal.

Despite the none too cheery prospect of having to repel another large-scale, determined Japanese attempt to reinforce Guadalcanal, there was room for optimism. Nearly 50 Navy and Marine aircraft were operational the morning of 14 November, including 16 SBDs. The big find of the routine morning search came at 0630 when a Dauntless discovered four enemy cruisers and six destroyers 140 miles west of Guadalcanal, well up the chain towards Bougainville. Major Sailer, quickly becoming the most experienced strike leader, took off at 0715 with five SBDs and six TBFs.

In 45 minutes Sailer's planes were on station, the SBDs delegated to the big cruiser *Maya* and the Avengers to *Kinugasa*. With that, Sailer rolled his Dauntless over and dropped down on *Maya*. The Marines got near misses which started fires along the cruiser's port beam but she showed no sign of slowing down. The TBF pilots fared better as four torpedoes slammed into *Kinugasa*, which was burning quite satisfactorily as the group turned for home, undamaged by AA fire.

Meanwhile, some two hundred miles southwest of Guadalcanal, *Enterprise* was running through heavy rain showers with all her SBDs still aboard. The task force commander, Rear Admiral T. C. Kinkaid, was concerned about the Japanese carriers reported further north—not to be ignored even if they hadn't been confirmed. It was decided to launch an economical scout force of ten SBDs, holding the others in readiness if something developed. The ten scouts, each carrying a 500-pound GP, had orders to attack any hostile vessels after reporting their positions. Launch began at 0620 from the "Big E's" rain-swept deck.

Shortly after 0700 one of the scouts, flown by VS-10 exec Lieutenant Bill Martin, reported ten unidentified aircraft 140 miles north of Kinkaid's task force. Kinkaid decided to launch his strike group upon this sketchy information, assuming the bogies were hostile, and by 0745 16 SBDs were airborne with ten F4Fs. The dive bombers were led by Lieutenant Commander James R. Lee, skipper of Scouting 10, with orders to attack any target he might find and then land on Guadalcanal. The planes reported by Martin were most likely friendly, as Japanese aircraft were inactive during most of the day.

But one of the "Big E's" search teams in the northwest sector did find something. The section was led by Lieutenant (jg) R. D. Gibson with Ensign R. M. Buchanan on his wing. Flying at 17,000 feet, the two VB-10 pilots made contact with an imposing surface force just south of Rendova at 0750. It was actually the same unit attacked earlier by Sailer's planes, but between the heavy AA fire and scattered low clouds, Gibson reported the Japanese force included battleships and a carrier. Though the identification was in error, the section remained high overhead for more than an hour, constantly sending updated information to *Enterprise*. Finally, with fuel running low, Gibson and Buchanan maneuvered into the sun, split their dive flaps, and singled out the damaged cruiser *Kinugasa*.

It was a familiar story to Gibson, who had near-missed a cruiser during the Eastern Solomons battle way back in August when he was with VB-6. But this time his luck was better as both he and Buchanan got direct hits with their 500-pounders, starting fires again on *Kinugasa*. The two SBDs landed safely at Henderson Field after a solid five hours in the air, despite an eight-inch hole in Buchanan's fuselage. A large-caliber shell had shot through his Dauntless without exploding.

Two other Bombing Ten pilots, Ensigns R. A. Hoogerwerf and P. M. Halloran, were searching the adjacent sector to the west and found the cruisers ten minutes after Gibson and Buchanan departed. They climbed to 17,500 feet and, not bothering to send a contact report, pushed over on two of the undamaged cruisers. Hoogerwerf's bomb hit 15 feet astern of one cruiser and he saw Halloran's explode on a light cruiser but then lost track of him. When Halloran failed to join up, Hoogerwerf set course for *Enterprise* by himself. Considering the intensity of the AA fire from so many ships, Halloran was probably shot down while recovering from his dive.

The Japanese cruiser force, already subjected to three air attacks that morning, received another about 1030. Lieutenant Commander Lee, keeping tabs on the 16-plane strike launched at 0800, had picked up one of Gibson's many reports not long after leaving the "Big E." Lee conducted a search of the area given by Gibson but found nothing and decided to check the opposite end of the sector, away from Guadalcanal, to the northwest. His hunch paid off when smoke from the burning *Kinugasa* appeared up ahead. In another 15 minutes the rest of the force was in sight. Only two of the ten Wildcats launched to cover the Dauntlesses had noticed Lee's course change but they were sufficient to deter an attempted interception by a pair of Rufes.

The 16 SBDs were organized into three divisions, one from VB-10 and two from VS-10. The skipper assigned the five Bombing Ten planes to the heavy cruiser and told his second division to take the light cruisers. Still mindful of the phantom carrier reported by Gibson some two hours before, Lee went below the clouds with his lead division to see if anything resembling a flight deck could be found. The ocean was empty so Lee climbed back to 7,500 feet and took his planes down on a light cruiser. Their aim was good, as four bombs splashed into the water so close to the drastically turning *Isuzu* that she was obscured by tall fountains of spray cascading down over her decks. Two bombs had failed to release but the cruiser had one boiler room flooded. The Bombing Ten division led by Lieutenant Commander Thomas bored down through the heavy and accurate flak to score a near miss on the lead ship, *Chokai*.

Isuzu had to proceed at reduced speed but she survived. It was another matter with *Kinugasa*, the sixth enemy warship sunk by SBDs in the Guadalcanal campaign. The Japanese force was further battered, as heavy cruisers *Chokai* and *Maya* and the destroyer *Michishio* all received bomb damage. The SBDs were safely on the ground at Henderson by 1315, after a search-strike mission of some five and a half hours.

As the strike group was landing at Guadalcanal, more of the "Big E's" scouts had been in action. A section composed of Lt(jg) Martin Carmody and Lieutenant (jg) Bill Johnson was patrolling The Slot and at last found the big transport group. Twenty-two ships, half of them escorting destroyers, were midway between New Georgia and Santa Isabel, just 120 miles northwest of Guadalcanal. They carried some 13,000 Japanese troops which simply could not be allowed ashore.

Well aware of the importance of their discovery, Carmody and Johnson climbed to about 10,000 feet and broadcast the contact until *Enterprise* acknowledged. Then at 1000 each pilot selected a transport and nosed over, immediately receiving the attention of every Japanese gun crew which could bring their weapons to bear. But the two scout pilots continued in their dives until they could see the enemy troops packed shoulder-to-shoulder on the decks.

The Dauntlesses dived past 2,000 feet, toggled their bombs, retracted the perforated dive flaps and pulled out close to the water. Their aim was good, if not perfect: Carmody got a very near miss off the stern of his transport and Johnson's bomb was thought to hit the fantail of his target. Then all at once the SBDs were swarmed by seven Zeroes, late arrivals on the scene. Carmody scooted for the clouds but his gunner caught a brief glance of a plane splashing into the water behind them. Carmody turned around just in time to see a pair of Zeros strafing Johnson's SBD, floating on the surface. Heavily outnumbered and critically low on fuel, Carmody set course for the "Big E." He got back with maybe five gallons to spare.

Henderson Field, meanwhile, long a hornet's nest to the Japanese, was also a beehive of activity. Strikes were being assembled and sent off without regard to squadron organization; just as soon as several planes were fueled and armed they were on their way up The Slot to attack the transports. The first full-scale dive-bomber formation, 19 SBDs under Joe Sailer of VMSB-132 and Bob Richard of VMSB-142, was taking off within 20 minutes of the time Carmody and Johnson dived on the transport force. By 1100 the strike was perched high on the stoop over the transports, which were heading steadily southeast in four columns. Sailer sized up the situation, detailed his tactical information, and led the attack as he rolled in from the right-hand side of the enemy formation. The VMSB-132 pilots split up and went for two ships; they hit one with two heavy bombs and staggered the other with four. Then Richard's VMSB-142 pilots gutted their target with a probable half-dozen hits.

Seven VT-10 Avengers were boring in from the opposite side of the same column of ships as the Marine SBDs pulled out of their dives. It was an exceptionally well-coordinated attack, as the big Grummans torpedoed two of the three damaged transports, sending them to the bottom. The third ship, *Sado Maru*, had no choice but to return to the Shortlands under escort of two destroyers. The Japanese force continued, minus nearly a quarter of its original number.

And so it went for the rest of the day. The transports doggedly plodding down The Slot, under almost constant air attack, the fliers and ground crews pushing themselves to the limit to keep up the pressure. There was a good deal of trading equipment and aircraft—somebody got away with Commander Lee's parachute—and each strike group took off without regard to squadron organization, led by whomever was senior.

The fliers named the shuttle missions they flew the Buzzard Patrol as the Dauntlesses and Avengers went out like birds of prey to scavenge off the fat transports. Pilots reported the decks literally ran red, and some became physically ill at the sight. Then they turned around to load up with more bombs and ammunition.

But not all the planes went out in formation. Ensign Chuck Irvine of VS-10, who had participated in a classic bounce on a light carrier on 26 October, found his Dauntless wasn't ready to go with an organized strike. Undeterred, he took off alone, worked his way through the Zero CAP, managed to avoid being hit by the ships' heavy AA fire, got a direct hit on a transport, and somehow returned safely.

The last strike, which began taking off at 1530, wasn't so lucky. Sixteen SBDs, half Navy and half Marine, went out with four TBFs and ran headlong into the stiffest aerial opposition of the day. Only five transports were left but the vengeful Zeros fought furiously to defend them. Lieutenant Glen Estes of VS-10 led three Marines from VMSB-142 in an attack which sank *Nako Maru*, leaving four transports and some half-dozen destroyers to press on. But Lieutenant Commander J. A. Thomas, skipper of Bombing Ten, had his flight of seven SBDs badly mauled. Zeros shot down three and two more had to turn back with heavy damage. Thomas wouldn't break off, however, and despite an attack by a Zero which ended only when his gunner flamed it at close range, he dived 12,000 feet through the still-formidable flak to make a direct hit. Of the two damaged SBDs, Lieutenant (jg) Gibson returned with 28 bullet holes in his plane and Ensign Len Robinson, chased almost all the way back, landed with nearly 70 holes in his plane.

The Naval Battle of Guadalcanal was over, and with it the major portion of the struggle for Guadalcanal. Major Sailer's Marines and the "Big E's" SBDs had flown some 90 sorties against the reinforcement convoy during the course of the day, which did not count other Navy and various Army planes. Dauntlesses sank four transports by themselves and shared three more with the other aircraft.

The last four transports, all damaged, were beached during the night to prevent them from being sunk but they were bombed to destruction the next day. Less than half the Japanese troops arrived on Guadalcanal, largely without weapons or equipment. Nobody knew it at Henderson Field, but the defeat of the transports convinced the Japanese high command that Guadalcanal probably could not be retaken.

Last of the old-line SBD units to depart Guadalcanal was VMSB-141 on 19 November. In two months, 141 had taken the heaviest casualties of any full-strength squadron in the campaign. Of the 39 crews sent up to Guadalcanal, 19 pilots and 14 gunners were lost to all causes, and others were wounded or otherwise evacuated. It all amounted to 45 percent casualties, including every senior officer.

In return, VMSB-141 and the other squadrons had done their job, and more. From August through November Henderson Field aircraft—largely SBDs—sank or wrecked 20 Japanese ships and damaged another 14.

The campaign for Guadalcanal was the first in history which saw a completely mutual dependence arise between flier and rifleman. The

CACTUS air force relied upon the Marine infantry to hold the small perimeter around the airfield. And at the same time the foot-slogging Leathernecks had to hope the aviators could sink enough ships to keep the number of Japanese on the island down to a manageable level. The small air force succeeded in that goal, thanks in no small part to the determined men who flew and maintained the pitifully few Douglas dive bombers which every day for over three arduous tropical months had operated from the fever-infested island with the strange-sounding name.

The game plan was understood.
Commander H. D. Felt

Six major naval engagements were fought in conjunction with the Guadalcanal Campaign, and two of them were exclusively carrier battles. The first of these—24 August 1942—occurred 17 days after the landings on Guadalcanal and passed into history as the Battle of the Eastern Solomons.

Admiral Yamamoto knew that the best way to knock the Marines off Guadalcanal was to eliminate American access to the Solomons by sea. The majority of supplies were delivered by transport vessels which required carrier-borne air cover. Henderson Field's capabilities were insufficient to do the job, owing to a lack of aircraft. During August the Marines' only offensive planes on Guadalcanal were Mangrum's dozen SBDs of VMSB-232. The muscle of American air power in the Solomons was concentrated in the three carriers of Task Force 61.

The Battle of the Eastern Solomons had all the makings of a classic carrier engagement. The Japanese were moving down from the north with three flattops, three battleships, nine cruisers, and numerous destroyers and submarines. The light carrier *Ryujo* was placed in the vanguard to act as bait for the American carriers. Once the Americans jumped *Ryujo* the enemy's reorganized First Carrier Division—built around *Shokaku* and *Zuikaku*—would be in position little more than 60 miles to the north with full deck-loads, ready to close the trap.

Enterprise, *Saratoga*, and *Wasp* were under the command of Admiral Frank Jack Fletcher, and as Nagumo headed the Japanese strike force, Eastern Solomons shaped up not only as a partial rematch of Midway, but as a contest between the most experienced combat carrier commanders in the world. Nagumo, of course, had been responsible for Pearl Harbor, the East Indies, Ceylon and Midway. Fletcher was entering his third carrier battle since Coral Sea in May, though neither commander was an aviator.

Believing the enemy forces were still at Truk in the Carolines, Fletcher detached *Wasp* on 23 August for refueling to the south. Thus, the seventh of the U.S. Navy's carriers was deprived of the only chance she would have to fight her own kind. Fletcher could have entered the battle on even terms with the Japanese, but owing to incomplete information he was outnumbered three to two, as at Coral Sea.

Scouting Five aboard the "Big E" was conducting Inner and Intermediate Air Patrol during the twenty-third and came up with an alarming number of submarine contacts. The first was at 0725 when Lieutenant Turner F. Caldwell spotted a surface sub heading south. He made a glide-bombing approach but his 500-pounder fell wide to starboard.

Less than an hour later Lieutenant Stockton B. Strong, acting VS-5 skipper, had another sub in sight 80 miles northeast of Caldwell's contact. Strong led his wingman, Ensign John Richey, to the attack in a glide from 1,000 feet as the sub crash-dived. Their two bombs forced the submarine back to the surface but it dived again and escaped.

That afternoon Ensigns Maul and Estes caught yet another submarine running surfaced and climbed for attack altitude. Though the Japanese vessel crash-dived, its conning tower was closely bracketed by both bombs, and the Dauntless pilots noted an oil slick on the surface after their target submerged. They claimed it "probably sunk."

But the twenty-third was just the beginning of the busiest period of antisubmarine activity *Enterprise* had seen since early December when Lieutenant Dickinson of Scouting Six sank *I-70*. During the next two days three more subs were attacked by Scouting Five; one on the twenty-fourth and two on the twenty-fifth. Estes was involved in both attacks

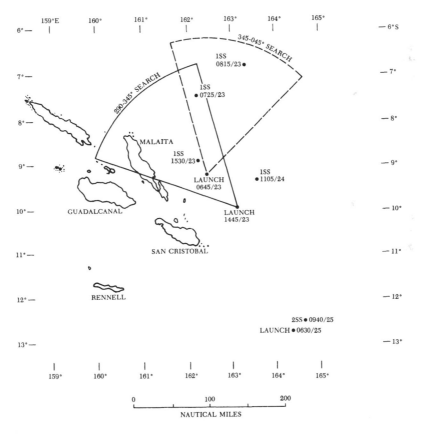

Scouting Squadron Five contacts with Japanese submarines while operating from Enterprise, *23–25 August 1942.*

on the twenty-fifth and received credit for a "definite sinking." Though three Japanese submarines were lost during August, all were sunk by allied destroyers in the last four days of the month. But it does appear that at least two and maybe three of the subs attacked by VS-5 received more than minor damage.

Saratoga's air group had not been inactive on the twenty-third, and Commander Don Felt led 31 SBDs and six TBFs in an afternoon hunt for the enemy transports, which were evidently headed for Tulagi. Heavy storms and poor visibility foiled the mission, however, so Felt led his formation into Henderson Field to spend the night. Two Dauntlesses stayed behind for minor repairs but the rest of the *Saratoga* group followed Felt back home next morning, landing aboard at 1130.

Shortly after 0900 on the twenty-fourth a PBY found the *Ryujo* task force and relayed the information. Two and a half hours later another PBY made contact, reporting the enemy force heading south at a point nearly 250 miles northwest of Fletcher's carriers. Scouting Five aboard *Enterprise* flew off seven SBDs, Bombing Six dispatched eight, and VT-3 launched seven Avengers. All had departed by 1315. The 23 planes were to search to a distance of 250 miles over nearly the entire northern perimeter: from 290° through due east.

Meanwhile, Don Felt's *Saratoga* air group was preparing for launch. The tempting bait offered in the form of *Ryujo* was too much for Fletcher to pass up, and at 1435 Felt led 37 aircraft out on a heading of 320° towards the enemy force, an estimated 216 miles away. Compared with other carrier strikes, both before and after, Felt's group was of only moderate strength. His 28 Dauntlesses consisted of 13 from VB-3, now led by Lieutenant Commander Dave Shumway, and 15 of Lieutenant Commander Lou Kirn's Scouting Three. The reorganized Torpedo Eight put up eight TBFs.

Felt was the only air group commander in the Pacific still flying an SBD. The other CAGs—except *Wasp*'s, who flew an F4F—had switched to TBFs by August because the Avenger had more range without ordnance than the SBD and, being larger, was better suited as a command aircraft.

Max Leslie, now a full commander after turning VB-3 over to Shumway, was the new *Enterprise* CAG, flying an Avenger. But Felt, who had skippered Bombing Two when it received the first fleet SBDs, was a confirmed Dauntless pilot. His pet airplane was SBD-3, BuAer number 03213, affectionately known as "Queen Bee." Felt was attached to his plane as only a combat pilot can become, and as an air group commander could fly it on nearly every mission. "Number 03213 and I were inseparable as long as I was Sara's CAG,"[1] Felt said, and now they were

Eastern Solomons was Saratoga's *only carrier battle, but her SBDs sank the Japanese light carrier* Ryujo. *(U.S. Navy)*

leading the first strike ever launched from *Saratoga*'s deck against the Japanese Navy.

While Felt was leading his 36 planes to *Ryujo* (a TBF had turned back with engine trouble) three of the *Enterprise* scouts made contact with various elements of the widely separated enemy surface forces almost simultaneously. Four of the search teams eventually found *Ryujo*—as they were meant to—and reported her in four slightly different positions due to navigational discrepancies. But two reports were almost pinpoint accurate.

Lieutenant Stockton B. Strong and Ensign John Richey, the same team which had jumped a submarine the day before, were in the 330° to 340° sector when Strong noticed three ships 15 miles ahead and dropped down to investigate. He identified them as two cruisers and a destroyer, but from that distance he could be excused the slight error. They were actually the heavy cruiser *Tone* and two destroyers, *Ryujo*'s escorts. Almost immediately the VS-5 skipper caught sight of *Ryujo* herself and approached to within five miles before sending his contact report: "Position Lat 06-25S, Lon 161-20E, Cus 180, Spd 15."[2] The message

Contacts in Sectors 310-330°
1. T-1 & T-6 at 1440
2. T-5 & T-13 about 1500
3. S-18 & T-14 at 1510
4. S-1 & S-2 at 1510

All four are sightings of the *Ryujo* group, with navigational errors making the differences. T-1 and T-6 made the most accurate report.

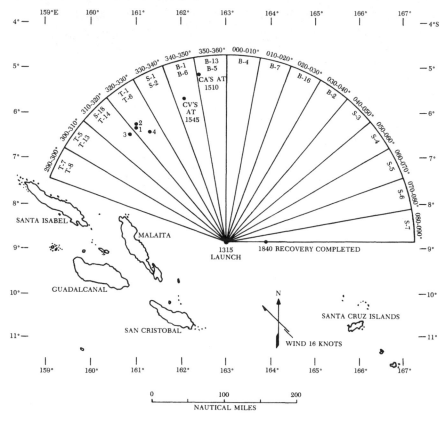

Enterprise *search pattern of 24 August 1942 (Battle of the Eastern Solomons).*

Plane and pilot assignments for Enterprise *search of 24 August 1942.*
(Squadrons involved were VB-6, VS-5 and VT-3.)

Plane No.	Pilot	Sector	Contact with enemy, if any
T-7	Lt(jg) Weissenborn	290-300	Brief engagement with Japanese aircraft near the U.S. task force. Landed 1830.
T-8	Ensign Mears		
T-5	Lieutenant Myers	300-310	Intercepted by Japanese VF near *Ryujo*. T-13 shot down, T-5 returned to *Enterprise*.
T-13	Machinist Corl		

132

Plane No.	Pilot	Sector	Contact with enemy, if any
S-18 T-14	Ensign Jorgenson Ensign Bingaman	310-320	Found *Ryujo* force at 1510, sent report. Returned to ship during attack, both ditched.
T-1 T-6	Lt. Cdr. Jett Ensign Bye	320-330	Found *Ryujo* force at 1440, made high-level bomb attack at 1510; no hits. Returned.
S-1 S-2	Lieutenant Strong Ensign Richie	330-340	Found *Ryujo* force at 1510, sent report and returned to *Enterprise.*
B-1 B-6	Lieutenant Davis Ensign Shaw	340-350	Found main enemy carrier force at 1545. Two near-misses on *Shokaku.* Returned 1840.
B-13 B-5	Lieutenant Lowe Ensign Gibson	350-360	Found cruiser force and attacked at 1510, two near-misses. B-5 ditched, B-13 returned.
B-4	Lieutenant Horenburger	360-010	Returning at 1730, attacked two Japanese VB without success. Landed at 1835.
B-7	Lieutenant Kline	010-020	Encountered five Japanese VB on return at 1730, attacked without success. Landed 1836.
B-16	Ensign Jaccard	020-030	No contact.
B-2	Ensign Pittman	030-040	No contact.
S-3	unknown	040-050	No contact.
S-4	unknown	050-060	No contact.
S-5	unknown	060-070	No contact.
S-6	unknown	070-080	No contact.
S-7	unknown	080-090	No contact.

Note: Plane numbers for the last five sectors are unknown and have been arbitrarily assigned.

was sent by key in plain language for six minutes but the "Big E" didn't acknowledge. It was just the first indication of maddening communications problems which plagued Fletcher's forces all day.

Strong and Richey were the only all-SBD search team to find *Ryujo.* Ensign J. H. Jorgenson, another Coral Sea veteran, had been a standby for the search mission and was launched when a TBF was unable to start. Jorgenson matched up with Ensign Bingaman's Avenger to scan the 310° to 320° sector, and just less than an hour out sighted a twin-float observation plane. It was obviously hostile, and the *Enterprise* pair gave chase but lost the quarry in a cloud. The SBD and TBF resumed the search and after another hour they were within visual range of the

Ryujo formation. It was 1510, exactly the same time Strong and Richey made contact in the adjacent sector.

The Japanese CAP was stationed as far as 30 miles out from the carrier, up to 3,000 feet. Jorgenson and Bingaman descended to 500 feet and began broadcasting a contact report, all the while working their way closer to the carrier by hopping from cloud to cloud. They were startled five minutes after the first sighting by splashes in the water just aft of *Ryujo's* stern. The origin of the near-misses could be seen at 12,000 feet as two TBFs made a horizontal bombing run. About this same time some of the nine Zeros circling over the carrier caught sight of the snooping Dauntless and Avenger. The fighters attacked but the two scouts headed south and got away. They returned to the task force at 1630 to find it under air attack. Bingaman's TBF and Jorgenson's Dauntless splashed with dry tanks about 1830 while preparing to land but both crews were rescued.

Strong and Richey also departed the target area after shadowing the *Ryujo* force and set course for *Enterprise*. They spotted a cruiser floatplane 40 miles south of the contact point but, being low on fuel, did not engage.

At the head of the 36-plane *Saratoga* strike, Don Felt was having trouble with his radio receiver. He had picked up Jorgenson's repeat of the contact report when still 55 miles south of the target and changed course to the north. But when he reached the reported position the Japanese ships were considerably further west, as the trail by then was nearly 40 minutes old and the thin, scattered clouds at 2,000 feet hampered the otherwise unlimited visibility.

Not long after he turned back to the original heading, Felt's receiver quit completely. He could still transmit instructions to his strike group but was unable to hear anything, so he throttled back and pulled up next to Lou Kirn leading the Scouting Three formation. Using standardized hand signals Felt indicated that he was turning the lead over to Kirn. But just a few minutes later, at 1606, *Ryujo* was sighted to the southwest, still doing 20 knots.

The *Saratoga* fliers weren't the only ones who had enemy ships lined up for targets that afternoon. Bombing Six's executive officer, Lieutenant J. T. Lowe, was in the northernmost search sector with his wingman, Ensign R. D. Gibson. Near the limit of their outbound leg Lowe and Gibson discovered the vanguard group of three cruisers with escorting destroyers. It was 1500 when the two SBDs circled east, climbing to

11,000 feet in order to make their approach out of the sun. Lowe and Gibson were on their way down, having picked out the largest cruiser, when antiaircraft fire opened up. The two 500-pounders bracketed the ship as she turned away to starboard, and there was nothing for the SBDs to do but clear out. Almost clipping the waves, they evaded heavy AA fire and retired south at full throttle. Lowe returned to *Enterprise* at 1820 but Gibson ditched near a destroyer when he ran out of fuel.

So far *Ryujo* had served her role to perfection. The *Enterprise* scouts had concentrated on her or the cruisers, thereby precluding detection of the real threat which lay out of sight to the north: the 25,000-ton veterans of Pearl Harbor and Coral Sea, *Shokaku* and *Zuikaku*. These two carriers, with full deckloads ready to launch, were finally·discovered at 1530 by Lieutenant Ray Davis, skipper of Bombing Six. Flying at 1,500 feet with Ensign R. C. Shaw, Davis noticed a pair of light cruisers and began climbing for an attack when the unmistakable yellow rectangle of a Japanese carrier deck appeared behind the screening vessels.

Davis began a steep spiraling climb at full power, broadcasting the critical news repeatedly. He knew he had made the most important contact of the day and that it was imperative Fletcher be warned of the hidden threat. Davis could see only one carrier, but he knew she was a big one and the activity among the planes on deck indicated she was preparing to launch. The force was headed south at 28 knots, obviously on urgent business.

Ray Davis was probably the most frustrated squadron commander since Max Leslie at Midway. As he gained altitude he could see *Zuikaku* trailing five miles behind her sister. Here were the two biggest enemy carriers operating in the entire Pacific, wide open to attack, and Davis had only one wingman. He earnestly wished for his squadron at his back, though an entire air group would have been better suited to the job.

About 15 minutes after sighting the light cruisers, Davis and Shaw were positioned at 14,000 feet, ready to pounce. They knew the 500-pounders they carried couldn't sink anything as big as a *Shokaku*-class CV, but perhaps they could at least knock one of the flight decks out of the battle. At 1545 Davis looked across at Shaw, noted his young wingman was ready, split his flaps and rolled into the familiar 70-degree dive.

It was a classic bounce as the two Dauntlesses plummeted on *Shokaku* from upwind, down sun, while the first tentative tracers curled upwards from the ships below. The big carrier was beginning a starboard turn as the SBDs plunged through 5,000 feet and the black bursts of heavy AA fire thumped nearby, occasionally jarring the planes in their dives. Almost literally hanging forward against their shoulder harnesses, Davis and Shaw had *Shokaku* well in their sights at 2,500 feet, while J. W.

Trott and H. D. Jones in the back seats watched for the Zeros they knew must be near.

Finally, at 2,000 feet, the pilots tugged their manual bomb releases, closed the dive brakes, and pulled out of the nearly three-mile plunge with a momentum which took them straight through a group of planes circling the carrier.

Shokaku had made a 60-degree right-hand turn during Davis' dive from 7,000 to 2,000 feet, and while it didn't throw off the pilots' aim by much, it was just enough. Both bombs hit close aboard the starboard side, Davis' 500-pounder missing by perhaps five feet. Shaw's bomb was close to his skipper's, 15 to 20 feet from the starboard quarter. The two SBDs passed so close to their target on the pullout that Jones in Shaw's Dauntless counted 20 planes on the flight deck.

The entire defensive screen concentrated its AA fire on the two dodging planes as they swept headlong through the tracers and flak that were turning the water white around them. The only Zero which made a pass at the SBDs never got in range as AA fire from a light cruiser slapped the fighter into the water.

Once clear of the enemy task force, Davis sent a second report telling of his attack and repeating the position on the possibility Admiral Fletcher hadn't received the first "flash." It turned out he hadn't heard either report, but other ships monitoring the frequency picked it up and after a lengthy delay the news was relayed to *Enterprise*. Fletcher tried to divert the *Saratoga* strike from *Ryujo*, which now was clearly a sacrificial decoy, to *Shokaku* and *Zuikaku*. But it was too late. *Ryujo*, the "Fighting Dragon," was already doomed.

Barely 20 minutes after Davis and Shaw went down on *Shokaku*, and about a hundred miles southwest of the main carrier force, Don Felt was sizing up the situation for his 36 planes. Though he couldn't receive on his radio he could still transmit, and from 14,000 feet he directed Kirn's 15 Scouting Three Dauntlesses and six of Bombing Three under Shumway to attack *Ryujo* with five of Torpedo Eight's Avengers. The other seven SBDs and two TBFs were to attack the heavy cruiser while Felt kept his "Queen Bee" overhead.

The four ships below the "Sara's" strike group were heading southwest, apparently to recover the attack launched earlier against Guadalcanal. Felt's planes maneuvered around to attack from two directions and hopefully split up the AA fire. Kirn led his scouts in from the northwest and Shumway's six bombers approached from the northeast, climbing to 16,000 feet. It took 15 minutes for the SBDs to position themselves after the sighting, but the enemy ships were surprisingly inactive. The sky was spotted with only a few scattered clouds so the group's approach could not have gone long undetected. There was no fighter opposition either, but the Dauntlesses didn't waste any time. At 1620, just 35 minutes after Davis and Shaw pushed over on *Shokaku*, *Ryujo* turned into the wind and began launching the Zeros still on board. At that moment 21 SBDs were diving on the small carrier as Felt circled high above by himself, watching the progress of the attack.

From where Felt sat it didn't look promising because *Ryujo's* right-hand turn and the resultant change in wind drift across the target threw off the aim of the first pilots. The CAG watched anxiously as the first ten bombs scored "nothing better than very close misses."[3] Felt decided the remaining SBDs still in their dives weren't enough to do the job and countermanded his distribution order, directing all aircraft to attack *Ryujo*.

But still he saw no hits, and as the other planes had apparently attacked unsuccessfully, Felt decided to do it himself. "The carrier was throwing up a curtain of automatic weapon fire, the cruiser was firing larger caliber AA, and five or six Zeros were jumping bombers as they pulled out of their dives," he reported.[4] But despite the fact Felt had no wingman on this mission and was attacking alone, he rolled into his dive and centered his crosshairs on *Ryujo's* flight deck. The flak was getting accurate—his radio mast was shot off—but Don Felt very professionally put his half-ton bomb squarely through the carrier's deck, slightly port and aft of dead center. You just couldn't do much better than that.

Felt strafed a destroyer on his pull-out and then his radioman reported a torpedo had struck the carrier's starboard bow. The Avengers, after aborting three approaches because of dense smoke, had finally made their run-in as Felt concluded his solo attack. They claimed two hits on *Ryujo* and one on the cruiser *Tone*, but the fish that struck the flattop was the only hit obtained by the TBFs.

The CAG moved out of the immediate vicinity to survey the situation. He orbited in some broken clouds until 1650, watching *Ryujo* run in circles to the right, pouring out black smoke, but maintaining an even keel.

Because of his understandable preoccupation with the carrier, Felt had not seen the attack on the cruiser. Fortunately his redistribution order had come just in time. Lieutenant Sid Bottomley was leading VB-3's second division in the push-over on *Tone* when Felt's order to shift the attack to *Ryujo* came through. The seven SBDs made high-altitude pull-outs, regrouped, and went after the flattop. Dive bombing Japanese carriers was nothing new to VB-3, for at least ten of the pilots on this strike had been at Midway. Bottomley was one of them, as were

Saratoga's *Air Group Commander H. D. Felt and his gunner, Snyder, with SBD-3, no. 03213, known as "Queen Bee." The Japanese flag represents the hit Felt scored on the carrier* Ryujo, *contributing to her sinking. (H. D. Felt)*

four other pilots of his division, and they set about proving they hadn't forgotten anything in the 11 weeks since 4 June.

The seven SBDs attacked from different directions from 15,000 feet and did the job up right; three direct hits and four near-misses. *Ryujo* lingered but was headed for the bottom, the sixth and last aircraft carrier sunk by Dauntlesses and the last sunk by any American aircraft for two years.

The *Saratoga* planes had been free of high-altitude interception but once low on the water, heading for the rendezvous, Zeros began attacking in earnest. Ensign W. A. Behr was the third VB-3 pilot to dive on *Ryujo*, scoring a near miss, and after pullout at 1,200 feet he found himself with a Zero fighter positioned on each side, ready to initiate simultaneous gunnery passes. Turning into the right-hand Zero, the SBD was hit 14 times by the left-hand fighter. As Behr popped his stick forward and made a run for the deck, the two Japanese made three more passes but failed to do further damage.

Behr was on course for *Saratoga* when he ran into three more Zeros at 1,000 feet. Repeating his previous tactics, he went down to wave-top level, depriving the Zeros of all but the shallowest of diving attacks. They gave up the chase and broke off.

It was 1845 when Behr finally landed, but not aboard the "Sara." She had planes spotted aft by then so Behr put down on the "Big E" after more than four hours in the air, an attack on a carrier, and a run-in with five Zeros. A very full day, indeed.

Behr wasn't the only *Saratoga* pilot to tangle with enemy aircraft, as Scouting Three claimed five Japanese planes. The first of these was a Kate shot down by Lieutenant Schroeder and his gunner about a mile from the *Ryujo* force early in the attack.

Lou Kirn was leading ten of his VS-3 Dauntlesses and three Bombing Three tag-alongs back home at 1725 when he sighted 30 Japanese aircraft at 8,000 feet, obviously with the same destination in mind. They were the second strike from *Shokaku* and *Zuikaku*. Kirn radioed ahead to *Saratoga* that the Japanese apparently knew where to find Fletcher.

It was well on towards evening when Kirn led his planes toward *Saratoga* for recovery, but Nagumo's strike was then attacking *Enterprise*. "Sara" was in no immediate danger, being several miles away, but her dive bombers got into the action. The SBDs came across four Vals at about 500 feet and, flying below them, pulled up and fired their fixed guns at the enemy's exposed bellies. The rear gunners then took their turn as the Vals passed overhead. The following sections finished up, as Ensign Hanson made a high portside attack on a Val at low level. His target began to smoke, then nosed into the water.

Lieutenant (jg) R. K. Campbell had been at 2,000 feet, above and behind these proceedings, and saw his chance. He dived on another Val, exploded the right wing fuel tank and watched his victim crash in flames —all in about five seconds.

Lieutenant William E. Henry of Scouting Three had seen two small groups of Vals during the return flight to *Saratoga* but had no opportunity to engage. His luck was no better with this last group, either, for most of them turned away and those which were caught were quickly dispatched by other SBDs. It was a frustrating experience for the aggressive Henry, who later became the Navy's top night-fighter ace.

Ensign H. R. Burnett had been launched early that afternoon on Inner Air Patrol and was returning to *Saratoga* when the attack developed. He took a position about six miles north of the ship and at 1715 made a beam run on an Aichi, opening fire with his .50 calibers. He

Japanese counterpart of the Dauntless was the Aichi D3A "Val." Like the Dauntless, it participated in all major carrier operations from 1941 to mid-1944. (Hideya Ando)

closed in, still firing, and the bomber hit the water burning. Besides these three Vals shot down, a fourth made off trailing a long plume of smoke.

Don Felt was over the ship at 1830, one of the last to arrive. He had led the first and perhaps the only air group attack on a carrier which cost not a single pilot or plane. Behr's Dauntless was the only one with any substantial damage.

"I found jubilation in the ready room," the CAG said, only then learning that Sid Bottomley's seven SBDs had received the order to shift targets, and consequently finished off *Ryujo*. Felt attributed his air group's success to the fact his crews were well trained and experienced, then added, "the game plan was understood."[5]

Two of *Saratoga's* SBDs were still in the game, however. Shortly before 1700 Lieutenant (jg) R. M. Elder, and Ensign R. T. Gordon had been launched in company with five Torpedo Eight Avengers. A Japanese surface force including a battleship and five cruisers was reported 200 miles to the northwest, and the seven planes spotted on "Sara's" flight deck were the only ones available.

Just over an hour after departure, the Japanese ships were spotted through a hole in the clouds. When they passed into a clear area, the planes were quickly sighted by the Japanese and the largest ship headed towards some low clouds while the other vessels closed up to concentrate their AA fire. The TBFs rushed in to the release point in swift power glides, their targets the cruisers of Admiral Kondo's advance force, but all five torpedoes missed.

Elder and Gordon, meanwhile, had climbed to 12,500 feet and were ready to attack what they identified as the battleship *Mutsu*. The two SBDs made their dives from the west through extremely heavy AA fire, released at 2,000 feet and bent on full throttle to the east. Remarkably, both got away unharmed except for a shrapnel hole in Gordon's dive flap.

Their aim was good—better than their recognition—as the "battleship" was in reality the large seaplane carrier *Chitose*. She was closely bracketed by both bombs, resulting in heavy flooding which nearly capsized her. Elder and Gordon returned safely to *Saratoga* with three of the TBFs, landing after dark. The other two TBFs ditched near San Cristobal but the crews were rescued.

The final episode in this confusing battle originated with the radio message Lou Kirn had sent upon sighting a large Japanese strike headed towards the American task force. In a hastily organized effort to fling all remaining aircraft at the Japanese carriers, *Enterprise* dispatched 11 SBDs (eight of VS-5, three of VB-6) and seven TBFs. They were launched at near-maximum range for combat loads, evidently with orders to strike *Ryujo*. Apparently the poor communications prevented the *Enterprise* air staff from learning that Felt's pilots had thoroughly dealt with her.

But it made sense to clear the "Big E's" deck for the incoming Japanese attack, and it was done not a minute too soon. Max Leslie was the last off, as his long-range TBF needed a full deck-run with its heavier fuel load. He lifted off at 1708, turned port to follow the others, and looked back in time to see a bomb explode on the flight deck. As Leslie's planes departed, *Enterprise* was burning and many Japanese planes were still attacking.

Leading the 11 SBDs was Lieutenant Turner Caldwell of Scouting Five. Miles out ahead of Leslie, cruising well above the torpedo planes, he only knew he was supposed to find the carrier that *Saratoga*'s squadrons had attacked earlier. The *Enterprise* pilots flew northwest for two hours and still hadn't sighted anything by the time the moon began to rise. Finally the Avengers jettisoned their heavy torpedoes and turned back towards the task force.

Caldwell decided against trying to return to a carrier which might or might not still be afloat, and might not be in range. After searching beyond the expected contact point he turned south for Henderson Field, hidden in darkness under low clouds. And there was no air-ground communication because the Navy and Marine radios worked on different frequencies. But Caldwell navigated to the strange field and signaled his intention to land.

Within minutes the Marines had set out kerosene lamps to roughly mark the runway and the SBDs began their approaches, skimming low over the palm trees and settling on the uncompleted runway. They all made it down safely. Caldwell's Dauntlesses, known to the "Big E's" operations schedule and to history as *Enterprise* Flight 300, would remain on Guadalcanal for a long, hard month.

The U.S. Navy learned a few things from the Battle of the Eastern Solomons, lessons which would show up later in the war. For the air groups in general it was a time for critical self-analysis. Avengers had scored no hits with bombs and only one with torpedoes, and Dauntlesses had dropped 36 bombs on enemy ships with only four hits—those on *Ryujo*. It was a disappointing 11 percent hit record, well under the performance of Coral Sea and Midway.

Consequently it was suggested in some quarters that emphasis be shifted from dive bombing to horizontal bombing. But Max Leslie had the right idea when he summarized the engagement in his report. He knew the problem rested not with the SBD, which was still the best dive bomber in the world, nor with the pilots who were largely veterans. Leslie simply realized that it had been nearly three months since many of the fliers had dropped a bomb in combat, and that limited time ashore precluded the opportunity for practice. "It is essential that our dive-bomber pilots get a maximum of training on moving targets when shore-based," he concluded.[6]

With the exception of several aviators, Eastern Solomons saw the departure of three extremely successful SBD squadrons. Bombing Three, Bombing Six, and Scouting Five were withdrawn from combat, having accounted—in whole or in part—for all six Japanese carriers sunk in 1942. With VB-5 these three units shouldered the major load of carrier warfare from Coral Sea through Eastern Solomons and they would be hard to replace. But several *Enterprise* pilots chose to stay on a bit longer for another cruise in the Solomons, another chance at combat.

The third carrier battle of history has most often been called indecisive or inconclusive. Admittedly, compared to Midway it failed to achieve spectacular results, but the U.S. Navy still retained strong forces in the Solomons area, thus protecting the beleaguered Marines ashore on Guadalcanal. Had the Japanese won the carrier duel they might have isolated the island long enough to recapture it.

For the Dauntless, the Battle of the Eastern Solomons was definitely a success despite the relatively poor bombing record. At a cost of two SBDs ditched at sea with no crew casualties, an enemy carrier had been sunk, a seaplane tender badly damaged, and at least five Japanese aircraft shot down. No matter what the strategists said about the battle as a whole, the SBD had a good day on 24 August 1942.

If blood be the price of admiralty, Lord God!
We ha' paid in full!
Kipling

The three carriers available to the U.S. Pacific Fleet in August—*Enterprise*, *Saratoga* and *Wasp*—represented the zenith of American naval air power for the rest of 1942. After the "Big E" departed the Solomons to have her bomb damage repaired, only two carriers were operational in the South Pacific, but it seemed as if every Japanese sub skipper knew where they were. *Saratoga* was torpedoed on 31 August, and after most of her planes were flown off for Espiritu Santo she headed for Pearl Harbor and repairs. She wouldn't return to South Pacific waters until December.

Hornet by this time was back in the Solomons, maintaining the carrier force at two, but not for long. On Tuesday, 15 September, *Wasp* and *Hornet* were cruising in company with the new battleship *North Carolina* and ten other escorts about 150 miles southeast of San Cristobal. It was *Wasp's* turn for providing antisub patrol, and at 1420 she turned into the wind to launch 18 SBDs. Captain F. P. Sherman had just turned to resume his westerly base course when lookouts shouted a warning of torpedoes already close aboard the starboard beam.

They were a spread of four from the Japanese *I-19* which had slipped through the destroyer screen. Sherman had barely begun to take evasive action when three torpedoes struck *Wasp* with tremendous impact. Aircraft on the flight deck and below on the hangar deck were flung around like toys, mangled into uselessness.

But the main damage, and the larger tragedy, occurred at *Wasp's* waterline where the three big torpedoes detonated. A dozen pilots were killed in their bunks. One of them was Ensign Dick Jaccard, veteran of Midway and Eastern Solomons, who had recently transferred from *Enterprise* with three other VB-6 pilots.

Despite early encouraging damage-control reports, the fires raged and gradually it became apparent that *Wasp* was past saving. The two-and-a-half-year-old carrier sank at 2100 that evening, taking 200 men and 46 aircraft to the bottom. But over two dozen of her planes landed aboard *Hornet* and eventually arrived at Guadalcanal.

Hornet twice narrowly escaped torpedoing, once when an alert SBD pilot dropped a depth charge in the path of a torpedo. She remained in the Solomons area awaiting the return of *Enterprise*.

The "Big E" was flying Air Group 10 when she pulled out of Pearl Harbor on 16 October, the first time since Midway that all her squadrons carried the same number. But though the air group was new, many pilots had stayed on from the previous tour. These included Lieutenant Stockton B. Strong and Lieutenant (jg) Harold R. Burnett, both veterans of VS-5 at Eastern Solomons, now under Lieutenant Commander James R. Lee in VS-10. Bombing Ten's skipper was Lieutenant Commander James A. Thomas. And even Commander Jimmy Flatley's Fight-

Fires rage on the carrier Wasp *(CV-7) after she was fatally struck at the waterline by Japanese torpedoes, 15 September 1942. Two hundred men and 46 planes were lost when the two-and-a-half-year-old carrier sank. (U.S. Navy)*

ing Ten included a couple of former SBD pilots who had made names for themselves at Coral Sea: John Leppla, formerly of VS-2, and Stanley "Swede" Vejtasa, late of Scouting Five.

When *Enterprise* linked up with *Hornet* on 23 October the two carriers were both staffed with experienced, well-trained aviators. *Hornet's* two SBD squadrons had both flown at Midway, as Lieutenant Commander William J. "Gus" Widhelm was now leading Scouting Eight. He had succeeded Lieutenant Commander Walt Rodee, who was now the new *Hornet* CAG. Bombing Eight was under the capable management of Lieutenant James E. Vose, also a Midway veteran. Vose was a relatively recent convert to aviation, having won his wings a little over two years before. A former *Wasp* fighter squadron and the reorganized Torpedo Six rounded out *Hornet*'s air group.

It was not known that the Japanese had regrouped after the abortive late August attempt to strangle Guadalcanal by sea, and had assembled an even more impressive task force. The two heavyweight flattops—*Shokaku* and *Zuikaku*—were joined by a pair of light carriers, *Junyo* and *Zuiho*, plus ten cruisers and nearly 30 destroyers. A large vanguard force of battleships and cruisers was also involved, so it was the same old story; the U.S. Navy was outnumbered and outgunned from the very start.

The Japanese Army and the Imperial Navy seldom worked in unison but this time the effort was made. By 22 October Henderson Field was to be under Japanese Army control while the Navy finished off whatever U.S. fleet units attempted to interfere. Though the U.S. Marines defending Henderson's perimeter repeatedly pushed back the enemy attacks, in the early morning of 25 October a handful of Japanese got through the lines and erroneously reported that Henderson was in their hands. It was the signal Admiral Nagumo had been waiting for, and his 47 warships turned south.

About mid-day on the twenty-fifth a PBY out of the Hebrides found two strange carriers heading southeast at high speed. *Enterprise* launched 48 aircraft, including 24 SBDs, to search west to north for two hundred miles. But nothing was found, as the Japanese were still too far north. This was one of the largest scouting operations undertaken to date, and the losses were proportionate: an F4F flew into the water and the rest of the planes arrived back over the "Big E" well after dark, low on fuel. Three Dauntlesses and three Avengers ran out of gas in the pattern and were forced to ditch, though destroyers rescued all the crews. Air Group Ten was getting a rapid introduction to operational flying, as it had been out of Pearl Harbor only nine days.

There was little doubt that sunrise would bring yet another carrier duel, and that night the *Enterprise* air officer, Commander John Crommelin, addressed the pilots. He spoke at length on the training which prepared them for combat, and of the Marines ashore who would be depending on them. But mostly he expected them to do their jobs properly, and his message could be reduced to three words: hit the target.

Crommelin's words had special meaning to Lieutenant S. B. Strong of VS-10. He was in an unusual position, having led Scouting Five at Eastern Solomons but now was under Lieutenant Commander Lee as flight officer. Lee characterized Strong and another VS-5 holdover, Lieutenant Harold Burnett, as "outstanding people who wanted another crack at the Japs before going home."[1] Strong and his wingman had found the *Ryujo* force on 24 August and remained on station, sending updated information which amplified the original report. But two months had passed, and Strong decided that if he got another chance he'd make it count.

The next morning 16 Dauntlesses left the "Big E's" flight deck 20 minutes before dawn in the opening move in what would become—excepting Midway—the bloodiest and most fiercely contested carrier battle of 1942. The SBDs were assigned to search from southwest by west through due north to a distance of 200 miles. Bombing Ten provided six planes to search the three southernmost sectors, 15 degrees each instead of the usual 10 degrees, while the scout squadron launched ten SBDs to the five northern sectors.

The sun rose about 0530 to reveal good carrier weather in the area of the U.S. task force, some 120 miles north of the Santa Cruz Islands. A light southeast breeze (six to ten knots) gave an advantage to the Japanese, as they could steam towards the Americans without turning out of the wind for flight operations. Ceiling and visibility were excellent as the only cloud cover was a layer of scattered to broken cumulus between 1,500 and 2,000 feet. The sun-tinged clouds covering 50 percent of the early morning sky were just the thing for scout pilots to hide in.

The first and only Bombing Ten team to make contact was Lieutenant V. W. Welch and Lieutenant (jg) B. A. McGraw, in the 266° to 282° sector. Their first indication of Japanese presence came 85 miles from point of launch when a Nakajima Kate, obviously on a similar mission, passed three miles to starboard on an opposite heading. Welch and McGraw continued their outbound course for about 20 more minutes before they sighted what was apparently a major enemy force. The two SBDs pulled up to 2,000 feet where they could take advantage of some cloud cover and, approaching from the east, circled around to the other side of the Japanese ships, closing to 10 miles.

Welch found the visibility unlimited except for a few squalls and scattered clouds at 1,300 feet but, try as he might, saw no carriers. There were in fact none to be seen, but Welch's contact report was fairly accurate, as at 0730 his radioman keyed: "Two BB, one CA, seven DD. Lat 08-10S, Lon 163-55E. Cus north, Spd 20."[2] This message was received in *Enterprise's* radio room. The enemy force actually comprised two battleships, four cruisers and seven destroyers, probably about 25 miles southwest of the reported position.

It remained for the "Big E's" scouts to locate the enemy carriers, and the skipper himself, Lieutenant Commander Lee, was responsible. Probing the 298° to 314° sector, Lee and Ensign Johnson picked up the flat-tops at 0750. The section was at 1,200 feet when the first sighting was

149

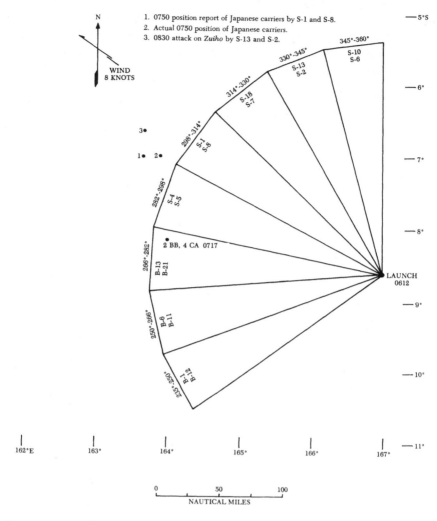

1. 0750 position report of Japanese carriers by S-1 and S-8.
2. Actual 0750 position of Japanese carriers.
3. 0830 attack on *Zuiho* by S-13 and S-2.

Enterprise *search pattern (VB-10 and VS-10), 26 October 1942 (battle of Santa Cruz).*

Aircraft assignments for Enterprise search, 26 October 1942.

Plane No.	Pilot	Search Sector	Encounter, if any
B-1	Lt(jg) Wakeham		
B-12	Ensign Stevens	235-250	No contact.
B-6	Lt(jg) Buell		
B-11	Ensign Hoogerwerf	250-266	No contact.

150

Plane No.	Pilot	Search Sector	Encounter, if any
B-13 B-21	Lieut. Welch Lt(jg) McGraw	266-282	Found battleships and cruisers at 0717, returned to ship.
S-4 S-5	Lt(jg) Burnett Lt(jg) Miller	282-298	Attacked cruiser *Chikuma*. S-4 shot down one enemy VT near ship.
S-1 S-8	Lt/Cdr Lee Lt(jg) Johnson	298-314	Found enemy carriers at 0750, shot down 3 VF and returned to ship.
S-18 S-7	Lt(jg) Ward Lt(jg) Carmody	314-330	Tried to attack CVs; gunners shot down one VF each. Returned to ship.
S-13 S-2	Lieut. Strong Ensign Irvine	330-345	0740 headed for BB/CA contact, turned towards CVs at 0805. Two hits on *Zuiho* at 0830. Returned to ship.
S-10 S-6	Lt(jg) Ramsay Lt(jg) Bloch	345-360	No contact.

Launch commenced 0612
Recovery finished 1030

made at about 35 miles. Identification was positively established within 15 miles of the Japanese force and Lee began a full-throttle climb to ensure his contact report was received aboard *Enterprise*. He also wanted a favorable position from which to make an attack, but the critical information had to be sent first. Lee's radioman, Chief I. A. Sanders, punched out the report four times: "Two CVs and accompanying vessels, Lat 07-05S, Long 163-38E."[3] Lee's navigation was excellent; the reported position was probably no more than ten miles off.

From the frenzied maneuvering of the ships below it was quite apparent that the SBDs' presence had not gone undetected. The Japanese vessels were rushing westward, attempting to cover themselves with a thick smokescreen. Lee and Johnson had *Shokaku* and *Zuikaku* in sight while the smaller *Zuiho* was out of view. The fourth carrier, *Junyo*, was operating independently and was not sighted.

By 0805 Lee and Johnson were climbing towards 3,000 feet, their gunners ready for action, when seven Zeros were seen above on a parallel course off the starboard beam. The fighters quickly forged ahead, turned and came back for a head-on approach. It was a typically wild, confused dogfight which started at relatively low level and worked its way lower. "Things happened fast," Lee related. "About the time my plane was hit in the windscreen with small caliber, I got off a burst of forward .50

caliber at the leading Jap and he exploded as he passed underneath me."[4]

Ensign Johnson went his skipper one better by splashing two Zeros, after which both SBDs made a run for the base of the rather sparse cloud cover. The aggressive Lee still wanted to press an attack on the carriers or at least get another good report on their activities, but Zeros were encountered every time the two scouts emerged from the clouds. "We finally got separated in these maneuvers," Lee said, "and each made his own way back to *Enterprise* since we had used up a lot of fuel."[5]

Lee's contact report had been heard by the teams in the two adjacent northern sectors. The Ward-Carmody team to the immediate north broke off and headed for Lee's position, hopeful of launching an attack. But, like Lee and Johnson, they were jumped by Zeros and had to shoot their way out of trouble. Each gunner claimed a fighter before the pilots managed to escape into the cumulus clouds and headed home.

Well to the northeast of Nagumo's main force of three carriers, the radiomen in Sail-13 and Sail-2 picked up Welch's report of 0730 about the battleships and cruisers. Garlow in the rear seat of Sail-13 notified his pilot, and Lieutenant Birney Strong went to work on the navigational problem.

Strong and Ensign Charles Irvine were at the limit of their search pattern, four sectors to the north of the contact, in the 330° to 345° segment. They were about as far away as any of Scouting Ten's planes since only Ramsay and Bloch were left, in the adjoining northernmost sector, and the latter team made no contact at all.

Strong was a good 150 miles from the reported position of the battleships. But after carefully considering the fuel situation he led Irvine in a turn to port and began climbing on a southwesterly heading. Even allowing for a leaned-out fuel mixture to reduce gas consumption, it was going to be awfully close getting home. Nearly a half hour after leaving their assigned sector to go after the battleships, Strong and Irvine got word of the carrier force by listening in on Lee's contact report.

Any dive-bomber pilot would rather have a carrier in his sights than a battleship, and Strong especially relished the idea of making up for his missed opportunity at Eastern Solomons. Lee's contact was just about a hundred miles from Strong's position, and a course change of about 30 degrees to starboard put the two Dauntlesses on Nagumo's trail.

The impromptu hunt called for a neat bit of navigating, the kind which fully justified the rigorous standards demanded of Navy pilots. In a case like this, when wind drift could only be estimated because of low clouds which obscured the sea, navigation became as much a matter of art and instinct as applied science. But Strong's problem was considerably simplified by the accuracy of Lee's report.

About 20 minutes after Strong heard the carrier contact, he knew that his navigation was accurate. The proof was emerging from under a cloud in the form of two Japanese flight decks which belonged to *Shokaku* and *Zuiho*. The third carrier, *Zuikaku*, was hidden under other low-lying clouds. Irvine also had the carriers in view and tucked his Dauntless in close formation with Strong's in case of interception.

For the next few minutes the lone pair of SBDs stalked the Japanese ships, occasionally losing sight of them as more clouds blocked the view. Curiously, there was a total absence of enemy action, but it was not because the Japanese were complacent. Strong and Irvine approached unopposed because the Zero CAP was at that moment chasing off Ward and Carmody, who had been unable to attack.

At 0830 Birney Strong looked over at Chuck Irvine and tapped the top of his cloth flying helmet with the "I've got it" signal. Irvine allowed his Dauntless to slide away from his leader's as Strong nosed up, moved the diamond-shaped flap selector lever and felt the plane decelerate. Then he pushed over into his dive on the nearer of the two carriers. Irvine followed, allowing plenty of space between both SBDs.

It was the perfect example of a scout-bomber attack. In the course of their 13,000-foot dive, the two pilots met not the slightest opposition. There was no flak to bounce their planes around, distorting the aim, and no Zeros firing their 7.7s and 20-mms from near-collision range. All Strong and Irvine had to do was concentrate on John Crommelin's plea to get that hit.

Strong tentatively identified his target as a *Shokaku*-class CV and noted that the flight deck was empty. The carrier was actually the 11,200-ton *Zuiho*—sister of the *Shoho* which had gone down at Coral Sea.

Strong was out of the cloud layer at 1,500 feet with a completely unobstructed view of the gleaming hardwood deck, making sure of his aim. Then he yanked the double-handled bomb release, retracted his flaps and careened out of his dive, just off the water, at full throttle. Irvine was right behind.

The two 500-pounders, with 1/100 second delay, both slammed into *Zuiho*'s stern, mangling the after portion of her flight deck and knocking her out of the battle. Her planes had already been launched but they would have to land on another carrier. Strong and Irvine's aim had been 100 percent deadly.

All at once a heavy AA barrage erupted from the screening vessels and a pack of Zeros came down on the snaking Dauntlesses as they cleared out to the west. They got out of gun range quickly but the Zeros weren't so easily evaded. Strong and Irvine knew their only chance of survival lay in close teamwork, precise flying, and the straight shooting of their gunners. The Dauntlesses weaved back and forth providing mutual support while Garlow and Williams in the rear seats traded machine gun fire with the swirling, slashing Zeros.

One Japanese pilot misjudged the range, ceased firing too far out and pulled around for another pass. ARM1/c C. H. Garlow needed only seconds to swing his twin .30s around for proper lead, rip off a burst into the Zero's undersides, and watch it flame into the water. E. P. Williams in Irvine's plane splashed another. But the Zeros scored, too. Irvine's tail was badly shot up and his starboard main fuel tank was holed. Even if they shook the Zeros there was no guarantee their fuel would last, so Strong radioed a message in the clear to *Enterprise,* stating that two hits had been obtained on a carrier.

At last, after a tail chase of 45 miles, both Dauntlesses found a friendly cloud. They plunged inside and emerged to find themselves happily alone in the bright blue sky. At reduced throttle and extra-lean mixture it took nearly an hour and a half to return to the "Big E," but by 1030 Strong and Irvine were safely aboard, though neither had enough fuel for a second circuit of the landing pattern. It was the end of a perfectly executed mission in every respect.

In fact, the search planes as a whole hadn't done badly. Burnett and Miller, in the 282° to 298° sector, had followed up Welch's sighting of the vanguard force, and attacked through heavy and accurate AA fire. They shook up the cruiser *Tone* with near misses and returned to Point Option only to find *Hornet* under attack from the enemy air group. Burnett in Sail-4 latched onto a Kate and shot it down for his second victory; he'd splashed a Val on 24 August.

All 16 scouts returned safely to *Enterprise* though five were damaged. Four of the search teams had some form of contact with the enemy. They had shot down seven Zeros, one Kate and disabled a light carrier. But the battle was just heating up.

The first of three American strikes launched during the morning was a 29-plane *Hornet* group of 15 SBDs from Scouting and Bombing Eight with six TBFs and eight F4Fs. It was led by VS-8's new skipper, Lieutenant Commander Gus Widhelm.

The next strike included every *Enterprise* plane which could be readied for launch by 0910, except Wildcats needed for CAP. Because of the heavy load imposed by scouting requirements and antisub patrol, only three SBDs could be scraped together. They were Bombing Ten planes flown by Scouting Ten "jaygees"—H. N. Ervin, C. G. Estes, and J. F. Richey. Eight TBFs and eight Wildcats filled out the formation with Commander Gaines in his CAG Avenger.

At almost the same time as the *Enterprise* strike was heading out, another 25 *Hornet* planes were dispatched. Commander Walt Rodee led this group, which included nine VB-8 planes under Lieutenant J. J. Lynch, plus nine TBFs and seven F4Fs.

The 73 aircraft of these three strikes (27 SBDs, 23 TBFs and 23 F4Fs) were launched under hurried and somewhat confused circumstances. It was a safe bet that the Japanese air groups were already on the way, so there was an urgent need to clear the carrier decks before bombs started falling. However, the range was optimal for a strike—200 miles—and there was no time or fuel to spare in organizing into a single formation. Each of the three groups proceeded independently, heading northwest and climbing slowly to conserve fuel.

Just 60 miles outbound at 5,000 feet Gus Widhelm's formation learned how close it had come to being caught on deck. The first Japanese strike was headed on a reciprocal course, bound for *Hornet* and *Enterprise*. Neither group took offensive action against the other—there wasn't enough gas to spare for such things.

A few miles to the southeast the Japanese saw the somewhat smaller *Enterprise* formation and figured the opportunity was too good to pass up. Nine Zeros moved around up sun and initiated a surprise attack, shooting down three Wildcats and three Avengers. Another F4F and TBF aborted with heavy damage, and though three Zeros were splashed, the "Big E's" strike was nearly halved to four Avengers, four Wildcats and the trio of Dauntlesses, which wasn't harmed. Later the pilots learned that John Leppla was in one of the missing F4Fs.

Up ahead, about 150 miles from point of launch, Gus Widhelm was looking at Japanese ships by 1025. Two cruisers and several destroyers were sighted off to starboard and some 20 miles further the pilots thought they recognized two battleships, two cruisers and seven destroyers on the port side. Nine Zeros paid instant attention to the *Hornet* group and were engaged by four Wildcats. The SBDs proceeded without seeing anything else and one of Widhelm's pilots radioed, "Gus, there's no carriers in sight here; let's return."[6]

But Widhelm wasn't so sure. He'd missed out on most of the action at Midway, as did all the *Hornet* SBDs, and decided to press on a bit further. Five minutes later a carrier group was sighted, "two CV, one CL and four DDs."[7] One carrier seemed to be damaged, as it was smoking noticeably, but Wildhelm didn't see anything wrong with the other one. He headed towards it.

It was 8 May at Coral Sea all over again. On that occasion *Zuikaku* had escaped attack by sliding into a squall line while *Shokaku* was left in the open. Now Widhelm chose the *Shokaku* for his target as *Zuikaku* remained unseen under some clouds.

The six Avengers of Torpedo Six had remained at 800 feet and subsequently failed to contact the enemy carriers. This meant that Widhelm's 15 SBDs had to handle the job entirely by themselves, as their four Wildcat escorts were busily engaged in fighting off the first group of Zeros. Two AA bursts near the Dauntlesses brought immediate reaction in the appearance of more fighters. The result was a 25-minute running gun battle at 12,000 feet with the dive bombers under continuous attack.

In a beautiful display of skill and teamwork the 15 SBDs turned as a group into the fighter attacks in order to present a more formidable defense. The Zeros lined up in echelon ahead of the tightly packed *Hornet* formation, and as they peeled off to initiate a gunnery pass they were confronted by the SBDs' massed firepower. The Japanese made repeated close and determined attacks but couldn't break up the tight defensive formation. Widhelm's plane was hit early in the battle and began to leak oil but remained in the lead.

The Zeros came again and again—nobody ever knew exactly how many there were—but it seemed apparent they outnumbered the Dauntlesses, and they began to take a toll. The first victim was Lieutenant (jg) Grant of Bombing Eight, followed by Lieutenant (jg) Fisher, who made a water landing but was never recovered. Lieutenant (jg) White's Dauntless was severely damaged and almost uncontrollable with the port aileron shot away. Though badly wounded in a shoulder and one hand, White held his plane in the air long enough to return to *Enterprise*, and succeeded in landing aboard.

The other SBDs pressed on to the target, faithfully following Widhelm's aggressive lead, even though his plane was now trailing smoke. His engine was losing oil and overheating, the Zeros were attacking as ferociously as ever, but Widhelm tenaciously held on, hoping to last just long enough to plant his bomb on the long, narrow flight deck now only a few miles away. But it was no use; with the last of the oil gone the engine froze up and the propeller stopped dead. Widhelm jettisoned his bomb and turned out of formation, beginning a long glide to the waves below. He turned over command to Lieutenant Vose, skipper of Bombing Eight, who smoothly took the lead.

One Zero peeled off from the pack and went after Widhelm's Dauntless, anticipating an easy kill. But Stokely in the rear seat fought the Zero almost all the way down before it broke off. Gus Widhelm dropped his landing flaps and tail hook, which would drag in the water and warn his when he was down to the last few feet, and pancaked the riddled SBD into the waves.

Lieutenant James E. Vose led the Hornet's *dive bombers in the attack that crippled the Japanese carrier* Shokaku *at Santa Cruz. (J. E. Vose)*

With the Dauntlesses so close to *Shokaku* the Zeros redoubled their efforts to knock them down but Widhelm's plane was the last they stopped. Though two gunners were badly wounded and two pilots had

157

lesser injuries, the Dauntless crews—and surely the *Hornet* fliers were dauntless that day—claimed "at least 15 Zero planes destroyed by fixed and free guns."[8] In retrospect Vose said that "fifteen seems a large number,"[9] and it is true that duplicate claims were made. Japanese records show five Zeros shot down, but the number is relatively unimportant. The gunfight couldn't go on much longer, and it didn't. Vose arrived over *Shokaku* with 11 aircraft, most of them damaged, and led them down in what would be the last air attack on a Japanese carrier for 20 months.

Despite heavy and accurate AA fire and several Zeros which tried to follow the SBDs in their dives, Vose and his pilots were not to be denied. One after another they dove on *Shokaku* as the big carrier twisted desperately to slide out from under the 11 bombs which were aimed for her flight deck. Nobody knows for sure how many bombs hammered into *Shokaku*, not even the Japanese, who said three to six hits were made. Vose saw at least three and Gus Widhelm, bobbing around in his liferaft not far away, jubilantly counted a half-dozen. He and his gunner were picked up by a PBY two days later.

The 11 Dauntlesses cleared the area and headed back to the task force, but when they arrived about noon they found *Hornet* badly hit and the friendly AA gunners not so friendly. The recognition signal for the day was left-hand turns, dipping the port wingtip twice. The shot-up Douglases performed the required ritual prior to landing aboard the "Big E" only to be greeted by a storm of antiaircraft fire. The ships had just been under heavy air attack and the gun crews were still jittery, but no damage was done.

The "Big E" had also been hit in the enemy strike which crippled *Hornet*, and when the orphan SBDs entered the landing pattern they could see they'd have no easy time getting aboard. *Enterprise*'s flight deck was smoking heavily up forward and there was a bomb hit aft. Even worse, the middle elevator was jammed in the lowered position, presenting landing pilots with the awesome spectacle of a giant square hole directly in the center of the flight deck, 300 feet from the stern. As the homing SBDs flew up the wake, nose high with arresting hooks dangling, it was essential for each plane to engage one of the rearmost arresting wires, which they all did. Then each pilot taxied very carefully around the edge of the elevator shaft to park his plane forward. Fortunately the elevator was only temporarily out of order.

"Moe" Vose was astonished by the souvenir one of his pilots brought back. Lieutenant Fred Bates, VB-8's flight officer, presented Vose with a piece of wood which was charred and jagged around the edges. It was a piece of *Shokaku*'s flight deck which had been blown into Bates' cockpit by the explosion of Vose's bomb. Bates had followed Vose in the dive,

158

and with his canopy open the unique souvenir had plopped in while Bates was still in his dive.

Both American carriers had been damaged, one severely, but *Shokaku* was also in trouble. The *Hornet* dive bombers had "opened her up like a sardine can" and she would be out of the war for nine months. But she didn't sink even though she'd probably taken as many hits as proved fatal to four carriers at Midway. She owed her survival to the fact that her aircraft were 200 miles southeast, mauling *Enterprise* and *Hornet,* when she was stricken. Without the highly combustable materials on deck which had inflamed *Akagi, Kaga, Soryu,* and *Hiryu* she would pull through. But there was no doubting she was finished as far as this battle was concerned, and the odds had dropped to two Japanese carriers against the limping *Enterprise.*

Meanwhile, the remnants of the *Enterprise* strike had the battleship and cruiser force in sight. The four Avengers and three Dauntlesses trailed the Japanese ships northwards for a few minutes, searching behind large cumulus clouds for the carriers they knew were in the area. But not finding the flattops, the "Big E's" pilots had to settle for the battleships.

The Scouting Ten trio picked out a large battlewagon they identified as *Kongo* class (they were right, she was *Kirishima*) and pushed over. Their aim was excellent—Ervin and Estes both reported direct hits and Richey near-missed to starboard—but two hits on *Kirishima's* well-armored 32,000-ton bulk barely made an impression and she steamed on unimpeded. The SBDs all escaped without damage.

The four TBFs had launched their torpedoes at a heavy cruiser which managed to avoid them all, and the *Enterprise* strike headed home, wondering if their carrier was still afloat. Shortly thereafter a single Zero appeared from nowhere and made a pass at the Dauntlesses. The gunners splashed him.

This left only the second *Hornet* wave to contend with the enemy forces and possibly finish off one of the damaged carriers. Lieutenant J. J. Lynch, leading nine SBDs, had heard the radio conversations between Widhelm's pilots which indicated no carriers were within range. He apparently didn't hear the contact report five minutes later which stated the presence of at least two flattops, but communications were nearly as much a problem in this battle as they had been in the previous one.

Lynch therefore radioed Commander Rodee that unless otherwise ordered he would attack the heavy cruiser which was already shooting at him. More radio trouble cropped up and Rodee never heard the transmission, so Lynch took the initiative. He readily identified her as a *Tone* class cruiser by her distinctive configuration; all four turrets mounted forward, none aft. She was *Chikuma*, second and last ship of the class.

The attack began at 1040 from 11,500 feet. Antiaircraft fire was heaviest during the initial approach and final dive, but no SBDs were badly damaged. The pilots claimed four hits on the big cruiser, and though the real score was one less, she was staggered. Lynch and his number three, Lieutenant (jg) J. C. Barrett, were both certain of hits and theirs were probably the bombs which demolished *Chikuma*'s bridge. A third bomb exploded belowdecks, two near misses rocked her badly, and the well-mauled cruiser was through for this battle. The Avengers attacked *Tone* with bombs but got no hits.

The formation returned to the task force at 1225 only to find *Hornet* dead in the water from five bombs and two torpedoes. The pilots were preparing to land aboard the "Big E" when more Japanese planes appeared. The nine SBDs broke off and went after them in a widespread free-for-all. Lieutenant (jg) Tom Wood claimed two Vals while the third section, led by Lieutenant Edgar Stebbins, combined to bag a Val and a Kate. The second *Hornet* strike landed aboard *Enterprise* at 1330.

The Battle of Santa Cruz was a tactical defeat for the U.S. Navy. The badly damaged *Hornet* was ordered abandoned and left in the path of the advancing Japanese, who finished her off with destroyer torpedoes—365 days after she was commissioned.

American and Japanese aircraft losses were fairly even, but though U.S. naval strength was severely limited as a result of Santa Cruz, the strategic situation remained unchanged. Just as Eastern Solomons was less than a resounding victory, the status quo was maintained and the last serious Japanese carrier threat to Guadalcanal was permanently ended at Santa Cruz.

Viewed strictly from the SBD's point of view, Santa Cruz was considerably more of a success than the overall picture showed. Over 20 Dauntlesses were lost to all causes, including 11 blown overboard or jettisoned from *Enterprise*. Yet of the 43 SBDs launched on the morning search and the three strikes, the only combat losses were the three *Hornet* planes shot down near *Shokaku*, two crews being lost. But Dauntlesses claimed no fewer than 23 Zeros, three Vals and two Kates shot down, even if the number of fighters destroyed was considerably less.

More importantly, however, was the comforting fact that bombing accuracy improved from 11 percent at Eastern Solomons to 40 percent at Santa Cruz, an unparalleled record at the time for U.S. Navy aircraft.

The various SBD formations had dropped 27 bombs on five enemy ships and made at least 11 hits on four of them. Three of the ships—a heavy and a light carrier and a heavy cruiser—were extensively damaged.

Between May and November 1942—from Coral Sea to The Slot—SBDs had sunk six Japanese carriers of 130,000 tons total displacement and badly damaged others on three occasions. A battleship, three cruisers, and four destroyers had also gone down under SBD bombs, though it must be noted that torpedo planes shared in the destruction of some of these ships. Even so, the Dauntless could claim over 140,000 combatant tons sunk unassisted and nearly 50,000 tons shared. Heavy damage to two carriers and four cruisers amounted to another 80,000 tons. This all added up to the staggering total of well over a quarter of a million tons of enemy warships sunk or substantially damaged. In simpler terms it meant that in six months very nearly 30 percent of Japan's prewar naval strength in carriers, battleships, and cruisers was sunk or disabled by SBD dive bombers.

The combatant ship figures do not include some 15 transports or merchantmen sunk, of which SBDs could claim eight exclusively. Nor does it account for the nearly 80 Japanese aircraft credited to Dauntless crews in the same period.

It is appropriately ironic that the most impressive statement about what the SBD meant to the Allied war effort in 1942 is not in terms of what it accomplished, but rather in what it did not do. Excluding submarines and small craft, from May through November in the Pacific the U.S. Navy sank one battleship, one cruiser, and 11 destroyers without any sort of assistance from SBDs.

The record seems clear enough in perspective: the Douglas Dauntless was the worst enemy of the Imperial Navy of Japan.

chapter 8
the other ocean

The deep, immense Atlantic.
Frederick W. Myers
Wind, Moon and Tides

Operation TORCH, the invasion of North Africa, was the first and only major campaign in which the Dauntless participated against the western Axis powers. Coming in early November of 1942, TORCH coincided with the climax at Guadalcanal.

American carriers were assigned only to the western portion of the three-pronged TORCH plan, with British flattops supporting the Mediterranean landings at Oran and Algiers. The main thrust of the Western Naval Task Force was Casablanca, on Morocco's Atlantic coast, but the operation was subdivided into Northern, Center and Southern Groups. Each group had its own carrier unit, with the Center Group being best protected. *Ranger* operated a hodge-podge air group consisting of two fighter squadrons and Scouting Squadron 41. The two fighter units boasted a total of 27 F4F-4s while Lieutenant Commander L. P. Carver's VS-41 had 18 SBD-3s on hand. The air group commander, Commander D. B. Overfield, flew the only TBF aboard the eight-year-old carrier.

Suwanee, one of the very first escort carriers, operated a mixed group of Wildcats and Avengers to supplement *Ranger,* but was assigned no SBDs.

The Northern Group, operating only 50 miles further up the coast from Fedhala where the Center Group would land its troops, had the escort carrier *Sangamon* for tactical air cover. Her composite Air Group 26 consisted of nine SBD-3s and nine TBF-1s under Lieutenant Commander J. S. Tracy while the fighter squadron flew a dozen F4F-4s.

Over one hundred miles to the southwest of Casablanca *Santee* was to support the landings near Safi. Like *Sangamon, Santee* had a mixture of aircraft with VGS-29 flying nine Dauntlesses and eight Avengers while VGF-29 numbered 14 wildcats. *Santee* in particular was short of experienced pilots, having fewer than a half-dozen to rely upon for leadership and know-how. Fortunately the Vichy French put up relatively few aircraft to contest the landings, and their antiaircraft fire would prove generally ineffective, though not always so.

Discounting antisubmarine patrols, the first air action of the North African invasion began at about 0700 on 8 November with the invasion transports laying off Fedhala. Lieutenant Commander Carver's 18 Dauntlesses dive-bombed Casablanca Harbor's submarine basin despite rather heavy AA fire from shore guns and those of the berthed battleship *Jean Bart.* All the SBDs landed back aboard, but *Ranger* was shortly called upon to launch a strike group to meet an unexpected threat.

Seven Vichy destroyers had departed Casablanca Harbor shortly after 0800, heading north with the obvious intent of attacking the vulnerable allied troopships off Fedhala. Spotter floatplanes informed the task force of the enemy vessels and SBDs with F4Fs initiated attacks. As the Wildcats went in low to strafe and hopefully suppress AA fire, the available Dauntlesses pushed over and dropped their bombs, but to little effect. One SBD was shot down, the pilot and gunner both lost.

American cruisers subsequently engaged the French ships, and a running gun battle developed. During this time *Suwanee* Avengers joined *Ranger's* Dauntlesses, which were still in action three hours after the trouble had started. Scouting 41 scored two direct hits on the destroyer *Albatross,* stopping her dead in the water. Three enemy ships, including the cruiser *Primauguet,* were beached where they presented easy targets to the SBDs. *Primauguet* took numerous hits between her bow and the bridge.

Sangamon's aircraft had little of *Ranger's* excitement on the eighth, operating with the Northern Group, but things picked up on the ninth. Lieutenant Commander Tracy's SBDs and TBFs were called in to clear various obstacles from the path of the advancing infantry, including tanks and roadblocks. Operating within easy distance of shore, *Sangamon* was capable of putting her aircraft over specified targets within minutes of a call for aid.

The inexperienced *Santee* pilots had more than their share of troubles. The *Santee* lost a total of ten Wildcats, four SBDs and seven TBFs during the four-day invasion. None of these losses could be definitely confirmed as caused by enemy action. However, the Scouting 29 pilots got in a few good licks on the ninth, attacking airfields and troop concentrations in support of the Safi operation. But forced landings, fuel exhaustion, and piloting errors plagued the *Santee* fliers for the remainder of the Western Naval Task Force operation, and their numbers amounted to half of the 44 carrier planes lost during TORCH.

On the third day, 10 November, the last major resistance in the Mehedia zone was blasted into submission by *Sangamon* Dauntlesses. This was the fortress Kasba, which had been bypassed by the landing teams but had refused to surrender. The air liaison party called in a strike on the fortress and Scouting 26's pinpoint bombing did the trick. The French defenders surrendered shortly after the SBDs pulled out of their dives, and by midnight resistance had ceased in the northern landing zone.

Ranger's air group was highly active on the tenth, flying numerous patrols and close-support missions against enemy strongholds and communications. A dive-bombing attack by Scouting 41 silenced antiaircraft guns at Ainsaba but that afternoon the moored battleship *Jean Bart* was back in action, firing at the cruiser *Augusta* offshore. *Jean Bart's* 15-inchers had been considered knocked out since the morning of the eighth but the French sailors had repaired one turret enough to commence firing again.

A Scouting 41 Dauntless lands aboard Ranger *prior to Operation TORCH in November of 1942. (Peter M. Bowers)*

Nine *Ranger* SBDs were directed to finish off the troublesome battle-ship, and arrived overhead at 1500. Of the nine 1,000-pounders dropped, two were solid hits and were enough to put *Jean Bart* out of the battle for good. Her hull opened up, she settled into the mud of the harbor. She was later raised and refloated. Counting the Japanese *Hiei* sunk near Savo Island three days later and half a world away, SBDs had sunk two enemy battleships in the same week.

Dive-bombing attacks continued on coastal batteries and a variety of other targets, but with the *Jean Bart* strike, Dauntlesses had largely con-cluded their major role in Operation TORCH. Nine SBDs had been lost —one-quarter of those engaged—but nearly all were operational losses unrelated directly to combat.

When American escort carriers became available for hunting U-boats in the mid-Atlantic in the early spring of 1943, TBF production was such that SBDs were not widely required. Capable of operating off CVEs as well as the Dauntless, the Avenger made a better antisubmarine aircraft for a variety of reasons. It had greater endurance, carried twice as much ordnance, and was much more adaptable to radar.

Therefore, the SBD's lack of success against German submarines is largely a reflection of its limited service with hunter-killer groups. The only escort carrier operating Dauntlesses in the Atlantic during the sum-mer of 1943 was *Santee*, still flying Composite Squadron 29's mixture of Avengers and SBDs. From June through August *Santee* had 13 TBF-1s

A VS-41 Dauntless off Ranger *(CV-4) provides antisubmarine protection to troopships during the invasion of North Africa in November 1942. The yellow ring around the fuselage star identified Operation TORCH. (R. M. Hill)*

and nine SBD-5s, plus 12 Wildcats, but every other CVE engaged in antisubmarine operations used exclusively Avengers as strike aircraft.

Land-based SBDs, still in the patrol and scouting role, continued to operate in the Caribbean well beyond shipboard Dauntlesses. Probably the last SBD unit operating in the Atlantic zone was Marine Scouting Squadron Three, based at St. Thomas in the Virgin Islands, and decommissioned in May of 1944.

The last and perhaps most interesting offensive assignment carrier-based SBDs drew in the Western Hemisphere came in October of 1943. Called Operation LEADER, this antishipping strike into Scandinavian waters was a joint American-British venture with *Ranger* being escorted by elements of the British Home Fleet. Air Group Four was assigned the task of clearing away enemy shipping from the Bodø roadstead and harbor, south of the Lofoten Islands. *Ranger* had operated with the Home Fleet before, but over half of her pilots had not yet flown a combat mission, and Operation LEADER was partially intended to introduce them to the shooting war.

Bodø was a small town on the Saltfjord near the 67th parallel, meaning *Ranger*'s aircraft would be operating north of the Arctic Circle. It was a far cry from the tropical climate most SBD crews came to know,

Dauntlesses over the Caribbean. These SBD-5s of Marine Scouting Squadron Three sport the Atlantic Theater insignia color scheme of white and gull gray, in May 1944. (U.S. Marine Corps)

but fortunately the weather proved not too severe for the occasion. The launch position was reached off the Vestfjorden before dawn on 4 October, but an 18-minute delay was imposed owing to insufficient wind. At length *Ranger* got 31 knots across her deck, but the first six of Lieutenant Commander G. O. Klinsmann's 20 SBD-5s were refitted with 500-pound bombs to lighten their takeoff weight. The other 14 retained their 1,000-pounders, and launch commenced at 0718, 150 miles from the target.

Escorted by eight F4Fs, Bombing Four flew in five four-plane divisions composed of two-plane sections. Most of the northeasterly leg was flown between 50 and 100 feet to avoid radar detection, as a masthead, 30-degree dive at 200 knots indicated airspeed was planned. Ten miles offshore the Dauntlesses climbed to 1,500 feet near the Myken Light and began looking for targets of opportunity.

One division was detached to scout an alternate lead into the fjord and found the 8,000-ton freighter *La Plata* a half-mile south of Aamno at 0824. The lead section broke off into a swift, shallow approach while two Wildcats dived down to suppress AA fire. Both Dauntless pilots released at extreme minimum altitude—Lieutenant (jg) Gordon toggled his bomb at only 60 feet—and both hit the target. One bomb exploded under the freighter's bow and the second hit amidships but bounced and exploded over 100 feet to port. The second section, seeing *La Plata* badly damaged, held its ordnance and proceeded towards Bodø to rejoin the main formation.

The other 16 SBDs and six F4Fs continued their search, passing up numerous fishing and cargo vessels obviously manned by Norwegians. But at 0830 three vessels were sighted in column heading north at about 12 knots—a tanker and a transport with a destroyer. As the F4Fs strafed, Lieutenant Commander Klinsmann led Lieutenant Weeks down on the leading ship, a 5,000-tonner. Klinsmann's bomb missed but Weeks put his just aft of the stack, apparently blowing a hole in her side. The third SBD's bomb failed to detonate and the fourth was wide of the target.

Two more sections, including the two planes which had withheld attacking *La Plata* shortly before, pressed their attacks on the 14,000-ton tanker *Schleswig*. She took one 500-pounder directly under the stern and another one aft. Listing to port, down by the stern, she wheeled hard over and grounded.

Eight Dauntlesses had not yet dropped their bombs and proceeded to Bodø Harbor while most of the others went to the rendezvous point. The four remaining two-plane sections each picked a ship in the harbor and followed the F4Fs down through the flak, indicating 220 knots, while Klinsmann's division circled nearby to draw off AA fire.

The first section attacked from the northwest. One bomb went wide but the other landed only 20 feet off the starboard beam, punching a hole in the ship. The second plane of this section, flown by Lieutenant (jg) C. A. Tucker, was hit by heavy caliber AA and crashed into the water from 200 feet.

Approaching from the east the second section released from 75 to 100 feet on a 3,000-ton vessel, gaining one hit on the tip of the bow and a near miss amidships. This vessel was burning spectacularly as the two SBDs raced from the scene, rear-seat men trading machine-gun fire with the shore batteries.

The last two sections claimed only minor damage to their targets. Lieutenant (jg) S. R. Davis, the last SBD pilot down, took a hit in the engine and indicated he was losing oil pressure. He ditched west of the harbor and launched his rubber life raft with his gunner while two Dauntlesses circled overhead. The pilots saw Davis signal that he and Radioman D. M. McCarley were all right, but neither was rescued.

A follow-up strike of ten TBFs and six F4Fs finished the destruction in Bodø Harbor, losing one Avenger on the way in. The tally for Operation LEADER was five ships totaling 23,000 tons destroyed and seven more damaged, four seriously. Bombing Four accounted for two ships by itself and another shared with the Avengers, plus damage to two more. This success cost VB-4 two aircraft and one crew with another crew missing in action. Four other Dauntlesses were damaged by light flak but returned safely to *Ranger*. When she sailed for the U.S. in early December, the SBD's tenure under American colors in the Atlantic Ocean had come to an end. The Dauntless would finish the war where it had started: in the Pacific.

Combat flying is hours and hours of dull routine laced with a few seconds of stark terror.

The crisis had passed on Guadalcanal by mid-November of 1942, but the campaign was still in full swing at Christmas. Certainly the straining, sweating ground crews and tired aviators had little indication that the end was in sight, for they still undertook operations almost daily, and a new threat was making itself known.

During the last week in November, the Japanese commenced work on a cleverly disguised field at Munda on New Georgia, only 175 miles north of Henderson Field. By 5 December a 2,000-foot runway was completed and a pack of Zeros was on the field by the end of the month.

One of the first in a long series of U.S. strikes was flown against Munda on Christmas Eve, when Wildcats escorted SBDs in an attempt to put the new field out of business. They got off to a good start: F4Fs shot down 14 Zeros while the Dauntlesses swooped down to bomb and destroy all 12 fighters still on the ground waiting to take off.

Munda would remain a hotly contested area for many weeks, as the Tokyo Express opened a feeder route there. But the Express maintained its old terminus on The Canal, and Marine SBD squadrons were engaged in contesting it as before. One of the Guadalcanal air force's great combat leaders was lost in the first week of December while leading a flight of SBDs against a force of 11 destroyers in The Slot. Major Joe Sailer of VMSB-132 was diving on one of the ships when his Dauntless was hit by antiaircraft fire and crashed in flames. Sailer's pilots achieved a measure of revenge by damaging five of the destroyers.

SBDs began their second full year of the war on 1 January 1943 when a flight of them bombed the area around Kokumbona where it was suspected the Japanese headquarters was located on Guadalcanal. The next day brought heavier activity when a force of ten destroyers came down The Slot in broad daylight, brazenly unconcerned about the B-17s which droned overhead at 20,000 feet. The Flying Forts dropped their loads but, as usual, failed to score any hits on moving targets. Late that evening, however, just before dusk a group of SBDs dropped in, their calling card a 1,000-pounder laid close aboard *Suzukaze*. The near miss slowed her to only ten knots and she turned back north. The remainder of the force was thwarted by PT-boats that night.

Another run of Japanese effort to reinforce troops on Guadalcanal was hit by Henderson Field SBDs in the early morning of 15 January as a group of destroyers scurried back north after the night's supply run. Fifteen Dauntlesses bombed and strafed the ships, damaging *Arashi's* rudder and putting numerous holes in another destroyer.

One week later, on the twenty-second, yet another new Japanese airfield was discovered. This one was located at Vila on Kolombangara and

An SBD-3 rolls into a steep right bank. Light control responses made the Dauntless a popular aircraft to fly, particularly when lightly loaded. (U.S. Navy)

boasted a 6,000-foot runway—long enough to accommodate bombers. It was necessary to hit the big field as soon as possible, and *Saratoga* was assigned the job. She had been out of combat with torpedo damage since 31 August, but on 23 January she launched most of her air group for Henderson Field in preparation for a heavy strike at Vila. Early the next morning "Sara's" 59 planes took off, including 24 SBDs and 17 TBFs. The Dauntlesses and Avengers dropped a total of 23 tons of bombs on the runway and facilities. And though it didn't put Vila out of business permanently, the Japanese were busy making repairs for several days.

175

By the end of January the Japanese high command at last admitted that the situation on Guadalcanal was irretrievable. Beginning on the night of 1–2 February the Japanese no longer strove to deliver troops and supplies, but to remove as many survivors of the six-month campaign as possible. Late in the afternoon of the first, a group of 20 destroyers was sighted heading down The Slot, apparently in the largest reinforcement attempt since the Naval Battle of Guadalcanal on 12–15 November.

At 1820 that evening, while there was still some daylight, 17 SBDs and seven Avengers went after the ships while 17 Wildcats tangled with some 30 Japanese fighters. Four U.S. planes were lost, but Dauntlesses stopped *Makinami* dead in the water with a direct hit. The other destroyers, generally unharmed, continued towards Guadalcanal and clashed with PT-boats that night, one of which slipped a couple of torpedoes into *Makigumo* and set her afire. Six SBDs attempted to finish her off around midnight but were unsuccessful. The Henderson Field planes had no better luck after dawn when more SBDs and TBFs attacked the retreating ships, but inflicted only minimal damage. The first evacuation attempt was a success, for 19 of the 20 destroyers returned with Japanese soldiers aboard.

The second evacuation mission came on 4 February, involving 22 destroyers and a heavy cruiser. With so much enemy firepower, the 33 SBDs and TBFs ran into stiff opposition when they attacked the Japanese that afternoon. Though ten Marine planes were shot down, Wildcats escorting the strike gunned down 17 Zeros while the Dauntlesses and Avengers broke through. Four destroyers were damaged, two seriously.

That night the 23 Japanese warships departed with their decks packed with troops. By the time the third evacuation run was completed a few days later nearly 12,000 hungry, exhausted, defeated enemy soldiers had been taken off Guadalcanal.

On 9 February 1943—173 days after Lieutenant Colonel Richard C. Mangrum's 12 SBDs landed at Henderson Field—Guadalcanal was declared officially secure. Dauntlesses had been largely responsible for Japanese shipping losses, which amounted to some four hundred vessels ranging from battleships to barges. But the Guadalcanal Campaign almost immediately evolved into the Solomons Campaign, and more Marine dive-bomber units were sent to Henderson and the newer fields in the area.

One of the new squadrons was VMSB-144, and its story may be typical of Marine SBD units arriving after the capture of Guadalcanal. Formed at San Diego in the fall of 1942, stateside training ended in December and the squadron's SBD-3s were loaded aboard a transport for shipment to the South Pacific. Ralph Kimble, a radioman-gunner at the time, watched the Dauntlesses being hoisted aboard but would later recall, "We never saw them again."[1]

Around the end of January the squadron arrived at Efate in the Hebrides, minus its aircraft, and helped a Seabee battalion build an airfield. After Guadalcanal had been secured, word came down that replacement crews were badly needed so VMSB-144 was split in two. One portion remained at Efate while the other half—18 crews—went up to Henderson Field to fill in until the rest could follow. Ralph Kimble was among the gunners temporarily assigned to other squadrons, almost none of which were operating at full strength.

At length VMSB-144 settled down to business and flew two tours from Guadalcanal in the opening phases of the Solomons aerial offensive. The squadrons flew so often, in fact, that many crews shared Kimble's feelings: "We flew and flew and flew until I hated to even see an airplane."[2]

The targets for Marine SBD and TBF squadrons were visited and revisited until their names could be repeated in a litany of boredom: Rabaul, Munda, Kahili, Ballale, Buka, Rekata, and still more. The five Japanese airfields at Rabaul were an exceptionally well-defended complex, and the Marines began picking away at the outlying bases, especially Munda. Over a hundred strike missions were flown there in four months, constantly holing the runways, but the industrious Japanese always had them repaired in a couple of days.

So went the long series of strikes which would form the longest aerial campaign of the Pacific War. Enemy air resistance was gradually beaten down by virtue of the arrival of a newer, faster and deadlier fighter at Guadalcanal. The SBDs' long-time stablemate, the Grumman Wildcat, was phased out in favor of the Vought F4U Corsair, introduced to combat in mid-February by VMF-124.

As Corsairs hunted down enemy fighters, antiaircraft fire increased in accuracy and quantity. It was difficult to eliminate AA guns with conventional bombs, but the Marines devised a devilishly ingenious method of coping with the problem. In place of a 1,000-pound bomb, a fuel tank was slung under an SBD's belly with a white phosphorous hand grenade taped to the tank. Using Knox gelatin from any handy mess hall, the Marine ground crews mixed aviation gasoline with the sticky gelatin in the fuel tank. When the tank was released the pin on the WP grenade was pulled, detonating the whole mess after a delay of several seconds. The gas-soaked gelatin clung to anything it touched on the ground and burned furiously. The Marines called their invention "hell jelly," but a more refined version came to be known as napalm, a combined form of the first syllables of its chemical composition: napthenic and palmitic acids.

177

Progress was slow, but it was perceptible nonetheless. Marine squadrons moved into the Russells in June of 1943 and were operating from fields on New Georgia, including Munda, by 24 July. Dauntless and Avenger squadrons at Munda began an intensive aerial siege against Kahili as a prelude to the landings on Bougainville, prompting some of the largest and most intensive raids of the campaign. Most squadrons flew as many as four missions a day, for weeks at a time, with a hundred or more planes participating in a strike. Vella Lavella began operation as a Marine air base in October and Bougainville, largest of the Solomon Islands, was captured and serving U.S. aircraft by early December.

With most of the important perimeter islands and their airfields in Allied hands by the end of 1943, attention turned almost exclusively to the Japanese bastion at Rabaul on New Britain. As the main Japanese anchorage in the Solomons, Rabaul carried double importance as an air and naval base. The Corsairs began clearing the sky of Zeros, and the SBDs and TBFs of Solomons Strike Command were able to concentrate on Japanese shipping.

The main target was Simpson Harbor, but the first serious attempts at attacking it in early January 1944 were badly hampered by weather. It remained for the Dauntlesses and Avengers to get in the first solid blow when they found eight cargo ships in the harbor on the seventeenth. Between the bomb-toting SBDs and torpedo-packing TBFs the Japanese ships were caught in a trap which was virtually escape-proof. Direct hits were registered on all eight vessels, three of which sank on

Lieutenant Leo R. Schall piloting one of VMSB-236's Dauntlesses on return from a long-range mission in 1944. Note the two drop tanks fixed to the 100-pound bomb racks. (R. M. Hill)

the spot and two more were last seen settling in the water as the Marines departed. The success cost 13 U.S. planes in exchange for 18 Zeros.

The Japanese could not sustain such heavy shipping losses, and recognized the fact. When the Imperial Navy pulled out of Rabaul in February 1944 it signaled an end to the last possible threat to Allied efforts in the Southwest Pacific. Enemy air and naval traffic had been choked off, leaving the garrison stranded. Nearly 250 ships had been sunk in and around Rabaul, plus 500-odd barges and small craft.

The air strikes continued well into summer before Allied planners at last decided that Rabaul was not worth the effort required to capture it. But even when the bypassed fortress was neutralized the Marines kept pounding away until AA fire almost vanished. This grind continued until the end of the war, when barely a structure was left standing at the once-impregnable bastion. In all, 33 Marine squadrons were involved at one time or another in blockading Rabaul, eight of which flew SBDs.

The tactical unit which would carry the majority of Marine aviation's operational chores in the Central Pacific was Air Wing Four, composed of two air groups. Formed in the latter part of 1942, MAW-4 was over a year reaching a combat zone because its squadrons were constantly being sent off to Guadalcanal or some other part of the Solomons. But with the advent of the Gilbert Islands invasion, MAW-4 moved out to the Ellice Islands to be within striking distance.

The wing contained ten squadrons within its two component groups, four of which flew SBDs. These were VMSB-151 and 241 in MAG-13 and VMSB-331 and 341 of MAG-31. Three-Thirty-One was the first squadron to stage through the newly captured Gilberts, flying a mission against the southern Marshalls in late December. But occupation of Eniwetok and Engebi Islands the next month effectively neutralized the remaining Japanese possessions in the Marshalls, thus setting the stage for yet another Marine aerial strangle. Air Wing Four moved a second time, from Tarawa to Kwajalein during March 1944 and dispersed its squadrons to outlying fields which were still being renovated by the intrepid Seabees.

The Japanese-occupied islands of Wotje, Maloelap, Mili, and Jaluit were almost totally lacking in air power after the Navy carrier planes departed. The enemy was cut off from outside supply sources but immune from invasion because the assault troops were needed elsewhere. Besides, as long as the Japanese on those islands were unable to sustain an offensive capability, they were pretty much out of the war.

But the enemy garrisons nurtured a stubborn failure to give up. As long as the runways and some facilities were maintained, their bases were potentially useful should they receive replacement aircraft. The Fourth Wing undertook the task of keeping the enemy off balance and his airfields unserviceable.

It wasn't entirely easy—Japanese AA knocked down 36 planes in the first six months—but destroyers and PBYs rescued half of the airmen downed in this opening phase. Inevitably, over a period of months, enemy opposition withered away as AA guns were knocked out or expended their ammunition. After that the Dauntlesses and Corsairs roamed at will over the small sun-blistered isles, machine-gunning, rocketing and bombing anything which seemed remotely worth the effort, often twice a day. The Marines' targets were all within 220 miles of Kwajalein.

Some 1,700 tons of bombs were dispersed liberally over the bypassed islands between March and September of 1944—a goodly portion by SBDs. The amazing Corsair was proving itself readily adaptable to dive bombing by this time, and could haul up to twice the bomb load of a Dauntless, but the Douglas would continue in service for many more months.

One of the best-known Marine squadrons still flying SBDs in the Central Pacific was VMSB-231. Famous for its "Ace of Spades" insignia, which had first appeared on biplane DH-4s in Haiti after Word War I, 231 was a combat-tested veteran of the Guadalcanal Campaign. The outfit's executive officer from Guadalcanal, Major Elmer Glidden, had also flown SBDs at Midway, which made him one of the most highly experienced dive-bomber pilots in the Corps. He had made 27 combat dives by the time he left Guadalcanal in late 1942, but he eclipsed that record during his stretch in the Marshalls as skipper of VMSB-231. With his radioman-gunner, Master Sergeant James Boyle, "Iron Man" Glidden rode his Dauntless down on island targets no less than 77 times. His total of 104 combat dives established the American record, yet Glidden and the crews who flew with him remained virtually anonymous.

At length the Corsair fully replaced the SBD in the Central Pacific, though some squadrons had grown so fond of their Douglases that they held farewell ceremonies in observance of their departure. One correspondent likened the SBD's retirement to sale of the family's trusty old Model T. By the end of 1944, after the SBD production line in California had closed down, it made sense to use Corsairs in the dive-bomber role. It meant a simplification of maintenance and spare parts since most squadrons within any group or wing would be flying the same aircraft.

The F4U wasn't quite as good a dive bomber as the Dauntless—after all, it wasn't built for that purpose—but most pilots thought it was better

Major Elmer Glidden (left), commanding officer of VMSB-231, points to mission insignia representing his dive-bombing attacks at Midway, Guadalcanal, and in the Central Pacific. He made more combat dives than any other American pilot. (U.S. Marine Corps)

than what followed. As the war progressed into 1945 and the dreary, boring milk runs continued, a number of Marine squadrons were re-equipped again, this time with the Curtiss Helldiver. A significant portion of the Marine Helldivers were not the SB2Cs the Navy was flying off carriers, but another model of the same plane, called the A-25. The A-25 was to the Helldiver what the A-24 was to the Dauntless—the Army version of a Navy dive bomber.

But the Helldiver failed to make much of an impression on the Japanese in the Central Pacific. Enemy survivors of the bypassed islands corroborated captured documents which stated that of all American strike aircraft the Japanese feared first the Dauntless and next the Corsair. Admittedly, without air opposition and only a minimum of flak, not to mention plenty of time to perfect their technique, Marine aviators became exceptionally proficient at the art of dive bombing. But even so, the enemy's evaluation of American aircraft still speaks in favor of the SBD dive bomber.

Marine Corps use of the Dauntless reached a peak in 1943–44 as numerous squadrons operated from land bases in the Solomons and Marshalls. By mid-1944 SBDs had flown a total of 1,190,000 operational hours, accounting for one-quarter of the Navy's carrier aircraft sorties and 26 percent of all sorties by Marine planes. But the Navy's carrier-building program caught up with combat requirements during this time, and the SB2C figured more and more prominently aboard ship. But when the Helldiver made its combat debut a year after the climax at Guadalcanal there was still a place aboard carriers for the SBD.

By June 1943 the Navy had placed nine new fast carriers in service; four CVs and five CVLs. The 27,000-ton *Essex*-class ships were the latest word in American carrier development. Laid down in 1941 and 1942, their design drew upon combat experience of the prewar carriers in such areas as construction and damage control.

The 11 *Independence*-class light carriers, displacing 11,000 tons each, were concessions to wartime expediency. Built on light cruiser hulls, they were fast enough to operate with the larger fleet carriers but had less space for aircraft. As CVL air groups consisted only of fighters and torpedo planes, Dauntlesses were not assigned to *Independence*-class ships.

The SB2C was slated for combat aboard the *Essex*-class carriers, but not until mid-1944 did it completely replace the SBD. While the new F6F Hellcat and the General Motors TBM joined the fleet in the summer of 1943, no immediate replacement was coming for the Dauntless. In fact, three of the first four new fleet carriers to enter combat operated SBDs during all or most of the first year of operations. They were *Essex* (CV-9) with Air Group Nine, *Yorktown* (CV-10) with Air Group Five, and *Lexington* (CV-16) with Air Group 16.

Bunker Hill (CV-17) was chosen to initiate the SB2C to combat, and VB-17 was her original bomber squadron. Skipper of Bombing 17 was Lieutenant Commander James "Moe" Vose, who had flown from the old *Hornet* with Bombing Eight at Midway and Santa Cruz. Bombing 17 nursed the new SB2Cs through their carrier qualifications, but not without difficulties. When the 2C made its debut in a strike against Rabaul in November of 1943 it was over a year late getting into the war.

Not that the Helldiver didn't do its job; it sank a good deal of Japanese shipping. The point was, it didn't offer much more than the aircraft it replaced. As Vose recalled nearly 30 years later, "The SB2C was of little improvement on the SBD . . . the SBD would be my choice."[3]

With the advent of an entirely new class of carriers came changes in the composition of air groups and the assignments of various aircraft. An *Essex*-class carrier stocked 100 or more planes while the normal comple-

An SBD-5 over Wake Island in October 1943. (U.S. Navy)

ment of a prewar carrier was 80. A major new feature was that scout squadrons completely disappeared from U.S. carriers during 1943, leaving the normal strength of an air group at three instead of four squadrons. The slack was taken up by greatly increasing the number of fighters in each ship, thus providing for stronger escort and CAP.

Consequently, the scout role passed largely from the Dauntless to the Avenger and Hellcat, as both had long-range capability, and allowed the dive bombers to be retained almost exclusively for strike missions. Dauntlesses were still flying inner air patrols as late as the Tarawa invasion of November 1943, but with the new year the SBD's role of scout was almost a thing of the past.

The Japanese carriers withdrew from operations for nearly two years after the Battle of Santa Cruz in October 1942. And while American flattops were hard-pressed to find enemy warships, they were increasingly active in other respects. *Enterprise* had been in almost constant operation since the war began, and she sat out most of 1943 undergoing refit and training a new air group. But during her absence the new *Essex* and *Independence*-class carriers had reverted to the tactics of early 1942 by again striking Japanese island bases. The difference was that the penetrations were much deeper and more carriers meant more planes. Now the only fleet carrier aircraft which had been in use on 7 December 1941, the Dauntless had started its way back across the Pacific.

Yorktown and *Essex* launched heavy strikes against Marcus Island on 1 September 1943. Bombing Five and Bombing Nine concentrated on the runways and oil storage depots even before the sun was fully over the horizon, and the day's final estimate was that the facilities on Marcus had been 80 percent destroyed or damaged.

And so it went—the big carrier raids on Buka and Rabaul, the invasion of the Gilberts, all in November. Then came the Marshalls in January 1944, with Kwajalein and Eniwetok Atolls being pounded by carrier-based Dauntlesses and Avengers in preparation for Marine amphibious invasion. SBDs did what they'd always done, only on a larger scale. They bombed Japanese airfields and facilities, flew countless anti-sub patrols, even shuttled VIPs back and forth between the newly conquered islands and the carrier task groups. When Admiral Marc Mitscher wanted to see how things were going he usually took one of *Lexington*'s Dauntlesses.

The new Essex-*class carriers took Dauntlesses deep into Japanese-held waters during the latter portion of 1943. Here two VB-5 planes return to* Yorktown *(CV-10) after a mission. (U.S. Navy)*

This Dauntless landed off-center and came to a stop in the gun gallery but no injuries resulted. The crash crew was immediately on hand. (U.S. Navy)

Enemy warships were sought out during the first half of 1944, but very seldom on the high seas. They preferred to hole up in their fleet anchorages, supposedly safe from attack. Task Force 58, the fast carriers, planned a two-day strike on Truk Atoll in the Carolines, hoping to smoke out the Japanese fleet. The raid, scheduled for 17–18 February, looked as if it might develop into the biggest naval battle to date.

Truk was indeed well-stocked with shipping, but not many were combat vessels. Some 200,000 tons of merchant shipping were sunk in the two-day raid, but nearly all was attributable to torpedo-armed TBFs. Dauntless squadrons had little opportunity to shine in this operation, for they mainly attacked land installations.

The "Big E's" frustrated dive-bomber pilots got a better shot at a Japanese man-of-war on 30 March during the attack on Palau. *Enterprise*'s reorganized Air Group Ten had instructions to hunt enemy ships, and sighted one about 50 miles north of the lagoon. It looked like a light cruiser in the dawn light but was actually a scaly 22-year-old destroyer, the 820-ton *Wakatake*.

Lieutenant Ira Hardman's 12 SBDs dived from 11,000 feet as VF-10 Hellcats strafed to suppress AA fire, while six Avengers bored in with torpedoes. One Dauntless was shot down early in the attack, and all the TBFs' torpedoes missed or ran too deep. *Wakatake* was churning up the water at 25 knots in a hard port turn, throwing up volumes of AA fire, when one of Hardman's pilots got a direct hit on her stern with a 1,000-pounder. Almost stopped dead in her tracks, the old destroyer was making less than ten knots when she took a second bomb well forward. *Wakatake* stopped, heeling over, burning, slowly sinking.

But some of the Japanese gunners kept up an accurate fire on the last SBD as it came down from starboard. At some point in his dive, Lieutenant (jg) Charles Pearson was apparently killed instantly by the AA fire for his Dauntless never wavered in its straight descent until it smacked into the water beside the doomed ship. The SBD's inherent stability had kept it on course, following the path its dead pilot had chosen.

As the Fast Carrier Task Force pushed ever westward, even some Navy pilots got a taste of the mundane backwater existence of the Marines who constantly bombed bypassed garrisons into nothingness. *Saratoga* still flew SBDs and her Air Group 12 remained in the Marshalls while the other large flattops went on to new adventures.

"Sara's" SBDs flew daily patrols far to the west in anticipation of possible Japanese intervention in the Marshalls but it never came. *Saratoga* had participated in only one carrier battle—Eastern Solomons in August of 1942—and now she would miss the biggest one of them all. The Imperial Navy was preparing to fight once more.

So faithful . . . and so dauntless in war.
Sir Walter Scott
Lochinvar

By June of 1944, two years after Midway, the situation was completely reversed in the Pacific. Now it was a Japanese outpost which was threatened by seaborne air power. Task Force 58 was knocking on the front door of the Japanese Empire.

Just as Admiral Chester Nimitz had been forced to risk his remaining naval forces defending Midway, so did the Japanese have to send their surviving ships of 1942 and the few which had been built since to defend the Mariana Islands. Guam, Saipan, and Tinian were about all that blocked the way to both the Philippines and the home islands. So there was no choice. The Imperial Navy, which hadn't engaged in a major battle since Santa Cruz, dispatched all its available carriers to contest the American thrust.

Admiral Yamamoto had taken four carriers to Midway. But Admiral Jizaburo Ozawa sailed with nine, including *Shokaku* and *Zuikaku*. Admiral Mitscher, *Hornet's* skipper at Midway, brought seven CVs and eight CVLs to the Marianas, so this time the U.S. Navy outnumbered the Japanese in both ships and aircraft.

Only two constants remained in American carrier aviation since Midway: *Enterprise* and the SBD. Veteran of every carrier battle except Coral Sea, the "Big E" was entering her fourth such engagement while no other flattop in the task force had ever launched a strike against enemy carriers. But the Dauntless had lost its numerical importance to the Helldiver. At Midway SBDs represented half of all U.S. carrier planes but now they were barely six percent of the total, and only a third of the dive bombers. Just two Dauntless squadrons totaling 57 SBD-5s remained with the Fast Carriers: those of *Enterprise* and the new *Lexington*.

Skipper of the "Big E's" Bombing Ten was tall, good-looking Commander James D. Ramage, better known as "Jig Dog." Even allowing for the increased fighter strength on each carrier, *Enterprise* carried 30 percent more Dauntlesses than VB-6 had in 1942. Ramage counted 23 SBD-5s on hand during the third week in June.

Enterprise's teammate in Task Group 58.3 was the *Lexington*, the last *Essex*-class carrier still operating SBDs. Bombing 16 numbered 34 Dauntlesses, very nearly as many as in a prewar air group. Lieutenant Commander Ralph Weymouth was skipper of the "Lex's" dive bombers, having flown with Scouting Three from *Saratoga* in the Eastern Solomons battle.

Bombing 16's personnel represented a typical cross-section of Americans under arms at the height of the Pacific War. They were 85 percent reservists averaging 23 to 24 years of age. The squadron's eager beaver by everyone's agreement was Lieutenant Cook Cleland. Cleland and his gunner, ARM2/c W. J. Hisler, had earned a reputation as an aggressive team which thrived on combat. During the raid on Mili Atoll, Cleland had spotted a Betty low on the water and pulled up alongside while Hisler fired away with his twin .30s. Exchanging broadsides in the manner of old sailing ships, the two antagonists continued a running gun battle until the Mitsubishi bomber went down.

As commander of the Fifth Fleet, Admiral Spruance was faced with much the same responsibility he had held at Midway. His job was twofold: stay within range of the islands to provide air support, and keep a constant watch for the approach of enemy carriers. There were three airfields on Saipan, plus more on nearby Guam and Tinian, which required the attention of the bomber squadrons. Spruance and Mitscher wanted to deprive the Japanese carrier planes of these fields, and during the afternoon of June 16 Task Force 58.3 launched strikes for this express purpose.

Commander Ramage led eleven of his Bombing Ten SBDs plus nine TBFs and a dozen Hellcats from *Enterprise* to hit Orote Field on Guam. The "Big E's" fliers put numerous holes in Orote's runway, destroyed some hangars and set afire numerous fuel storage tanks. The *Lexington* strike achieved similar results on the Agana airstrip, but the Japanese retained land-based airpower in the Marianas even though the Hellcats were beginning to cut a swath through it. The eighteenth saw a repeat of the previous day's activities while long-range Avengers searched over three hundred miles to the west for the enemy carriers, still without result.

Monday, 19 June was to be a highly successful day, but not for the dive bombers. Task Force 58 remained about a hundred miles west of the invasion beaches as aviators bemoaned the orders which tethered them to the islands. Carriers had to be free to move and seek out the enemy. But now with the biggest sea battle of the war to date shaping up, TF-58 was still held back. As before, the search pilots returned badly disappointed—there was nothing to report. It was widely heard aboard *Enterprise* that Captain Matt Gardner had thrown his cap across his cabin and stomped on it in frustration.

The Japanese weren't being passive, and evidence of that was not long in coming. Beginning at mid-morning American radar scopes picked up the first of the day-long series of Japanese air strikes, and F6Fs scrambled to meet the threat. The Hellcats outfought the enemy at a ratio in excess of ten to one, protecting the task force from all but a few Japanese which slipped through. Even those did very little damage.

Bombing Ten launched 11 aircraft shortly after the first radar contacts and the "Big E's" SBDs orbited 20 miles east of the task force, awaiting instructions. Ramage's squadron watched three futile air attacks on Mitscher's battleships and another on Task Group 58.3, which was equally ineffective. Half an hour after launch VB-10 was directed to initiate a 250-mile search for the Japanese carriers to the west, as Ozawa's Mobile Fleet remained undetected. The 11 Dauntlesses had barely set out when they were recalled and told to return to their original station, though no explanation was given. Finally, at 1300, orders came through to attack the airfields and facilities on Guam. Bombing Ten swung around and approached the Orote Peninsula from the southwest at 10,000 feet.

Despite intense AA fire, Ramage's planes suffered no significant damage, and all met at the rendezvous to return to *Enterprise*. "The airdrome looked well worked over," summarized the action report.[1] Several *Lexington* SBDs also bombed Orote and Lieutenant G. L. Marsh's plane was hit during its dive. With the engine running rough, Marsh glided four miles out to sea and made a successful water landing. The crew spent a half-hour in the water before a pair of SOC floatplanes arrived. Marsh's was the only SBD lost on the nineteenth.

By dusk Admiral Ozawa had lost most of his planes and two carriers. But U.S. submarines, not aircraft, were responsible for sinking the flag-

A pair of Bombing Ten Dauntlesses over Enterprise *in early 1944. Air Group Ten had previously flown from* Enterprise *in late 1942, participating in the Santa Cruz carrier engagement and the Battle of the Slot. (R. M. Hill)*

ship *Taiho* and the old familiar *Shokaku*. Like the "Big E," *Shokaku* had participated in every carrier battle but one—she'd missed Midway because of damage inflicted by SBDs at Coral Sea. Only her sister *Zuikaku* remained afloat of the six carriers which had launched strikes against Pearl Harbor.

Mitscher's ships maintained a westerly heading all through the night of the nineteenth and into the early hours of the twentieth, hoping to arrive within range of the enemy for a dawn search. If Ozawa's seven remaining carriers weren't brought to battle on the twentieth it looked as if they would get away without even being sighted by U.S. aircraft, as Spruance couldn't allow his ships to stray too far from the Marianas.

Enterprise had provided the scouts at both Eastern Solomons and Santa Cruz, and she repeated the role again. The difference was that two Avengers and a Hellcat comprised each search team instead of two SBDs. Four teams were launched at 1345 on the twentieth but not until 1540 did one of the Avenger pilots sniff out the Japanese Mobile Fleet.

The original contact placed Ozawa's force at Latitude 15° 00' North, Longitude 135° 24' East, proceeding west at 20 knots. Commander Gus Widhelm, who had flown SBDs at Midway and Santa Cruz, leaned over *Lexington*'s chart table, figuring the distance. It didn't look good. Rule of thumb for a maximum range strike was 250 miles, and if the contact was accurate, it meant a 237-mile flight out and nearly that much back. Furthermore, it was apparent that those aircraft which did manage to return would do so in darkness, and few air groups were fully qualified for night operations.

Mitscher anxiously asked his staff, "Can we make it?" After a lengthy silence Widhelm said, "We can make it, but it's going to be tight."[2]

For "Uncle Pete" Mitscher, there was but one reply: "Launch 'em!"[3] It had been nearly two years since any of his pilots had seen a Japanese flattop and this was the opportunity they wanted more than anything else.

Below decks, in Bombing 16's ready room, Lieutenant Commander Ralph Weymouth's crews plotted the contact on their navigation boards, then filed out of the room to man their planes. Observers noted the usual banter and jostling was missing.

Over on the "Big E," Commander Jig Ramage told Bombing Ten the best power settings for the long flight. "We're going to be gas misers," he said, to allow any chance of making a round trip.[4] Privately, Ramage doubted very seriously that his planes could return from such a lengthy strike. Settling in the cockpit of the lead dive bomber as the carrier swung into the wind, Ramage's remaining hopes almost completely vanished. Word came through that the original contact was in error by one degree of longitude; the Japanese fleet was 60 miles further west. Ramage pulled out his plotting board and figured the range again—297 miles. No matter how he looked at it, he didn't see how his planes could get back. But, he recalled, "there was no tenseness or nervousness . . . we were ready, we were good, and we knew it."[5]

That same kind of optimism was found on *Lexington*'s flight deck, too. Weymouth cautioned his junior pilot, 20-year-old Ensign Gene Conklin, against making another extra-low release. Lieutenant "Cookie" Cleland was heard telling his gunner Bill Hisler, "This is the job the SBD was made for—fleet action. Watch our smoke!"[6]

Cleland was flying "his" airplane, old number 39, for which he had developed a strong affection. After a raid on Palau, number 39 had been badly damaged and Cleland had landed aboard *Enterprise*. The deck crew had wanted to push his bird over the side, saying it was too badly shot-up to be repaired. But Cleland talked them out of it and flew old 39 back to *Lexington* where she was patched up.

Leading VB-16's second division was Lieutenant Don Kirkpatrick, who also considered the numbers angle as he prepared for launch. Kirkpatrick had, like Widhelm, flown at Midway and Santa Cruz; a total of 41 missions to date. He'd been shot down once and returned with damaged aircraft 18 other times. He and his gunner, AOM2/c R. L. Bentley, were assigned the squadron's number 13 plane; surely not a good omen.

Lieutenant Commander Weymouth, as senior *Lexington* pilot on the mission, would lead the Air Group 16 strike. Launch commenced at 1621 into the brisk east wind, which was the opposite direction from the Mobile Fleet. Weymouth brought his SBDs around at low level until they were headed into the late afternoon sun.

Bombing 16 had launched 15 SBDs but shortly after departure one of Cleland's wingmen in the last section had to abort with fuel leakage. Unknown to anyone else, Cleland was having similar problems. Fearing he'd be ordered back if he informed Weymouth of his situation, he pressed on, flying with one eye on the fuel gauge.

Enterprise had launched 12 SBDs, five Avengers, and 12 Hellcats, all of which swung onto a magnetic heading of 286 degrees immediately after launch. Flying a "guest appearance" with Bombing Ten was Lieutenant (jg) Jack Wright of VB-16. The day before, Wright's Dauntless had sprung an oil leak and he'd put down on the first carrier in sight. It turned out to be *Enterprise*, and before he could return to *Lexington* the "Big E's" air group was put on continuous alert. Unable to depart, Wright had stayed the night and obtained permission to fly with his hosts.

Overhead view of a formation of SBDs, outlined in flight against the Pacific. The Dauntless proved to be the thoroughbred workhorse of the Navy's air fleet throughout World War II. (U.S. Navy)

The SBDs climbed slowly, at an indicated 115 knots. As they passed through 10,000 feet the pilots and gunners fastened their oxygen masks; "We wanted clear heads when we found the Japs," said Ramage.[7] Breathing pure oxygen at 16,000 feet the pilots scanned the horizon for some indication of Ozawa's carriers.

From scout reports the attack groups knew the Mobile Fleet was deployed in four units; northern, center and southern carrier divisions with an oiler group trailing the carriers. Ralph Weymouth at the head of *Lexington's* dive bombers noticed a large oil slick on the water at about 1815, but it wasn't just a blob showing where a ship may have sunk. It formed an irregularly defined trail which led off towards the northwest —evidence that a Japanese tanker had a broken oil line trailing in the water. Weymouth turned slightly to starboard, taking a bearing on the oil slick.

Up ahead a little way was Bombing Ten, which made visual contact at 1830. There were six oilers and six escorting destroyers, which to Ramage looked "mighty fat, but not for us; we were after bigger meat."[8] The *Enterprise* Dauntlesses hadn't come nearly three hundred miles to drop their bombs on tankers when carriers were around. They continued several miles to the northwest when Ramage heard another pilot call out the tally-ho. "I could see many dots on the ocean about 40 miles ahead," the skipper reported.[9] The dots came into focus as the silhouettes of enemy warships.

Ramage had the center group picked out for his attack. It was Ozawa's Carrier Division Two which consisted of *Ryuho, Junyo,* and *Hiyo,* with two heavy cruisers and eight destroyers. As he turned off his base course the VB-10 skipper could plainly see two flattops, which made the attack disposition simple—one for each of his divisions.

The bright red sun was low on the horizon, leaving the upper air relatively clear with good visibility, but three miles below dark was falling. Though other air groups were attacking, the two carriers appeared untouched as he nosed down from 16,000 to 12,000 feet in preparation for the dive. As Bombing Ten drew nearer to the Japanese ships, the sky magically blossomed with hundreds of black puffs 200 yards off to starboard. As the 12 SBDs glided lower towards pushover altitude they were subjected to thicker AA fire but the formation remained intact.

Ramage wiggled his wings and Bombing Ten broke into attack disposition. The first division would take the nearest carrier while Lieutenant L. L. Bangs' second division proceeded on course to the other. No mix-up this time in diving order, such as had nearly foiled the *Enterprise* SBDs at Midway. The skipper pulled up and over Lieutenant (jg) De-Temple in the lead section and had just dropped his nose when Cawley in the back seat called out, "Zekes overhead." Ozawa had managed to put up 75 aircraft to intercept the incoming attackers. Ramage turned to watch the first fighter make a half-hearted run at the SBDs and bank away. "No guts," Ramage thought to himself.[10]

Then the CO was directly over the carrier he had identified as a "Zuiho class" ship. She was actually *Ryuho*—very similar in appearance and dimensions to the late *Shoho* and her sister *Zuiho*; small with no island and a long bow. Ramage dipped his left wing and came around, encountering more antiaircraft fire. The aviators had never seen it so thick or spectacular—the multi-colored tracers and bursting shells combined with the cherry glow of the low sun to form an unforgettable panorama. But then the carrier disappeared from view under the nose of Ramage's Dauntless and he popped his dive flaps, rolling into his attack from a left-hand turn.

Ryuho stopped turning momentarily, straightening out on an easterly heading as the skipper's SBD came down nearly vertical from stem to stern, downwind to the west. "The whole flight deck was outlined by tiny candle light flickering, punctuated with numerous large-caliber gun bursts," Ramage said. "The dive seemed forever, and at 8,000 feet I opened up with my twin .50 caliber nose guns. The tracers disappeared into the deck, however the Japs not for a second left their guns."[11]

As his plane screamed past 4,000 feet, Ramage was steadying his sight on the ship's forward elevator. The AA fire, which was becoming more intense as the small-caliber weapons chimed in, was still accurate in altitude. Those gunners were tracking him well all the way down, but the shells were exploding behind and to port. It caused little distraction, though the tracers seemed headed straight into his gunsight. But Ramage hung on: "I was determined to ride this bomb down to make certain of a hit."[12]

At 1,500 feet Ramage released his 1,000-pounder and simultaneously saw *Ryuho*'s stern swing out to starboard as she began a careening turn to port. He moved his flap selector lever and started his pull-out, but before the dive brakes were closed he was startled by the sound of Cawley firing. Glancing over his shoulder, Ramage found himself face to face with an astonished Zero pilot perhaps 15 feet away. The Japanese fighter stood on its tail and scrambled for the nearest cloud, "climbing at an impossible angle."[13]

Still at low level, Ramage's SBD was jarred as his bomb exploded. Behind him he could see black smoke at the extreme aft edge of *Ryuho*'s flight deck. His bomb hit mere feet from the stern. Ramage's wingman, DeTemple, put his bomb almost on top of his skipper's, close aboard the stern in the churning white wake. Third down was Lieutenant (jg) Hubbard, with a very near miss on the port beam, while Schaffer's bomb hung up and didn't release. Lieutenant (jg) Fife was a bit wide off the starboard quarter but the sixth and last pilot in the lead division, Lieutenant (jg) Schaal, claimed a hit. He thought his heavy bomb went through the aft port corner of the flight deck, right near the edge. A giant puff of white smoke seemed to erupt from the hangar deck, but as *Ryuho* is known to have escaped heavy damage it is probable that Schaal's bomb penetrated the deck overhang and detonated in the water.

The attack finished, Ramage's division then had to run the incredible gauntlet of concentrated AA fire from the massed escorting ships. A heavy cruiser loosed an entire broadside at Ramage as he streaked along at 300 feet, but the eight-inch shells exploded far behind. The light automatic weapons were more accurate, and tracers criss-crossed in front of the fleeing Dauntlesses. It took Ramage and his pilots a full five minutes to emerge from the withering fire of flak and tracers from destroyers, cruisers, and carriers.

The Zeros which appeared just before Ramage pushed over had been timid in the face of concentrated return fire from the gunners, and were loath to plunge into the seething mixture of light and heavy AA. But they were waiting for the six Dauntlesses to get clear of the carriers and were set to swoop down from above when *Enterprise* Hellcats hit them. Fighting Ten F6Fs splashed two Zeros on the first pass and the other Japanese left Ramage's section alone.

When Ramage had broken off to attack out of his port turn, the second division of Bombing Ten continued on course to the northwest. A "*Hayataka* class" carrier—misnomer for *Hiyo* class—had been picked up about ten miles ahead and Lieutenant Lou Bangs took his six planes towards it. Nearing the pushover point, the lead section extended flaps in preparation for the dive. But Lieutenant (jg) Grubiss, leading the second section, mistook this as an indication that a third carrier, almost directly below, was Bangs' intended target.

The result was that two sections of three SBDs each attacked a carrier. Bangs, Mester and Lewis dived on *Junyo* while Grubiss, Bolton and the *Lexington* tag-along, Jack Wright, went down on *Hiyo*. Bangs took his two wingmen in a high-speed run from 16,000 down to 9,000 before pushing over in a steep dive on the northernmost carrier. All three pilots strafed continuously until release at 2,000 feet. Bangs, the first to drop, got a direct hit well aft on the fantail, blowing about half a dozen planes overboard. Lieutenant (jg) C. R. Mester put his bomb to port of that one, compounding the damage. And Lewis made the section's record 100 percent with a hit immediately aft of the island. As the section recovered at 1,000 feet the carrier was seen burning. But there was no time for sight-seeing in the midst of heavy flak, and Bangs led Mester off to the west, while Lewis took a circuitous course to the southeast before turning due east for the rendezvous point.

Junyo was last reported dead in the water, down by the stern and listing to starboard. Surely, the pilots thought, she was headed for the bottom. But so, apparently, were Bangs and Mester. Just past the destroyer screen they were jumped by several Zeros, one of which closed to minimum range on Mester's plane. A 20-mm cannon shell holed one wing and machine gun bullets shattered the glass canopy between pilot and gunner. But the two rear-seat men put up a spirited defense and kept the rest of the Zeros at maximum range until they turned back towards the main battle area. Bangs and Mester were well past the rendezvous spot and set course for *Enterprise* on their own.

Grubiss' section, meanwhile, dived on an "unidentified light carrier," actually *Hiyo*, strafing all the way down from 9,000 feet. The three pilots could see their tracers penetrating the empty flight deck and were spared the violent antiaircraft fire their squadronmates encountered. Grubiss got a bomb hit just aft of the stern and Wright of VB-16 got a near miss to port. The last *Enterprise* SBD pilot to ever drop a bomb on a Japanese carrier was Lieutenant (jg) Bolton. Unfortunately for history's sake, the result was not observed by Bolton or anyone else. The section headed east at 400 feet, still undamaged.

Jig Ramage circled at the designated meeting spot and counted nine planes joining up in formation. That meant three were missing. "Remembering back," Ramage said, "my heart sank as I recalled a dive bomber aflame at about 4,000 feet over the Jap carrier. Could it have been one of my missing ducklings?"[14] It was actually an SB2C, but there was insufficient fuel remaining to wait around and find out. Ramage had no way of knowing Bangs and Mester had already started home, but correctly figured that Jack Wright of VB-16 had rejoined his *Lexington* friends.

Approaching the expected contact area at 1823, Ralph Weymouth at the head of Bombing 16 heard an F6F pilot call "ships ahead." Twelve minutes later, Lieutenant Thomas E. Dupree noted several ships about 20 miles off to port. Lieutenant (jg) George Glacken in Cleland's tail-end section thought they looked like carriers and wondered why Weymouth remained on course. But the skipper recognized them as oilers and he was looking for "the fighting navy."

Swinging ten degrees north to clear an immense flat-topped cumulus cloud, the *Lexington* strike had the Mobile Fleet in sight. Weymouth's wingmen, "jaygees" J. A. Shields and T. R. Sedell, were entranced. Like most pilots on the strike they had never seen any Japanese carriers, let alone so many other enemy ships.

Bombing 16 apparently did not sight Ozawa's Carrier Division Three, which was a good ten miles south of the center group, CarDivTwo, as Weymouth led his strike on a course between *Zuikaku* of CarDivOne to the north and the three flattops of CarDivTwo to the south. Heading west, the 14 *Lexington* Dauntlesses were delegated by their skipper to hit a "*Hayataka*-class" carrier which was moving almost precisely downwind. Such identification errors were largely owing to poor translation of Japanese into English, for the "*Hayataka*" was *Hiyo*, name ship of her class.

The *Lexington* pilots could see that attacking Ozawa's carriers would be no easy job; the flak was thick and spectacular. But AA gunners were the least of VB-16's problems at the moment, for a cluster of Zeros had swept down on *Lexington*'s Avengers from above and behind, shooting one out of formation. The Zeros continued on to the SBDs, nearly catching them by surprise before the Hellcats intervened. Weymouth's gunner, Radioman W. A. McElhiney, spotted the strange planes directly behind the squadron, opened his canopy, deployed his twin .30s and opened fire. The Dauntlesses nosed down to gain speed.

Several other gunners had also seen the Zeros coming and were ready for them, but others were not. Radioman R. L. Van Etten in Ensign

Moyers' plane was leaning over the side of his cockpit, engrossed in photographing the spectacle below, when a gleaming stream of tracers flashed by. Van Etten turned to catch a glimpse of a Zero flashing past his rudder. Abandoning his photography, the gunner unlimbered his twin .30s just in time to turn them on another Zero overhead. He watched his tracers hit the nose of the fighter and then it was gone below.

Another three Zeros ganged up on Ensign Gene Conklin's Dauntless but his gunner, AOM3/c Jim Sample, got a good burst into the engine of one Zero, and hit it again as it went under the starboard wing. Two more gunners hit a fighter with their combined fire, causing one of its landing gear wheels to extend.

Lieutenant (jg) W. L. Adams' SBD took three hits in the right main fuel tank but the self-sealing liner held up. Three bullets through Cleland's rudder was the only other damage to Bombing 16.

Reaching the push-over point at 11,500 feet, the squadron was subjected to a vicious pounding by heavy caliber AA guns from both the northern and center carrier groups. Bringing his planes around in a slow port turn, Weymouth signaled for attack formation by holding up his right fist, then dipped his wings as if to say "Now." The inside plane of each section executed a cross-over turn to starboard so the three-plane elements were staggered in right echelon.

Bombing 16 was now heading east, the sun behind and low on the horizon with the two carriers in sight beginning evasive action by turning port from north to nearly due east. Weymouth had the absolutely perfect setup: he could dive directly upwind, the length of the ship's flight deck from bow to stern, and the bright setting sun would glare in the AA gunners' faces as he pulled out. Rolling into his dive at 1904, Ralph Weymouth realized that he had a dive-bomber's dream.

All the way down, through extraordinarily intense flak, Weymouth concentrated on putting his heavy bomb through *Hiyo*'s flight deck, mindful that he'd near-missed *Ryujo* at Eastern Solomons 22 months before. At 1,500 feet he released and began his high-G pullout, recovering at around 800. McElhiney in the rear seat saw a black puff of smoke belch from the flight deck beside the island.

Behind and above the lead SBD, Bombing 16 was unwinding in rapid sequence over the carrier, which had just put her rudder hard over. The bombs were falling so fast that it was nearly impossible to tell who got the hits, but Lieutenant Harry Harrison, ninth to dive on *Hiyo*, saw only three splashes in the water and assumed five hits had been made. His own bomb hit about 40 feet off the starboard quarter. Ensign Conklin aileron-rolled part of the way down to keep the carrier in the illuminated circle reflected in his Mark VIII sight. Forgetting Weymouth's pre-launch advice about going in too low, Conklin bored down until he either had to release or plunge into the deck. But during the mind-blurring high-G pullout neither pilot nor gunner observed the result.

The last two planes down on *Hiyo* both claimed direct hits. Lieutenant "Pinky" Adams' gunner, Kelly, reported the bomb went directly through the center of the flight deck and said Ensign Hank Moyers also scored. Van Etten in the back seat of Moyers' SBD thought the hit was from one of the last two VB-16 planes, but neither of them had dived on *Hiyo*.

Lieutenant (jg) George Glacken was the fifth pilot to dive, but when he pushed over the first four Dauntlesses blocked his view of the carrier. He jinked around trying to get his sights on it, but by the time he located the target again, it was directly under him. If he persisted in the dive at such an angle he knew he'd probably miss. Just then he caught sight of *Hiyo*'s sister *Junyo* off to the left and came back on the stick and settled his dive on her. But just as he pushed the red button marked *B* on top of the stick, *Junyo* started a hard evasive turn and the bomb fell wide.

The section of Lieutenant Cleland and Ensign J. F. Caffey was one plane short after the number three man had aborted following launch. Seeing Glacken's attack, Cleland and Caffey diverted from *Hiyo* to *Junyo* in hopes of helping out. They were the last of the squadron to attack, and came down through the vicious, spectacular AA fire alone.

As Cleland swooped down on *Junyo* his SBD took a succession of hits from light-caliber weapons. First a 20-mm shell hit the starboard wing tank and a 40-mm put a two-foot hole in the same wing. Then another 40-mm blasted the floor out of the rear cockpit, knocking the Dauntless off course. Cleland rolled back on target, took careful aim again, and pushed the button with his thumb. His bomb hit *Junyo*'s flight deck about ten feet forward of the stern.

Cook Cleland had claimed the last hit an SBD would ever score on a carrier, but "Irish" Caffey was the last pilot to roll a Dauntless into a dive over an enemy flattop. Shrapnel banged against Caffey's plane, all during that last dive, and though he released low the result was not clearly seen.

Pulling out of his dive, Cleland was attacked by a Zero in a high side run from the starboard quarter. Bill Hisler put about 60 rounds of .30 caliber into the fighter's belly as it swung around. The Zero smoked, dropped one wheel and glided for the water to ditch by a destroyer. It sank almost immediately. But then a Val came in from port firing at Cleland, who was reluctant to make an abrupt turn with such a big hole in his starboard wing. Caffey swung his nose towards the intruder and opened fire. The enemy dive bomber turned away.

After the attack on *Hiyo*, Lieutenant Commander Weymouth was faced with a thorny problem. His fuel was running low but the most direct route home was straight through the milling Japanese task force with its fearfully thick AA fire. But fuel was the critical problem, so Weymouth led eight other VB-16 planes through the deadly gauntlet of enemy guns. It was a nightmarish journey made at high speed despite the low fuel level, with rear-seat men swapping gunfire with Japanese destroyers, cruisers and even battleships.

Glacken, Cleland, and Caffey made a more or less direct line to the rendezvous, but Dupree and Kirkpatrick swung south to avoid the worst of the AA fire. Dupree had just turned away from a heavy cruiser when a Zero began a gunnery pass from starboard. The SBD turned into the attack and Dupree pressed the trigger for his .50 calibers. Nothing happened; they were jammed. He quickly pulled both charging handles and squeezed the trigger again—still nothing. The Zero had him for sure. But inexplicably the Japanese pulled up and over the SBD without shooting.

The two Dauntlesses joined up with two TBMs of Torpedo 16 only to be further harassed by more Zeros. The pilots had to rely on bluffing their way out of the situation since Dupree couldn't fix his jammed guns. Three Zeros barreled down on Kirkpatrick, shooting off the top of his rudder and holing his wings, fuselage, and canopy. He dove for the waves, evading his pursuers in the gathering darkness. Things got better when some F6Fs came upon the beleaguered bombers.

The Zeros had also hit Weymouth's nine planes. Eight fighters came down almost vertically so the gunners had to unlock their rotating seats and lean all the way back to get a bead on them. The first two dived past with such speed that the Americans expected them to plunge headlong into the water but both pulled out. The third Zero started a run on Weymouth, then moved over to Shield's plane which presented a better target. Three gunners concentrated their fire on this fighter, which triggered a single expert burst before it zoom-climbed, stalled and fell into the water. But that one burst was enough to send Jay Shields into the water. Radioman Leo LeMay was still firing when the SBD crashed.

Most of the *Lexington* planes had regrouped by this time, including Lieutenant (jg) Wright, who had broken off from his newfound VB-10 companions. But the larger formation only seemed to attract more Zeros, not scare them off. Cleland counted 18 Zeros against four VF-16 Hellcats and wondered why the Japanese concentrated on Weymouth's lead section when there were plenty of cripples around. With that big hole in his wing Cleland couldn't maneuver adequately to evade many fighters. It looked like the *Lexington* group would have to shoot its way out of trouble if it was going to get home at all. Then quite unexpectedly several strange F6Fs jumped into the dogfight and quickly routed the Zeros.

As *Lexington's* 27 surviving planes headed east, the sun behind them dropped further under the horizon.

It was 270 miles back to Task Force 58, and after the sun set around 2000 most of the pilots had to rely entirely upon instruments for reference. With Mitscher's carriers steaming northwest at 20 knots the compass course home was 100 degrees, and though some fliers became disoriented in the dark, at least they knew Task Force 58 was somewhere to the east. What they didn't know was whether they had enough fuel to get there. Commander Ramage, leading Bombing Ten, had an advantage. His squadron, like the entire *Enterprise* air group, was one of the few units fully qualified for night operations. But even so, that didn't make it much easier flying on a moonless night through tropical rainsqualls.

Nearly two hundred planes were heading eastward in the inky darkness, some with their squadrons, some singly or in pairs. Roughly 90 minutes after the attack, while approaching the task force, fuel began to run dry. Helldivers, Avengers and Hellcats ran out of fuel, their engines sputtering, propellers windmilling uselessly. But remarkably, somehow, the Dauntless pilots kept their planes in the air. Ramage and Weymouth's squadrons milked every last drop from their tanks, nearly allowing the engines to quit entirely before switching over to the fourth and last tank. Some ran their engines at dangerously lean fuel mixtures, but kept boring eastward.

Lieutenant Dupree was one of the first *Lexington* pilots to pick up the task force's ZB homing signal, about 75 miles out. Soon other aviators detected the high-pitched hum in their headsets, concentrating with hands pressed against earphones to get as precise a steer as possible. Bombing 16 discovered it was north of the task force and turned right to get on the beam. Ramage and VB-10 made the same discovery, but not by human assistance. From the corner of one eye Ramage had detected a strange flash of light. He turned towards it, swinging 20 degrees to starboard. As he closed the distance Ramage thought it was a large searchlight from one of the carriers, but they weren't visible until later. Bombing Ten had been guided home by a bolt of lightning.

As Ramage neared the task force his fuel gauge showed 15 gallons remaining. Remarkably, every ship was brightly lit up—a juicy invitation to prowling submarines. Admiral Marc Mitscher, in a decision steeped in risk for his ships and love for his aviators, (he was Naval Aviator No. 33 himself) had given his most famous order: "Turn on the lights."[15]

The *Enterprise* strike was over the task force at 2130 and found the "Big E." But Bombing Ten's first planes received wave-offs because a *Lexington* SBD flown by Lieutenant Harrison had missed the wires and crashed on deck, preventing landing operations for ten minutes. The night sky was a madhouse, split by the whine of low-flying aircraft and the white fingers of innumerable searchlights. Mitscher had ordered all aircraft to land on any available flight deck, hence Harrison's Dauntless on *Enterprise*. Only two VB-10 pilots landed aboard the "Big E" that night. Bangs almost made it but his fuel gave out right in the landing pattern and he splashed down close by.

The rest of Bombing Ten was scattered among three other carriers, none of which were even in the *Enterprise* task group. Five put down for the night aboard *Wasp*, one got aboard *Bunker Hill*, and Ramage found safe haven on *Yorktown* with Lieutenant (jg) Lewis. "We were made most welcome," Ramage said, "we were glad to be alive."[16] He'd been in the air nearly six hours.

Most of Bombing 16 returned to Task Group 58.3, with six planes each landing on *Lexington* and *Enterprise*. But the ratrace in the darkness had everyone's nerves on edge after the long flight, the unbelievable AA fire over Ozawa's carriers, and the trying circumstances of finding a deck to land upon. None of the first six planes which put down on *Lexington* were from Air Group 16. An SB2C crashed, fouling the deck while other planes ran out of gas and splashed. But the hard-working deck hands had the wreckage out of the way in ten minutes, allowing Ralph Weymouth and five others to come aboard. Dupree came close—he ran out of fuel only 200 feet from *Lexington*'s flight deck.

Over on the "Big E" things were even more confused. After Harrison's SBD crashed and was pushed overboard, five more VB-16 planes landed. One of them was flown by Jack Wright, who was amazed to find himself back aboard "the same old bucket" he'd started from over five hours before.[17]

Cleland had led Wright and Caffey down towards the task force but didn't get aboard as quickly as they. Forcing himself to concentrate, Cleland made two approaches at the light carrier *Princeton*, two more on *Lexington* and even one on a destroyer. Ship types were hard to distinguish in the dark with only lights for reference. The sixth landing approach, on *Enterprise*, was aborted and Cleland went around the pattern, finally landing on his seventh attempt of the night. Taxiing up the deck, his engine died of fuel starvation. It had been that close. Old number 39 had brought him back again.

Deck hands pushed the battered Dauntless the rest of the way forward, amazed that it could have flown so far with such extensive damage. They gawked at the jagged hole under Hisler's seat. He'd been able to look straight down at the water since the 40-mm shell exploded in the belly during the dive on *Hiyo*.

Deck space was at a premium that night, and shot-up aircraft were being pushed overboard to make room for those in the air. A plane captain scrambled up on the wing, nervously urging Cleland and Hisler to get out. "Step on it," he yelled, "we've got to push this thing overboard!"[18] The weary pilot recalled the first time he'd nursed number 39 to *Enterprise* and persuaded the crew not to give her the deep six. But now the plane captain retorted that there was no room for a badly damaged aircraft and repeated the demand to get clear.

That did it. Nobody was going to push old 39 over the side, not after all she'd been through. Cleland reached for his service pistol: "Damn you, this plane stays aboard."[19] He won his argument.

By 2300 the last planes that were coming back were all aboard.

It took a major portion of 21 June to sort out all the air groups and tally up the score. Of the 216 aircraft launched in the late afternoon of the twentieth, 104 were shot down, ran out of fuel, or were jettisoned—48 percent of the entire strike. Those planes that succeeded in getting aboard a carrier took on very nearly an entire load of gas when refueled. Ramage's SBDs, for instance, had an average of only four gallons remaining. Bombing 16's planes had a bit more leeway, but not much. They had consumed an average of 230 gallons from their 254-gallon total capacity. Considering that Ramage had fully expected to swim back from the strike, it was amazing SBD losses were so light.

The two Dauntless squadrons had launched a total of 27 aircraft, losing one in combat and three operationally. Bangs' ditched plane was the only Bombing Ten loss. The four missing SBDs represented 15 percent of those launched.

By comparison, over a quarter of the F6Fs and nearly 60 percent of the Avengers went down during the mission, but even these figures were small compared to the attrition among SB2C squadrons. Over half of the Helldivers splashed with dry tanks, and most of the others were shot down or discarded with extensive battle damage. Only five of the 50 launched on the twentieth were back aboard carriers the next day—a 90 percent loss rate. Though many fliers were rescued, the SB2C losses were the worst for any U.S. carrier aircraft in any battle since Midway.

The results achieved during the 20 minutes spent over the Mobile Fleet were disappointing to the aviators who had waited so long for a shot at Japanese carriers. Bombing Ten claimed six hits on two flattops, though the figure was later reduced to four. Bombing 16 thought fully nine hits had been made on two carriers, while *Lexington* Avengers claimed damage to a third. In all, Air Group 16 figured it had sunk *Hiyo* and *Junyo* plus damaging *Ryuho*. But *Ryuho* was not hit, *Junyo* was not sunk, and *Hiyo* was finished by *Belleau Wood* torpedo planes. The SBDs of VB-10 and VB-16 could therefore share the credit for damaging three enemy carriers to varying extents. *Hiyo,* though sunk by torpedoes, took at least a couple of bombs and *Junyo* suffered two bomb hits and six damaging near misses. *Ryuho* was rattled by several near misses but escaped significant damage. Considering that TBMs also dropped bombs on these ships, the two SBD squadrons' combined claim of over a dozen hits was clearly optimistic, though certainly understandable in the midst of such fury and confusion.

Bombing Ten had little chance to shoot at Zeros but the *Lexington* Dauntlesses had much more opportunity than anyone desired. They shot down at least two and damaged nine more, expending over 6,000 rounds of machine gun ammunition. Japanese aircraft losses were, for all practical purposes, 100 percent. Admiral Ozawa had only 35 flyable aircraft among his six remaining carriers on 21 June. It was the effective end of Japanese naval aviation; the remaining carriers had neither trained fliers nor enough replacement aircraft for further offensive operations.

The Dauntless flew its last mission with the Fast Carrier Task Force on 5 July, when VB-10 attacked targets on Guam. It was also the last combat operation of Air Group Ten, and upon returning to *Enterprise* the pilots staged an impromptu airshow to celebrate. Dauntlesses, Hellcats, and Avengers entertained the task group by buzzing ships, rolling at low level, crews whooping at the joy of being alive.

The SBD remained the only American aircraft to fly from flattops in all five of history's carrier battles. The F4F Wildcat had participated in all of the 1942 engagements but by 1944 it was relegated to escort carriers in the improved FM-2 variant. Grumman's versatile Avenger, of course, was introduced to combat at Midway but had flown from a land base. So the Dauntless maintained a completely unique record as the only U.S. carrier plane to see combat all the way from the Coral Sea in May of 1942 to the Philippine Sea in June of 1944.

The SBD no longer flew from carrier decks, but if the Navy saw fit to replace the Dauntless, at least the Marines still clung to theirs. And the last time the Douglas dive bombers participated in an offensive campaign was under the direction of the First Marine Air Wing in the Philippines.

The First Wing had seven dive-bomber squadrons in its two air groups, MAG-24 and MAG-32, which left their South Pacific staging bases in December 1944. Their destination was the Lingayen beachhead where they would fly in support of General McArthur's infantrymen.

The "Diving Devildogs of Luzon," as war correspondents were wont to dub the Marines, flew their first mission two days after arrival in late January 1945. The squadrons had trained intensively in the Solomons, perfecting the technique which would become known as close air support, but the Army foot-sloggers were at first uncertain whether they wanted Marine aviators dropping bombs within rock-throwing distance. Consequently the First Wing began the campaign by flying ordinary bombing missions and patrols.

The Army men needn't have been so hesitant about the Marines, as all seven squadrons were highly experienced in training, if not in actual combat. But two of the SBD units, VMSB-142 and 241, had been around the Pacific for a long time. The former had flown from Henderson Field in late 1942 and the latter had assisted in the defense of Midway. The other squadrons were VMSB-133, 236, 243, 244 and 341. The month of February would solidly convince the riflemen they could bet their lives on the Marine dive bombers.

The Luzon-based SBDs possibly achieved a first in military history by guarding the flank of an infantry division from the air. The First Cavalry Division made a headlong sprint of a hundred miles towards Manila with at least nine Dauntlesses always on patrol over their left flank, destroying strongpoints with precision bombing. By the end of the first week in February the Army commanders were convinced and called upon SBDs more and more frequently for a variety of missions. A flight of Dauntlesses proved the real meaning of tactical air power on one occasion

A First Marine Air Wing SBD-6 lines up for takeoff against Japanese positions on Luzon during the Philippine Campaign, late 1944. (U.S. Marine Corps)

by rescuing a trapped infantry patrol, laying heavy bombs within 300 yards of their position to drive out encircling Japanese.

Antiaircraft fire during the drive on Manila was formidable in its quantity but caused few losses, and aerial opposition was nonexistent. During February the First Wing Dauntlesses flew 4,000 sorties, during which three fliers were killed in action. The Japanese had had nearly three years to fortify the Philippines but quickly learned to appreciate the accuracy of the Marine dive bombers. Prisoners confessed that some guncrews were afraid to open fire on U.S. aircraft for fear of retaliation by the Dauntlesses.

Bit by bit the two Marine Air Groups moved from one field to another as the Army troops captured more territory. And a new feature was added to the Army-Marine blitz when it was discovered that pilots needed an airman's description of the terrain in order to pinpoint hidden targets. An infantry platoon leader had little or no idea of what features were prominent from the air, but a pilot in a radio-equipped jeep could easily tell his airborne friends what to look for.

Eventually the Marine Dauntlesses moved to Mindanao and took up where they left off at Luzon, finishing the Philippines Campaign in the same expert style with which they began it.

When the Second World War ended, a few Marine SBD squadrons were still pounding away at bypassed garrisons in the Solomons. But most Dauntlesses had been relegated to training or utility status by then, and the last ones reported in operational service were SBD-6s on 30 September 1945.

The Dauntless had fought a truly international war. New Zealand airmen had flown ex-Marine SBDs in the Solomons and Free French squadrons used SBDs and A-24s in Europe after D-Day. The French, in fact, made good postwar use of their Dauntlesses. Operating from American-built light carriers with British-built Seafire fighters, SBDs were probably the first U.S. aircraft engaged in the Indo-China conflict. As late as 1949 French-flown Dauntlesses were carrying out bombing attacks against Communist terrorists, almost as though in anticipation of the time two decades later when other Douglas aircraft would be similarly engaged.

But the SBD made its name and its mark on history over the broad blue curve of the Pacific, from Pearl Harbor to V-J Day. It established the lowest loss rate for American carrier aircraft of the entire war, a tribute to the airframe and the oft-maligned Wright Cyclone engine.

For an airplane supposedly vulnerable to fighters, the Dauntless outshone every other naval strike aircraft. In all, 138 Japanese planes were credited to Dauntless pilots and gunners: 106 to carrier-based and 32 to land-based SBDs. Incomplete record-keeping during the Guadalcanal Campaign makes precise figures nearly impossible, but it is almost certain that fewer than 80 Dauntlesses were shot down by Japanese aircraft from 1941 to 1945.

Over 300,000 tons of enemy shipping went down under SBD bombs, including at least 18 warships ranging from submarines to battleships. During 1942, the Dauntless established itself as the premier carrier-killer of all time, sinking six flattops almost entirely without assistance.

Thus did the Douglas Dauntless pass into history. A classic aircraft in both design and utilization, it performed its mission supremely well. Though almost never popularized and possibly never fully appreciated outside its immediate sphere, the SBD's contribution to winning the Pacific War was unexcelled by any other American or Allied aircraft.

Seven SBDs or A-24s are known to have been licensed for civilian use following the war, but 30 years later only four remained intact. A fifth Dauntless, an SBD-6, was retained by the National Air and Space Museum of the Smithsonian Institute in Washington, D. C. It had been used by the Flight Test Division of Patuxent River Naval Air Station until 1948.

The civilian Dauntlesses found their wartime roles of bombing and reconnaissance turned to more mundane but nonetheless useful purposes. The City of Portland and Multnomah County, Oregon, operated a pair of A-24s for many years as spray planes to combat mosquitos. Both aircraft were based at the Troutdale, Oregon, airport where they were maintained by E. H. Fletcher of Aero Flite, Inc.

In 1965 the Navy acquired Portland's A-24A as it had been sold under a conditional sales contract when released by the government. It was disassembled and sent to the Naval Aviation Museum at Pensacola, Florida, where it received a 1941–42 color scheme and markings.

Portland's remaining aircraft was an A-24B, and served for a total of 17 years as a sprayer before being released in 1971. Three antique airplane pilots working as Pacific Aeronautical Corporation acquired the dive bomber, which was then the only Dauntless flying in the world. A solid year of restoration work returned it to SBD-5 configuration with Bureau of Aeronautics paint and markings specifications for early 1943.

The second Portland Dauntless was restored in 1971–72 and flown by J. H. Tillman of Athena, Oregon. In configuration and markings of an SBD-5, it may be seen at the Marine Corps Museum, Quantico. (B. Tillman)

The only Dauntless which still flies regularly is owned by the Confederate Air Force in Texas. It displays the markings of an SBD-3 during early 1942. (Confederate Air Force)

It was flown by J. H. Tillman of Athena, Oregon, until obtained by noted aircraft collector Douglas Champlin of Oklahoma in the spring of 1974. This aircraft, factory serial number 17421, was the last Dauntless ever privately owned and has been in the Marine Corps Museum at Quantico, Virginia, since March of 1975.

The only other flyable Dauntless is maintained by the "Confederate Air Force" in Texas. It came from Mexico and was obtained from the now-defunct Planes of Fame Museum at Buena Park, California, in 1971. The CAF had previously purchased an A-24B from Aero Flight at Kent, Washington, in 1965 but lost it in an accident en route to Texas.

Another Mexican A-24B was part of the Tallmantz Aviation collection at Santa Ana, California. It was purchased by a private party in the Tallmantz auction of 1968, but sat badly neglected at San Fernando for many years. Finally in 1972 the Admiral Nimitz Center of Fredericksburg, Texas, obtained the A-24 and transported it to a trade school in Waco for restoration. The once-neglected dive bomber is now a non-flying exhibit at the Nimitz Center's mall in Fredericksburg, configured as an SBD-3. An Aichi Val, the SBD's long-time antagonist, will eventually be displayed with the Dauntless–a most unusual and commendable project.

Numerous SBD or A-24 fuselages may be found throughout the U.S. but very few of them retain empennages and none have wings. Two or three could be made into relatively complete airframes if wings were available, but that possibility is so remote as to be virtually nonexistent. No intact SBDs or A-24s are known to remain in any foreign country though the types were operated by New Zealand, France, and Mexico. Barring some totally unexpected discovery in the future, the five surviving Dauntlesses are now all found in the southern and eastern United States.

Type	Serial No.	FAA Registry	1975 Location	1975 Status
A-24A	42-60817	Ex-N9142H	Naval Aviation Museum Pensacola, Florida	Static display as SBD-3
A-24B	42-54532	N54532	Confederate Air Force Harlingen, Texas	Flying in SBD colors
A-24B	42-54582	N17421 Ex-N4488N	Marine Corps Museum Quantico, Virginia	Airworthy as SBD-5
A-24B	42-54682	Ex-N74133	Admiral Nimitz Center Fredericksburg, Texas	Static display as SBD-3
SBD-6	BuAer 54605	————	NASM, Smithsonian Inst. Washington, D. C.	Under restoration

appendix b
dauntless specifications
for all models
(navy and marine)

	XBT-2	*SBD-1*	*SBD-2*
Wingspan	41 ft 6 in	41 ft 6 in	41 ft 6 in
Length	31 ft 9 in	32 ft 2 in	32 ft 2 in
Height	12 ft 10 in	13 ft 7 in	13 ft 7 in
Wing area	320 sq ft.	325 sq. ft.	325 sq. ft.
Empty weight	5,093 pounds	5,903 pounds	6,293 pounds
Gross weight	7,593 pounds	9,790 pounds	10,360 pounds
Engine	Wright XR-1820-32	Wright R-1820-32	Wright R-1820-32
Rated power			
Top speed	230 knots, 265 mph	220 knots, 253 mph	219 knots, 252 mph
Cruise speed	135 knots, 155 mph	125 knots, 142 mph	131 knots, 148 mph
Rate of climb	1,450 ft per min	1,730 ft per min	1,080 ft per min
Service ceiling	30,600 feet	29,600 feet	26,000 feet
Maximum bombing range	604 st. miles	860 miles	1,125 miles
Maximum scout range	1,485 st. miles	1,165 miles	1,370 miles
Pilot's armament	2 fixed .30s	2 fixed .30s	2 fixed .30s
Gunner's armament	1 free .30	1 free .30	1 free .30
Maximum bomb load	1,200 pounds	1,200 pounds	1,200 pounds
No. of model built	1	57	87
Delivery began		June 1940	November 1940

SBD-3	SBD-4	SBD-5	SBD-6
41 ft 6 in	41 ft 6 in	41 ft 6 in	41 ft 6 in
32 ft 8 in	32 ft 8 in	33 ft 0 in	33 ft 0 in
13 ft 7 in	13 ft 7 in	13 ft 7 in	13 ft 7 in
325 sq ft	325 sq ft	325 sq ft	325 sq ft
6,345 pounds	6,360 pounds	6,533 pounds	6,554 pounds
10,400 pounds	10,480 pounds	10,700 pounds	10,882 pounds
Wright R-1820-52	Wright R-1820-52	Wright R-1820-60	Wright R-1820-66
1,000 h.p.	1,000 h.p.	1,200 h.p.	1,350 h.p.
217 knots, 250 mph	212 knots, 245 mph	219 knots, 252 mph	229 knots, 262 mph
135 knots, 152 mph	130 knots, 150 mph	119 knots, 139 mph	124 knots, 143 mph
1,190 ft per min	1,150 fpm	1,700 fpm	1,710 fpm
27,100 feet	26,700 feet	24,300 feet	28,600 feet
1,345 miles	1,300 miles	1,115 miles	1,230 miles
1,580 miles	1,450 miles	1,565 miles	1,700 miles
2 fixed .50s	2 fixed .50s	2 fixed .50s	2 fixed .50s
2 free .30s	2 free .30s	2 free .30s	2 free .50s
1,200 pounds	1,200 pounds	1,200 pounds	1,200 pounds
584 to USN, 168 to AAF	780 to USN, 170 to AAF	2,965 to USN, 675 to AAF	450
March 1941	October 1942	May 1943	

SBD-1	57	A-24	168
SBD-2	87	A-24A	170
SBD-3	584	A24-B	675
SBD-4	780		1,013
SBD-5	2,965		
SBD-6	450	SBD's	4,923
	4,923	A-24's	1,013
			5,936

notes

chapter 1

1. Interview with Colonel Bruce Prosser, Salem, Oregon, October 1972.
2. Correspondence with Admiral H. D. Felt, 9 November 1972.

chapter 2

1. Lieutenant A. R. Buchanan, ed., *The Navy's Air War*, Harper, New York, 1946. Page 12.

chapter 3

1. Pat Frank and J. D. Harrington, *Rendezvous at Midway*, Warner, New York, 1967. Page 71.
2. Ibid. Page 72.
3. Norman Polmar, *Aircraft Carriers*, Doubleday, Garden City, 1969. Page 199.
4. Frank and Harrington, page 78.
5. Scouting Squadron Two action report for 8 May 1942.
6. Ibid.
7. Stanley Johnston, *Queen of the Flattops*. Ballantine, New York, 1970. Page 165.
8. Scouting Squadron Two action report for 8 May 1942.
9. Johnston, page 177.
10. Robert D. Loomis, *Great American Fighter Pilots of WW II*. Random House, New York, 1961. Page 33.
11. Johnston, page 196.
12. Interview with Admiral Wallace C. Short, October 1974.
13. Ibid.

chapter 4

1. Correspondence with Admiral Murr E. Arnold, June 1973.
2. Walter Lord, *Incredible Victory*. Harper and Row, New York, 1967. Page 97.
3. Ibid. Page 121.
4. Correspondence with Captain James E. Vose, June 1973.
5. Lord, page 140.

6. Vose, op. cit.
7. Lord, page 156.
8. Correspondence with Admiral Max Leslie, 16 November 1972.
9. Commander Edward P. Stafford, *The Big E.* Dell, New York, 1962. Page 94.
10. Lieutenant C. E. Dickinson, *The Flying Guns.* Scribner's, New York, 1942.
11. Lord, page 166.
12. Correspondence with Lt. Cdr. R. H. Best, 15 November 1972.
13. Leslie, op. cit.
14. Interview with Admiral John S. Thach. San Diego, California. September, 1971.
15. Lord, page 197.
16. *Yorktown* action report for 4 June 1942.
17. Ibid.
18. Leslie, op. cit.
19. Best, op. cit.
20. Stafford, op. cit. Page 94.

chapter 5

1. Thomas G. Miller, *The Cactus Air Force.* Harper and Row, New York, 1969. Page 24.
2. Correspondence with Lt. Gen. R. C. Mangrum, October 1972.
3. Ibid.
4. Ibid.
5. Ibid.
6. Ibid.
7. Ibid.
8. Ibid.
9. Interview with Col. Bruce Prosser, Salem, Oregon, October 1972.
10. Ibid.
11. Mangrum, op. cit.
12. Ibid.
13. Ibid.
14. Miller, page 58.

chapter 6

1. Correspondence with Admiral H. D. Felt, 9 November 1972.
2. Scouting Squadron 5 action report for 23–25 August 1942.
3. Felt, op. cit.
4. *Saratoga* Air Group action report for 24 August 1942.
5. Felt, op. cit.
6. *Enterprise* Air Group action report for 23–25 August 1942.

chapter 7

1. Correspondence with Admiral James R. Lee, 23 January 1973.
2. Bombing Squadron 10 action report for 26 October 1942.
3. Scouting Squadron 10 action report for 26 October 1942.
4. Lee, op. cit.
5. Ibid.
6. Bombing Squadron 8 action report for 26 October 1942.
7. Ibid.
8. Ibid.
9. Correspondence with Capt. James E. Vose, 8 January 1973.

chapter 9

1. Correspondence with Capt. Ralph R. Kimble, USMC, 11 September 1972.
2. Ibid.
3. Correspondence with Capt. James E. Vose, USN, 8 January 1973.

chapter 10

1. Bombing Squadron 10 action report for 19 June 1944.
2. Lieutenant Commander Joseph Bryan, *Mission Beyond Darkness*. Duell, Sloan and Pearce. New York, 1944. Page 15.
3. Ibid. Page 15.
4. Rear Admiral James D. Ramage. Personal account written in June 1944.
5. Ibid.
6. Bryan, page 28.
7. Ramage, op. cit.
8. Ibid.
9. Ibid.
10. Ibid.
11. Ibid.
12. Ibid.
13. Ibid.
14. Ibid.
15. Bryan, page 73.
16. Ramage, op. cit.
17. Bryan, page 97.
18. Ibid. Page 96.
19. Ibid. Page 96.

bibliography

Official Sources

The Navy's Operational Archives Branch in the Washington Navy Yard holds the after-action reports for nearly all carrier squadrons during World War II. Dr. Dean C. Allard's office provided some 300 pages of action reports and other pertinent material for the preparation of this book, including those reports for all air groups and SBD squadrons involved in the five carrier duels of the war: Coral Sea, Midway, Eastern Solomons, Santa Cruz, and the First Battle of the Philippine Sea.

The SBD units involved in these five engagements were Bombing Squadrons 2, 3, 5, 6, 8, 10 and 16; and Scouting Squadrons 2, 3, 5, 6, 8 and 10. The Operational Archives also provided a copy of *Ranger's* Air Group 4 action report for the Bodø raid in Norwegian waters of October, 1943. Torpedo Squadrons 2, 3, 4, 5, 6 and 8 operated in conjunction with SBD squadrons in these operations and their reports were also studied. Additionally, a somewhat incomplete but very useful history of VB-3 was also made available.

Particularly illuminating about the prewar aspects of dive-bomber evolution was a series of excellent articles by Lee M. Pearson in the Naval Aviation Confidential Bulletins of 1949–50. Titles included "Dive Bombers: the Pre-War Years," "Development of the Attack Concept," and "The Attack Bomber: the War Years."

The builders of the SBD, now McDonnell-Douglas Long Beach, made available a useful chart showing the evolution of the Dauntless from XBT-1 through SBD-6 as well as a large amount of "nuts and bolts" technical material. For this wealth of data, special thanks are extended to Mr. Harry Gann of the American Aviation Historical Society.

Unofficial Sources

In order to fill out the framework provided by official documents, frequent reference was made to interviews and correspondence with former SBD pilots, and to previously published material.

Interviews and/or correspondence with each of the persons listed in the contributors' section following resulted in a large volume of first-hand accounts and recollections. Private papers and records were loaned or otherwise made available by Colonel Bruce Prosser, Rear Admiral James D. Ramage, and Rear Admiral Wallace C. Short. Admiral Ramage kindly sent a copy of the personal account he wrote of VB-10's dusk attack on the Mobile Fleet only a few days after the First Battle of the Philippine Sea, and Admiral Short retains a wealth of material from his days as skipper of Bombing Five.

Mr. Richard M. Hill, Milwaukee, Wisconsin, himself a former Naval Aviator, contributed many photographs which would have been otherwise mostly unavailable.

Mr. Douglass Hubbard, Executive Director of the Admiral Nimitz Center in Fredericksburg, Texas, proved most helpful in obtaining addresses of retired Navy personnel. A good deal of the credit for getting this book off the ground belongs to him. Detailed information on Japanese aircraft losses in the carrier duels of 1942 came from naval historian John B. Lundstrom, who made possible an accurate revision of long-standing claims from Coral Sea, the first carrier battle.

Each of the following contributors is listed with his rank at retirement, except Mr. Haizlip who served as a civilian.

RADM Murr E. Arnold, *Yorktown* Air Officer at Coral Sea and Midway.

LCDR Richard H. Best, CO of VB-6, *Enterprise*, at Midway.

ADM Harry Don Felt, CO of VB-2, *Lexington*; *Saratoga* CAG at Eastern Solomons.

Mr. James G. Haizlip, Douglas factory test pilot.

LCDR William E. Henry, VS-3, *Saratoga*, at Eastern Solomons.

CAPT Ralph R. Kimble, Rear-seat man of VMSB-144 in the Solomons Campaign.

RADM James R. Lee, CO of VS-10, *Enterprise*, at Santa Cruz and The Slot.

BGEN W. C. Lemly, Marine Corps aerial photography.

RADM Maxwell F. Leslie, CO of VB-3, *Yorktown*, at Midway.

LTGEN Richard C. Mangrum, CO of VMSB-232 on Guadalcanal.

COL Bruce Prosser, Operations officer of VMSB-232 on Guadalcanal.

RADM James D. Ramage, CO of VB-10, *Enterprise*, at First Philippine Sea.

RADM Wallace C. Short, CO of VB-5, *Yorktown*, at Coral Sea and Midway.

ADM John S. Thach, CO of VF-3, *Yorktown*, at Midway.

CAPT James E. Vose, VB-8, *Hornet*, at Midway and CO at Santa Cruz.

Books

Brazelton, David. *The Douglas SBD Dauntless*. Profile Publications, UK, 1967.

Bryan, Joseph, III. *Mission Beyond Darkness*. New York: Duell, Sloan, Pearce, 1944.

Buchanan, A. R. *The Navy's Air War*. New York: Harper Bros., 1947.

DeChant, John A. *Devilbirds*. New York: Harper Bros., 1947.

Dickinson, C. E. *The Flying Guns*. New York: Chas. Scribner's, 1942.

Frank, P. and Harrington, J. *Rendezvous at Midway*. New York: Warner Books, 1968.

Jensen, Oliver. *Carrier War*. New York: Simon and Schuster, 1945.

Johnston, Stanley. *Queen of the Flattops*. New York: Ballantine, 1970.

Loomis, Robert D. *Great American Fighter Pilots of WW II*. New York: Random House, 1961.

Lord, Walter. *Day of Infamy*. New York: Holt and Co., 1957.

———. *Incredible Victory*. New York: Harper and Row, 1967.

Miller, Thomas G., Jr. *The Cactus Air Force*. New York: Harper and Row, 1969.

Mizrahi, Joseph V. *Dive and Torpedo Bombers*. Canoga Park, Cal.: Sentry, 1967.

Morison, Samuel Eliot. *A History of United States Naval Operations in World War II*. Volume IV: Coral Sea, Midway and Submarine Actions. Boston: Little, Brown and Co., 1969.

———. *A History of United States Naval Operations in World War II*. Volume V: The Struggle for Guadalcanal. Boston, Little, Brown and Co., 1969.

Polmar, Norman. *Aircraft Carriers*. Garden City: Doubleday, 1969.

Stafford, Edward P. *The Big E*. New York: Dell, 1964.

Toland, John. *The Rising Sun*. New York: Random House, 1970.

Watts, Anthony J. *Japanese Warships of World War II*. Garden City: Doubleday, 1969.

index

The Naval Institute Press is the book-publishing arm of the U.S. Naval Institute, a private, nonprofit membership society for sea service professionals and others who share an interest in naval and maritime affairs. Established in 1873 at the U.S. Naval Academy in Annapolis, Maryland, where its offices remain today, the Naval Institute has members worldwide.

Members of the Naval Institute support the education programs of the society and receive the influential monthly magazine *Proceedings* and discounts on fine nautical prints and on ship and aircraft photos. They also have access to the transcripts of the Institute's Oral History Program and get discounted admission to any of the Institute-sponsored seminars offered around the country. Discounts are also available to the colorful bimonthly magazine *Naval History*.

The Naval Institute's book-publishing program, begun in 1898 with basic guides to naval practices, has broadened its scope to include books of more general interest. Now the Naval Institute Press publishes about one hundred titles each year, ranging from how-to books on boating and navigation to battle histories, biographies, ship and aircraft guides, and novels. Institute members receive significant discounts on the Press's more than eight hundred books in print.

Full-time students are eligible for special half-price membership rates. Life memberships are also available.

For a free catalog describing Naval Institute Press books currently available, and for further information about joining the U.S. Naval Institute, please write to:

Customer Service
U.S. Naval Institute
291 Wood Road
Annapolis, MD 21402-5034
Telephone: (800) 233-8764
Fax: (410) 269-7940
Web address: www.navalinstitute.org